convicted

convicted

A Scientist Examines the Evidence for Christianity

Brad Harrub, Ph.D.

PRESS

Dedication

This book is dedicated to Melinda—a living
example of a Biblical virtuous woman (Proverbs 31).
I am thankful for your strong convictions.

CONVICTED
Published by Focus Press, Inc.
2nd Printing, November 2009
3rd Printing, April 2010
5th Printing, 2014

© Copyright 2010 Focus Press, Inc.
International Standard Book Number 978-098218157-7
Cover and interior design by MTWdesign / Marc Whitaker
Cover image by: Shutterstock
Interior images by: Shutterstock

All Scripture quotations are from the New King James Version, copyright 1979, 1980, 1982, Thomas Nelson, Inc., Publishers, unless otherwise noted.

Printed in China

For information or to order copies of *Convicted*, contact the publisher:

FOCUS PRESS, INC.
625 Bakers Bridge Avenue, Suite 105
Franklin, Tennessee 37067

Library of Congress cataloging-in-publication
    Brad Harrub (1970-)
Convicted
Includes Biblical references
ISBN: 978-098218157-7
    1. Science and religion.   2. Creation.   3. Apologetic's and Polemics.
    I. Title

Acknowledgments

This book has been a labor of love—but a labor that would be impossible were it not for the dedication, support, time, energy, and sacrifice of so many others. While my name may grace the cover, rest assured that many people helped "behind the scenes" to make this a reality. I want to start by thanking God. My studies have taken me many directions; through good times and bad—but His love is steadfast. Thank you God for giving us the evidence! Second I want to thank the incredible staff at Focus Press. This team routinely amazes me at the way they continue to set the bar extremely high and give so much of themselves. (I would also thank their families for their sacrifice). As we have talked about at the office, "the world sees what you do, but God sees why you do it!" Thanks for your servant hearts. I would also like to thank Tonja McRady for her assistance and patience. She has encouraged me and put up with me as we flooded one another with tweaks and corrections to the manuscript. I spent many hours in various airports combing through her suggestions and sending her more material. A big thanks goes out to Clay Young and Marc Whitaker for producing such an incredible book! I appreciate so much your "we'll get it done" attitude. In addition thanks to Apologetics Press, the source of some of the material in this book. Also thanks to Nancy Stewart and her eagle eyes!

I also want to shine a special light on the Birdwell Lane congregation in Big Spring, Texas, and the Hillsboro congregation in Hillsboro, Tennessee. The church needs more visionary congregations like yourselves. You all don't just talk the talk—you also walk the walk! Thank you for your leadership and example. Also many thanks to Rod & Cindy Wilson.

And finally, thanks to my wife and family. God has blessed us so richly, and I am so thankful to have each one of you in my life. It would be a joy to be a "fly on the wall" in our house, but I am blessed to have more than a spectator's view. I get to experience firsthand the love and energy in the Harrub household. Melinda, thanks for your never-ending support, your encouragement to finish this project, and your love. Will, Reese, Claire, and Luke, thank you for your smiles, your love, your laughter, your sacrifice, and your encouragement. I love you all very much.

Introduction

contents

Contents

Contents

Introduction

Ever since I was a young boy, I have been inquisitive. I want to know how things work and why they work that particular way. My mind is constantly spinning as I observe nature and the world around me. Science for me was an obvious choice when I was picking a major in my undergraduate studies. By that point in my life, I was determined to study how the human body worked. I had so many questions: How were new blood cells formed? Where were memories stored? How did the nervous system or muscular system work? The answers to many of my questions came from two sources: (1) Book knowledge from hours spent in classrooms and libraries; and (2) "Hands-on" training from Vanderbilt University Medical Center, human dissection labs, and research labs. During my formal training, I formed a "love-hate" relationship with my academic environment. I loved the fact that with each passing day I was able to fill my mind with answers to my questions (even though often those answers led to additional questions!). But I did not like the political and often atheistic environment in which I was being trained. There was no question that many of the professors under which I was training had little or no belief in God. In fact, upon formally entering the department of neurology, I discovered many of the doctors had God-complexes—viewing themselves as a god.

Many students have followed a similar educational path with a different outcome. They attend classes taught by atheistic professors and slowly buy into the notion that all intelligent people believe evolution—and that religion is simply a crutch for the weak-minded. Having listened as teary-eyed parents share the story of their own children abandoning a belief in God, I realized that I needed to fight back in the language that modern-day students understand: **evidence**. Thus the reason for the book you are holding. The primary difference between my own personal experience versus the experience of those who have abandoned their faith is that I took the time to critically evaluate the evidence. I turned the lens of my scientific training onto the Bible and the existence of a Supreme Creator. What I discovered was not a crutch or mythological story—but rather a **belief so founded by evidence that I concluded blinders were necessary in order for one not to believe.** Sadly, those blinders exist and they are handed out in many universities today under the guise of biology, genetics, microbiology, chemistry, ecology, anatomy, geology, molecular biology, evolutionary biology, physics, etc. These blinders have created a barrier between science and religion—a barrier that appears to many individuals insurmountable.

Given the history of science and theology, it would be expected that a conflict might arise. Prior to the 16th century, most individuals viewed science and medicine with fear and trepidation. Oftentimes the survival rate of humans was markedly **decreased** when an individual sought medical treatment from those within the scientific field. This was long before Louis Pasteur revealed his Germ Theory for Disease. Thus, it was still common for a physician to treat a sick patient, then walk right over and begin examining another patient without washing his hands. During this time theologians were sought after for their wisdom and knowledge and were often given preeminence among the people. These were scholars who could read and who could accurately detail the will of God. These were men with answers. The pendulum was firmly on the side of religion.

But with the advent of antibiotics and vaccines, the pendulum started to swing in the other direction. Suddenly, science was thrust into the spotlight, as men listened to the latest offerings from the fields of geology, astronomy, microbiology, genetics, and physics. Where people once sat at the feet of theologians for wisdom and understanding, they now found their attention drawn to scientists. As more and more discoveries were made, questions began to ripple throughout society about the real need for religion—after all, much of science was now allegedly disproving the creation of man by an Almighty Creator. The pendulum did not stop in the middle. Its arc was fairly swift and it shifted completely to the other side. Today, a large percentage of the population place their faith in science. It has become a modern-day Baal that many worship—either consciously or subconsciously. As I mentioned, during my training religion was cast as an "activity" for uneducated imbeciles. How many souls have been forfeited as young people run off to college or out in the work-a-day world and end up embracing the humanism, atheism, and evolutionary teaching, all because the intellectual "elite" have pronounced it as truth. I fear that many have forgotten, "If you tell people a lie long enough and loud enough they will believe it."

Real truth can stand up to scrutiny. **Real truth has evidence to back it up and not merely speculations or probabilities.** This book is my effort to uncover the truth and to bridge science and the Bible. While some may still choose to wear blinders, this book holds solid evidence for New Testament Christianity. I have authored or coauthored several books in the past—but this one is different. This one is personal, and it is aimed at those like myself who have inquisitive minds—those in search for the Truth. Some will find many chapters challenging, as it may very well upend their entire worldview. But I ask that you focus your attention on the evidence and logic contained therein. Having spent twenty-three years in school, I have examined the evidence and I am **convicted!** It's time for the pendulum to shift back!

*"For since the creation of the world
His invisible attributes are clearly seen,
being understood by the things that are made,
even His eternal power and Godhead,
so that they are without excuse."*

– Romans 1:20

Chapter

Worldviews and the Whole Duty of Man

The young man woke and smiled to himself. He felt different. Much of the guilt and discomfort he had been burdened with the last several years had melted away. For the last seventeen years of his life, he had conducted himself to please his parents. He dressed neatly, finished his homework, attended church every week, and even went on a mission trip two years ago. But a conversation with some close friends over the past three days had led to a paradigm shift—an epiphany that would forever alter his behavior and his life. Prior to this "epiphany," the young man had always conducted himself—somewhat in fear and trepidation—with the belief that there was a God, a Supreme Being, who would one day judge the world. Having spent several hours talking with his friends and listening to their arguments, this young man no longer believed in or feared that God. He no longer worried about "judgment." He awoke this morning to the guilt-free realization that his actions no longer mattered. He believed there was much more "gray" in the world than he had previously believed. In a solitary weekend, this young seventeen-year-old went from holding doors for the elderly to being more concerned about himself and his own desires. His views on relationships with females changed dramatically. He would continue to abide by the laws of the land, but he would no longer worry about others the way he once did. From this point forward, he would only worry about #1. A new day and a new era were dawning, and he was eager to face it, so he looked into his closet for something to wear.

Whole Duty of Man

There is no question of greater importance than whether or not God exists. The answer to this single question affects **ALL** other questions. If there is a Supreme Being, then life has inherent purpose and some form of meaning. The very existence of a Creator logically indicates there was a "plan" that included mankind. If not, then our very presence on this earth is simply the result of a cosmologic explosion, and we are the beneficiaries of climbing our way to the top of the evolutionary tree of life. Without an Intelligent Designer, humans are the end result of naturalistic changes that have occurred through time. Consider the following proposition:

1. Only bodies in which a component (e.g., the spirit) is eternal and endless can have meaning. (E form: No finite lives have meaning).
2. If there are no gods, then there are no endless lives. (A form: If there are no gods, all lives are finite).
3. If there is no God, then no lives have meaning.

This meaning does not equate with happiness, as non-believers and believers alike can experience worldly happiness. However, the core meaning for our lives shapes our attitudes and often dictates how we conduct ourselves while on this earth. For many, the whole duty of man is to "fear God and keep His commandments" (Ecclesiastes 12:13). For others, the duty of man is to eat, drink, and be merry, similar to the seventeen-year-old described previously.

My scientific training took place in an atmosphere devoted to naturalism. The notion of anything supernatural was shunned and ridiculed. We were routinely trained that if you could not taste, touch, smell, hear, or see "it," then "it" was not real. Sure, as scientists we recognized there were things such as love or memory that might exist outside the realms of our normal senses, but we held fast to the notion that, given enough time and the right technology, everything had an explanation that could be traced back to naturalistic causes. This  notion was reconfirmed in textbooks, which strove diligently to give naturalistic explanations for everything. They strove…but routinely came up short. Naturalism struggled to explain altruism in mankind, the tendency of man to worship, and even the very existence of life and matter. While vague promises were made that the data

> *There is no question of greater importance than whether or not God exists.*

for these areas would be forthcoming, what did the evidence really reveal about a Supreme Being? Was science too pre-committed to Darwinian evolution to fairly evaluate the answer to this question? Since this question is the most important, it is the place we must begin. Before proceeding, take a second and consider the difference the answer to what "the whole duty of man" makes for mankind and our offspring. To answer this question, I want to employ not only scientific skills of observation, but also logic and reason.

Something From Nothing

Any logical person would be hard pressed to defend that nothing exists today. The very fact that you are reading this book indicates that something exists. (Some might contend that this is all a hallucination—but I would still ask where did the hallucination come from, and exactly how do you know it is a hallucination? In order for something to be acknowledged as a hallucination would mean that one can know reality.) Since it is an absolute truth that something now exists, it demands that **something has existed forever.** *Otherwise, one would be forced to argue that something came from nothing—a position that is weak and illogical.* It is a self-evident truth that something can't come from nothing, thus something has to have existed forever. This truth does not prove a Supreme Being, but rather it establishes that something has "eternal" properties. The essence of being **eternal** can be defined as "existing without a beginning or end"—sometimes considered to be outside of time. Since something exists today, it is a reasonable scientific observation to then go one step further and deduce that something has existed forever.

But how do we go about identifying that eternal "something"? This is where naturalistic science meets philosophy. All of our scientific observations exclude anything being "eternal" in nature. (Some might argue that the universe holds an eternal

potential, i.e. Heni Poincare's work would argue that given a sufficient length of time, it will reorder itself into its original arrangement without any loss of usable energy. However, the evidence for such a "theory" is grossly lacking and would be a faith-based assumption in itself.) Everything that man is currently aware of obeys the Second Law of Thermodynamics, which states that things are running down and wearing out (a concept also shared by writers of the Bible; see Hebrews 1:11; Isaiah 51:6; Psalm 102:26). If something is eternal it would indicate that something is not running down and had no beginning. Consider the following equations:

1. *Something* exists today—THUS—*something* must be eternal and has always existed.

2. *Something* is eternal (Doesn't Wear Down and Was Not Created)—THUS—*something* violates scientific laws (specifically the Second Law of Thermodynamics).

3. *Something* violates scientific laws—THUS—*something* exists outside the observable laws of naturalistic science.

From these we can conclude:

4. **Something eternal is THUS outside the observable laws of naturalistic science!** While many may not like this "math," it is inescapable. To argue otherwise would be to deny our very existence. We can logically conclude that something has existed forever—something that is not explainable by naturalistic science. Now the question becomes: what is that something?

A Lot of Bang for Your Buck

Most textbooks begin the question of origins "mid-bang." Students are routinely taught that the universe is the result of the Big Bang explosion, but textbook writers never reveal where the matter for the "bang" originated. (In fact, they also never explain who or what pulled the trigger!) We have proven that "something" has eternal properties, but

"Big Bang cosmology is probably as widely believed as has been any theory of the universe in the history of Western civilization. It rests, however, on many untested, and in some cases untestable, assumptions. Indeed, Big Bang cosmology has become a bandwagon of thought that reflects faith as much as objective truth."
–Astronomer Geoffrey Burbidge, 1992, *Scientific American*, p. 96, Feb.

was that "something" responsible for the creation of the universe? Was that "something" responsible for the creation of man?

Within science, there is a hierarchy that has been built upon knowledge. Scientists commonly offer hypotheses or postulate about what they expect to observe in various research studies. From their observations, they offer theories about how things will behave. At the pinnacle of this hierarchy are scientific laws. Scientific laws differ from hypotheses and theories in that they are empirically determined to be constant—never violated. One such scientific law is the **Law of Cause and Effect.** The Law of Cause and Effect recognizes that for every material effect there must be an adequate cause that existed prior to the effect.

There has never been a known exception to this law (otherwise, it would immediately lose its status as a scientific law). No one would ever believe that a mole dug the majestic Grand Canyon. Anyone who has viewed the canyon firsthand would recognize the foolishness of such a suggestion. This cause (the mole) is insufficient to explain the effect (the Grand Canyon). One can easily surmise that a bigger cause must be responsible for the canyon. As such, we can rationally apply this scientific law to the universe. Consider how big a cause would be required to make that kind of effect. Truly we can conclude that something massive (a Supreme Force or Being) was needed to cause the universe. In later chapters, we will identify characteristics of this Supreme Being. For now, it is sufficient to conclude that the evidence demonstrates that something is out there, and has been for eternity.

> ## *We know an enormous and complex universe exists today, so what caused it?*

Skeptics might be quick to question, "Okay, then what caused God?" Take a closer look at this scientific law of cause and effect. It states that for every **material** effect there must be an adequate cause. The Bible describes God as a spirit (John 4:24), and thus this law would not apply to Him. This entire line of argument—frequently used by atheists such as Richard Dawkins—is an argument of infinite regression. Should someone offer "X" as an explanation for where God came from, the next logical question would be: Where did "X" come from? This line of questioning would then go on forever, until the skeptic comprehends the concept of "eternality". Just because a scientist cannot grasp eternality doesn't mean that God does not exist. It simply reveals that the scientist has not come to terms with the fact that matter exists today and it had to come from something. Plainly put, something has to have eternal characteristics.

The evidence is adding up for the existence of a Supreme Being—a Being that is outside the normal scope of scientific measurements—**a Being that should change the very way we conduct our lives.** Now one might question why the existence of a Supreme Being would alter our behavior, given that man is superior to insects and that rarely changes their behavior. The answer can be found in the reality that man possesses a consciousness and soul—insects do not. In chapter two, we look at several ways we can prove there is a God. Once you have evaluated the evidence for the existence of an eternal Supreme Being, one is better equipped to answer those nagging questions of life.

Does Your Worldview Contain a Supreme Being?

What is our ultimate purpose in life? From the dawn of man until the present, individuals have been searching for the answer to this question and other major questions of life. The answers to these questions are not altered by your bank account or position at work. It matters not whether you are male or female, young or old. They are questions asked by religious individuals as well as atheists. Mankind has spent years pursuing the answers to:

- Who am I (and what am I worth)?
- Where did I come from?
- Why am I here?
- Where am I going when I die?

How would you answer these questions?

Worldviews

The approach we take to answering these questions is greatly shaped by our **worldview.** Worldview can be defined as the overall perspective from which we view and interpret the world and the events around us. Our worldview is often shaped by our parents, educational experiences, and the environment in which we live.

While many different worldviews exist, below are the five most common:

Naturalism (atheism, agnosticism, existentialism) is the belief that everything around us can be explained through processes of nature. Most who hold this view believe the "scientific method" (hypothesize, predict, measure in laboratory setting, test, repeat results) is the only correct and effective way to evaluate the world around us.

Pantheism (Kabbalistic, Taoism, New Age, Buddhism) is the belief that nature, the universe, and God are one and the same. Any concept of God is normally very abstract. Most of these belief systems view God not in a personal way, but rather as some vague cosmic force.

Theism (Christianity, Judaism, Islam) is the belief in and worship of a supreme deity (monotheism–the belief in one God). Commonly, this form of divinity is considered omniscient, omnipotent, and omnipresent. Simply put, most who hold this view believe that God exists and is able to interact with nature or the universe.

Polytheism (Greek mythology, thousands of religions) is the belief and worship of multiple gods. Firmly held by many Romans and Greeks, this philosophy identifies gods for many material objects (e.g., sun, moon, water, etc.).

Postmodernism (comprised of believers and non-believers) is the philosophical belief that truth cannot be known. This recent belief system urges a change in thinking with the notion that past beliefs (whether theistic, naturalistic, etc.) are incorrect because we have a more complete under-standing. This view holds that dogmatic lines cannot be drawn on things like morals and truth.

Due to the extreme differences in these worldviews, it is easy to understand why there are so many different beliefs and so much confusion out there. University class-rooms are in turmoil as tenured professors feel safe to promote their own personal preferences. **However, is there one worldview that can be considered "correct"?**

Tolerance vs. Intolerance

What makes one worldview better than another? Why should we accept one while rejecting the others? Simply put, if one system is superior to the others, then it should stand up to scrutiny. A thorough examination of the evidence should expose the flaws and inconsistencies of inferior worldviews. **This book will examine the evidence for a <u>theistic worldview</u>**—specifically the Christian religion.

A gentleman once asked me what was so wrong with children being educated about atheism or the Muslim religion in the public school system. If these worldviews and belief systems were correct, then there would be nothing wrong with it—but if not, then he is ultimately asking if I mind if my children learn false doctrine or lies—a false worldview. His question mirrored the sentiments of many living today. Simply put, many people want everyone to be tolerant of everything. In fact, many schools are now teaching that the only real sin is the sin of intolerance. But is tolerance and embracing multiple religions the answer?

> *A thorough study of both Bible and the science reveals that intolerance is not a sin.*

A thorough study of both the Bible and science reveals that intolerance is not a sin. Consider that the very first commandment of the Ten Commandments was "Thou shall have no other gods before Me" (Exodus 20:3). Our God is a jealous God (Exodus 20:5; Deuteronomy 4:24), and He will not tolerate you accepting or embracing other gods. As we look through the Bible, we see multiple examples of individuals who were intolerant of unrighteousness. We know Elijah was intolerant of Jezebel (1 Kings 19). Paul was intolerant of witchcraft books (Acts 19:11-19). Peter was intolerant of the un-repentant Jews (Acts 2:37-39). Jesus, the Son of God, was intolerant of moneychangers making the temple into a den of thieves (Mark 11:15-18). Jehovah God was intoler-ant of the vile homosexual behavior in Sodom and Gomorrah (Genesis 19—Don't forget, He even overthrew the inhabitants of the all the Cities of the Plain: Admah and Zeboim, v. 22 with the exception of Zoar Deu. 29:23). These people didn't embrace the worldviews of those in error. Intolerance is not held captive within the pages of the Bible.

Many of the same people who are crying for mankind to tolerate everything have overlooked examples of intolerance that have utterly reshaped the country in which we live. For instance, what would this country be like if George Washington had toler-ated British troops? Where would we be today if Thomas Jefferson had tolerated King George III? Or what if Fredrick Douglas had tolerated slavery, or Martin Luther King Jr. had tolerated segregation? What would America be like if Winston Churchill had tolerated Adolf Hitler or if Susan B. Anthony tolerated only men voting? **Part of what made these individuals great was that they were strong enough to stand up for their convictions.** They recognized something as "wrong," and they didn't tolerate it.

"I had motives for not wanting the world to have meaning; consequently assumed it had none, and was able without any difficulty to find satisfying reasons for this assumption….The philosopher who finds no meaning in the world is not concerned exclusively with a problem in pure metaphysics; he is also concerned to prove there is no valid reason why he personally should not do as he wants to do…. We objected to the morality because it interfered with our sexual freedom."

–Aldous Huxley, 1966,
Report: News of the Month in Perspective,
Vol. 3, p. 19

This is not a question of tolerance of one person's beliefs versus another's. It is a question of can we discern right from wrong? Can we know where we came from and where we are going? **Can we evaluate the evidence and develop a belief system that is harmonious with the evidence?**

Acceptance of Truth vs. Embracing a Lie

For many, the notion of developing a worldview centered around a Supreme Being is distasteful. To do so requires a healthy dose of humility along with a conscience of right and wrong. Some would rather embrace a lie than even consider the remote possibility that there is indeed a God. Sadly, many individuals have accepted the truth that Darwinian evolution cannot explain the existence of life or the universe, but they have stiffened their necks against the notion of an eternal Supreme Being. Instead, they have adopted a godless worldview in which they can "eat, drink, and be merry."

At what ultimate cost? If indeed there is a Supreme Being whom we should obey, then the consequences of our belief system do not suddenly vanish upon our deaths. Rather, they are held against us at Judgment. Blaise Pascal was a brilliant scientist who helped provide the foundation for fields like hydrostatics and differential calculus. He was also the man who came up with the famous "Pascal Wager," which simply says that if there is no God and you are an atheist, you lose nothing. Likewise, if you are a Christian and there is no God, you lose nothing. But if there is a God and you are an atheist, you lose everything. The question becomes what will you do if the evidence doesn't fit your own personal preference? **This book is not concerned with preferences. It is concerned with stripping away blinders to reveal the Truth. In answering the questions of life, it is time we evaluate the evidence and stop blindly accepting secular propaganda.**

The Importance of Evidence

Today more than ever the word *evidence* is used to defend one's beliefs. Centuries ago, the general populace believed that theologians possessed sufficient evidence and therefore held the answers to their questions. It was during this historical period that many viewed science and medicine as little more than witchcraft. The pendulum has swung and now the majority of individuals place their faith in science, often ridiculing religion. Thanks to help from the mainstream media, the Biblical worldview has been painted as ignorant or radical—a crutch for those who can't handle life. They would espouse that there is insufficient evidence for God. **Nevertheless, the reality is we all have the same evidence. The difference is in the interpretation.** What bias do you bring to the table when you evaluate something? How has your interpretation of the evidence shaped your worldview?

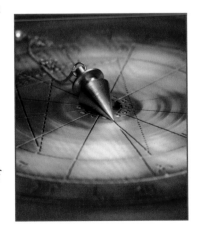

> *Today, most biology textbooks teach organic evolution as fact. At the very foundation of this anti-God theory is the teaching that all living creatures have evolved from a common ancestor.*

Just how important is your worldview? Consider the difference between someone growing up with a God-centered, Biblical worldview versus someone who grows up with a "self-centered," secular worldview. What are some differences that you would expect to see in their perception of the world?

Take a moment and consider how the world influences your worldview. The media is telling you that you need more "stuff." The judicial system is telling you that certain abominations (e.g., abortion, same-sex marriage) are legal. The work force is telling you that climbing the corporate ladder is the only thing of real importance. Scientists are telling you that everything in existence is the result of a Big Bang cosmic explosion, and that man is the product of evolutionary changes over time. However, does any of this coincide with the available evidence? Does it help you answer the questions of life?

Today, most biology textbooks teach organic evolution as fact. At the very foundation of this anti-God theory is the teaching that all living creatures have evolved from a common ancestor that evolved from non-living material. It does not stop with science books. Fingerlike projections from this godless theory have entered into history, English, social studies, civics, and even math books. Suddenly, instead of learning a math problem about two trains leaving the train station at the same time, teens are presented with a math problem that spotlights the evolution of Neanderthal man compared to a timeline of when "Lucy" allegedly roamed the earth. Hiding under the guise of "education," these anti-God beliefs can be found in just about every subject. It is time we are honest with ourselves and admit that many public school classrooms have abandoned true education only to embrace a naturalistic worldview and a teaching style of mindless indoctrination that is hazardous to our children's spiritual well-being.

Children are told repeatedly that one cannot know the Truth. If true, then how would one know that statement is true? Obviously, many philosophers do not comprehend the inspired words found in 1 John 5:13. "These things I have written to you who believe in the name of the Son of God, **that you may know** that you have eternal life, and that you may continue to believe in the name of the Son of God." It is as if activist groups such as the ACLU have corralled Americans onto ships of liberalism and have ferried us to a totally new island—a landscape that does not resemble the America of years gone by. And sadly, many parents and grandparents are so busy looking at the scenery and cramming their new grass huts with wonderful new goods and gadgets that they never realize their children are lost. It is time we examine our world views (and the news being taught to our children) and the consequences of such beliefs.

Conclusion

Something exists today, thus something has always existed.
Does the concept of an Eternal Being fit into your worldview?

Questions:
1. What are some factors that affect your worldview?
2. Consider the question: "How Old is the Earth?" How does your worldview change the answer to that question?
3. What are some examples of individuals who rejected theism in the Bible?
4. What does it mean to have the Word engrafted (James 1:21)?
5. Why is the idea of tolerance so appealing to the world?

Scriptures to Study:
Acts 5:29 • Acts 17:2-3, 11 • Hebrews 5:12 • Jude 3

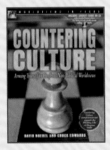

Resources:
Noebel, David and Chuck Edwards (2004), *Countering Culture* (Nashville, TN: B&H Publishing).

Hamken, Britt Beemer and Todd Hillard (2009), *Already Gone* (Green Forest, AR: Master).

References
Burbidge, Geoffrey (1992), "Why Only One Big Bang?," *Scientific American*, February.
Huxley, Aldous (1966), "Confessions of a Professed Atheist," *Report: News of the Month in Perspective.*

"Be still and know I am God.
I will be exalted among the nations,
I will be exalted in the earth!"
— **Psalm 46:10**

Chapter

You Can't Prove Him in a Lab:
The Evidence for the Existence of God

Most individuals can still remember using Bunsen burners in high school science class. While the experiments were often a flop, for many it was the first real taste of the scientific method. The scientific method is often described as a body of techniques that allow for observation of a particular phenomenon. With each passing school year, students are introduced to new ways to measure or observe things. They begin to utilize microscopes and spectrometers. Students discover that the scientific method is used in all fields of science, no matter what type of inquiry or experiment is being made. By their junior year in college, the scientific method has been thoroughly ingrained. The understanding is that if you can't measure it using the five senses and replicate your results, then it is not real. By introducing the scientific method at a young age, students never think to question how this would affect the existence of God. The scientific method is not considered by students as evil or dangerous–and as a tool to acquire knowledge about the observable universe it is not evil. But by the time young people are able to think for themselves, most have bought into the concept that this is the only way to determine whether something is true or not. They have been intimidated into thinking that anyone accepting in something outside the scientific method (e.g., the supernatural) is ignorant. And so by the time they graduate from college, they have placed their allegiance firmly in "science" and are often repelled by the notion of "God."

I doubt that there is any way to accurately gauge the number of pews that remain empty today because of worldly intimidation, doubt, and the scientific method. The forces of atheism, humanism, and evolution have been extremely successful in convincing thousands of people that either God is dead or He never existed in the first place. But is this truly the case? The mainstream media is quick to declare and recycle propaganda against Christianity or the existence of a Creator (e.g. April, 2009 *Newsweek*). A close examination reveals that this is nothing more than poor journalism and misinformation.

This doesn't stop Web sites from boldly declaring that God does not exist and encouraging young people to "live free and responsible—debaptize yourself!" (I've often wondered: Would this require a hair-dryer?) But seriously, our children are taught (sometimes not so subtly), to eat, drink, and be merry—and only be concerned with "self." This paradigm is now being reflected in how young people treat one another and their expectations in life. It is reflected in the physical and emotional health of many humans. A vocal minority of atheists have the media's attention and our children's ears. Sadly, this propaganda has also taken a major toll on God in the courtroom. While black robes and ornate courtrooms cannot diminish or eradicate the existence of God, that has not stopped them from trying.

> *The forces of atheism, humanism, and evolution have been extremely successful in convincing thousands of people that either God is dead, or He never existed in the first place.*

Modern Courts Outlawing God

In the 1892 ruling of the *Church of the Holy Trinity v. United States* (143 U.S. 226), the United States Supreme Court went on record noting that the United States was a "Christian nation." While they were using the term *Christian* very loosely, the point was made that most individuals in the United States identified themselves as believers in God and Jesus Christ. In the 117 years since that declaration was made, the landscape of this great country has changed dramatically. For instance, in 2002, the radically liberal 9th Circuit Court of Appeals in California ruled that the phrase "under God" in the Pledge of Allegiance was unconstitutional. With atheist Michael

Newdow leading the charge, the court observed:

> In the context of the Pledge, the statement that the United States is a nation "under God" is an endorsement of religion. It is a profession of a religious belief, namely a belief in monotheism.... A profession that we are a nation "under God" is identical, for Establishment Clause purposes, to a profession that we are a nation "under Jesus," a nation "under Vishnu," a nation "under Zeus," or a nation "under no god," because none of these professions can be neutral with respect to religion (Judge Alfred T. Goodwin).

Arrayed in black gowns and effusing an air of arrogance, the court single-handedly proclaimed that Jehovah God had not done enough for mankind to be singled out—and as far as they were concerned, He was equal with the Greek god Zeus.

Fast-forward fifteen years, and consider the difference we would face if a similar decision were handed down by our Supreme Court. All public declarations of God, the Bible, or Christianity would have to be removed, including our national motto. Schools would not be the only place from which God is silenced. Military cemeteries would no longer be able to use crosses for headstones. Religious ceremonies for all government officials and military would cease. Public prayers before sporting or civic events would be outlawed. Public crosses or steeples would soon fall under attack. The President would no longer be sworn into office with his hand on the Bible. And if this verdict were handed down by our own Supreme Court, there would be no appeals. In essence, they could proclaim Almighty God dead and gone in the United States.

Enter Atheists Stage Left

One of the reasons atheists have been so successful in emptying church pews is because they have convinced at least two generations that everything must be proven using the scientific method. From an early age, students are taught that if you cannot see, touch, taste, smell, or hear it, then "it" does not exist. Those who have stiffened their necks against God recognize that He exists beyond scientific measure—and thus, our young people feel that it is impossible to prove His existence. Case in point—just before I was to teach 700 students about Christian evidences in a Christian academy, one of the seniors got up and offered a prayer. During his prayer, he made a statement that, while they didn't know for sure God was real and couldn't prove He existed, they had faith and believed in Him. Many Christian parents find themselves dismayed when their children return home from school only to pronounce they no longer believe in a God. They become another statistic and another empty pew. However, the story does not have to end this way.

> *During his prayer, he made a statement that, while they didn't know for sure God was real and couldn't prove He existed, they had faith and believed in Him.*

While it is true that God is a spirit (John 4:24), and we cannot prove His existence using the five senses, we can use other intellectual means, such as logic and reason, to prove His existence. Consider how many church pews would be empty if every single child reared in a Christian home were diligently taught the following proofs for God's existence.

Seven Ways to Prove the Existence of God

1. Every Creation Must Have a Creator (cosmological argument)

It doesn't take a special telescope to prove that the universe exists. An upward glance on a clear night is a concrete reminder of this scientific fact. The reasonable question remains: "From whence did the universe originate?" In reality, there are only three options: (1) it is eternal; (2) it created itself from nothing; or (3) it was created.

Atheists and evolutionists would have students believe that the universe is eternal; however, that does not fit the scientific data. We know today that the universe is expanding, which is a clear indication it had a beginning. As evolutionist Robert Jastrow admitted: "The lingering decline predicted by astronomers for the end of the world differs from the explosive conditions they have calculated for its birth, but the impact is the same: **modern science denies an eternal existence to the universe, either in the past or the future**" (1977, p. 30, emp. added). Even the weak Big Bang theory recognizes the universe had a beginning.

Additionally, any sane, unbiased scientist will further admit that it is ludicrous to suggest that all of the matter in the universe created itself from nothing. It is a self-evident truth that something cannot come from nothing. (If someone wants to argue this fact, I would love to sell him some "nothing.") Since something now exists, this indicates that something has existed forever. These truths leave only one possibility—**the universe was created.** An eight-year-old child can recognize that something now exists. As such, it must follow that something has existed forever. That "something" must therefore be responsible for creating the universe. **That "something" was God.** In 1995, NASA astronomer John O'Keefe declared, "We are, by astronomical standards, a pampered, cosseted, cherished group of creatures.... If the universe had not been made with the most exacting precision we could never have come into existence. It is my view that these circumstances indicate the universe was created for man to live in." (From an interview with Fred Herren in *Show Me God).*

2. Every Design Must Have a Designer (teleological argument)

If design is found in nature, then by definition there must have been a designer. As such, Nobel Laureate Francis Crick, co-discoverer of the molecular structure of DNA, admonished, "Biologists must constantly keep in mind that what they see was not designed, but rather evolved" (as written in *What Mad Pursuit).* The reason they must keep that in mind is because the design we observe today is one more proof that God exists.

Staunch atheist Richard Dawkins observed in his book *The God Delusion*: "Thanks to Darwin, it is no longer true to say that nothing that we know looks designed unless it is designed. Evolution by natural selection produces an excellent simulacrum of design, mounting prodigious heights of complexity and elegance" (2006, p. 79). He goes on to refer to the "pseudo-design" of the nervous system. Then he painstakingly (with utter failure) tries to discount the design observed in unique structures like the wing and eye. While Richard Dawkins claims that small incremental steps—what he deems as climbing "Mount Improbable"—through natural selection explains the design in the universe, the truth is, natural selection is not a "designer."

Consider the design of the earth. How can chance (or Dawkins' "incremental steps") explain the earth's position in the following: (1) the right type of galaxy; (2) the right location within that galaxy; (3) the odds of being near the right sun; (4) being the right distance from the sun; (5) having the right rotation rate and proper tilt; (6) possessing enough water; and (7) having the right atmospheric conditions

to sustain life? And that is just the beginning! For instance, in 1981 *Science Digest* reported that the earth moves in its orbit around the sun, departing from a straight line by only **one-ninth of an inch** every eighteen miles. If it departed by one-eighth of an inch, we would come so close to the sun that we would be incinerated; if it departed by one-tenth of an inch, we would find ourselves so far from the sun that we would all freeze to death. An honest evaluation of the universe quickly reveals design. Design demands a designer. (For more information on design see my book on the design of the human body *Dissecting the Truth*, 2008).

3. Codes Require Someone to Program the Code

Think logically…we spend millions of dollars on the SETI (the Search for Extra-Terrestrial Intelligence) project looking for some type of code or sign of intelligence from outer space. Scientists (i.e. Carl Sagan) contend that any code or signal from space would indicate that there is intelligent life out there. Yet our own DNA is disregarded as just a product of evolution. Our own DNA code, which required more than 13 years, hundreds of labs, and millions of research dollars to unravel is chalked up as merely a byproduct of some cosmological explosion. The very existence of such complex DNA demonstrates that we must have had a code-programmer.

> *Scientists contend that any code or signal from space would indicate that there is intelligent life out there. Yet our own DNA is disregarded as just a product of evolution.*

4. Laws Require a Lawgiver

Anyone reading these words has experienced firsthand natural laws such as the law of momentum. Every morning when we get out of bed, we never question whether our feet will go up or down, thanks in part to the law of gravity. These laws were put into place at creation, and their very existence allows us to live in an ordered and somewhat predictable environment. No one can honestly argue that these laws exist, but the question remains from whence did they come? Laws require a lawgiver. It is illogical to ascribe time and chance as the causative factors for producing these laws. Once again, their very existence points toward a Creator. "There is one Lawgiver, who is able to save and to destroy" (James 4:12).

5. The Law of Cause and Effect

For every material effect, there must be an adequate cause that existed prior to that effect. Imagine walking through the ruins of a massive tornado, only to hear a news reporter blame all of the destruction on a butterfly that was flying out of control. No one in his right mind would believe such foolishness. A butterfly is not an adequate cause to leave that kind of effect. The universe exists, so the question becomes what was the cause? Hebrews 3:4 records, "For every house is built by someone, but He who built all things is God." Some might question, "Alright, then what was the cause of God?" As stated earlier, this scientific law demands that for every material (or physical) effect there must be an adequate cause. God is a spirit and is therefore not bound by this law.

6. The Existence of Morals (anthropological argument)

Mankind, unlike the animals, has a moral code. Where did it come from? Imagine visiting more than ten different island populations who were completely isolated from one another…and learning that they all possessed laws regarding murder and adultery. Furthermore, each group viewed things like lying and stealing as wrong. Where did these independent groups come up with such a similar moral code?

It is impossible for matter—by itself—to evolve a system of moral "right" and "wrong." Yet, man recognizes right and wrong. The question then arises, from whence did morals originate? One of the very first questions I routinely ask atheists with whom I correspond is, "Would you have a problem if I came to your house, murdered your family, and robbed you blind?" Without fail, every single one has answered in the affirmative—this behavior would be wrong. In 1967, George Gaylord Simpson admitted, "Morals arise only in man." However, in order for something to be "right" or "wrong," there must be an absolute standard for morality. What is that standard? There are really only two options that could adequately explain the existence of morals—either they were conjured up and created by man, or they originated from God.

Why are these behaviors recognized as wrong?
Lying, Stealing, Rape, Pedophilia, Assault,
Abortion, Cheating, Killing, Beastiality, Arson,
Drunk Driving, Infanticide

Consider the plight of an atheist. They are forced to admit morals exist—otherwise they wouldn't have a problem with your murdering their family members. However, they refuse to acknowledge a belief in God. As such, they **must** contend that morals arose from man. The question then becomes who gets to decide which behaviors are right and which are wrong? For instance, Hitler felt annihilating Jews was right. Isn't evolution all about the "survival of the fittest?" So if I decide a certain behavior will allow me to survive better, shouldn't I participate in it—even if it hurts you? For instance, what would be the problem with slicing a coworker's tires before an interview if both individuals were applying for the same job?

The only option that makes logical sense is that humans have adopted God's standard for right and wrong. God's unchanging nature allows our morals to be

"My road to atheism was paved by science . . . . But, ironically, so was my later journey to God."

– Journalist/author Lee Strobel, 2004, *The Case for the Creator.*

recognized as absolute standards for all situations. Only God is eternal (Psalm 90:2; 1 Timothy 1:17). Only God is holy (Isaiah 6:3; Revelation 4:8). Only God is just and righteous (Psalm 89:14). And only God is forever consistent (Malachi 3:6). The existence of a worldwide system of morals is excellent proof that God exists.

7. Communication Requires a Communicator

Consider that every single day humans all over the world look at symbols (which we call letters) and use those symbols to form words. We then string those words together in both the written and spoken form—allowing humans to communicate and build on knowledge. How is it that man is the only animal with this unique ability? In fact, a quick examination of Genesis 2 reveals that God created man with the ability to communicate before Eve was even created. Communication is yet one more example that there is a God.

The Ballots Are In

While individuals may not want to accept that there is a God, the evidence points to the contrary. The question is not "what do you and I prefer or desire," but rather, what we can know. The seven evidences above prove there is an eternal God who played a major role in creating the earth and mankind. While one might be able to dismiss one or two of the evidences above with some mental gymnastics, an honest heart seeking the truth recognizes there is far too much evidence for God's existence to ignore. This evidence demands a voice in our society and a response.

Conclusion

I've heard it said many times that it takes more faith to be an atheist than a Christian. Given the amount of evidence we have for God, I would agree. Ask yourself: "Do I have enough faith to be an atheist?"

Brad Stine once mused: "Who is more irrational? A man who believes in a God he doesn't see, or a man who's offended by a God he doesn't believe in?" I would take that even one step further: "Who is more irrational? A Christian who believes in a God but doesn't teach his child about Him, or an atheist who doesn't believe in Him but takes the time to teach the child his beliefs?"

God does exist. All of the best-sellers in the world espousing otherwise will not change that fact. But if we really expect our children to believe and follow the One True Living God, we must start thinking outside the box! Sadly, the atheists of this country are doing their job better than we Christian parents are. It's time someone states the obvious: What we've done in the past hasn't worked. If you do not believe this, just walk into a church building and inquire if anyone there has children who have abandoned the Faith. But be prepared—the line that forms before you may be much longer than you ever expected. Far too many young people are leaving the Church only to turn around and embrace secular humanism, or even worse, atheism.

Now think: How many of those children who have left the Church can name most of the state capitals? How many of those children know the value for pi, *or how to solve for* x *in an algebra problem? How many of those children can name bones of the body or describe the water cycle? How many of those children know every word to their favorite songs or can tell you verbatim lines from their favorite movie? How many of those children have studied for hours to take tests over meaningless material? As you sit there considering how much time these young people have spent cramming for standardized tests, ask yourself this one simple question: How much time have they spent actually studying Christian evidences or logical arguments to prove God's existence? If we are going to reverse this trend, we must start thinking outside the box as to what is "normal." It's time we expect more from ourselves and more from our children. Their worldview is hanging in the balance.*

Questions:

1. Why do young people today need evidence for Christianity more than in times past?
2. What can the average Christian do in an effort to defend the existence of God?
3. Why is it illogical to believe in an eternal or self-creating universe?

Scriptures to Study
Hebrews 3:4 • Colossians 1:16 • Isaiah 42:5

Additional Resources

Geisler, Norman and Ronald M. Brooks (1990), *Come Let Us Reason* (Ada, MI: Baker).

Geisler, Norman and Frank Turek (2004), *I Don't Have Enough Faith to be an Atheist* (Wheaton IL, Crossway).

Strobel, Lee (2005), *The Case for a Creator* (Grand Rapids, MI, Zondervan).

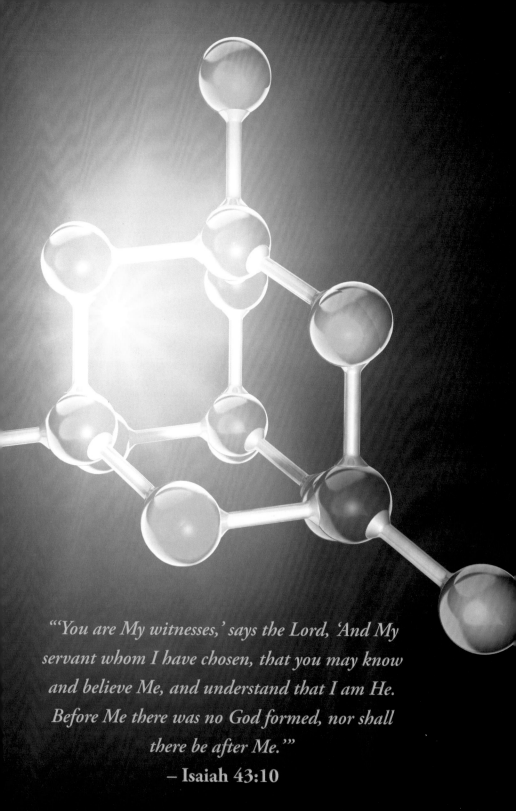

"'You are My witnesses,' says the Lord, 'And My servant whom I have chosen, that you may know and believe Me, and understand that I am He. Before Me there was no God formed, nor shall there be after Me.'"

– Isaiah 43:10

Chapter

One God, a Multitude of Gods, or No God?

There was a peculiar trend throughout my training as a scientist. During my initial undergraduate years, as I sat through General Biology and General Chemistry classes, I remember studying large textbooks that spoke in generalities and gave credit to evolution for the origin of living things. However, as my scientific training continued and narrowed, my textbooks remained large (and expensive!), but they would focus on only one particular field-for instance, neurobiology—demonstrating the complexity and diversity in science. Then, as I pursued my doctorate, the textbooks were still incredibly long and detailed, but at this stage they were only dealing with one aspect of a particular system. For instance, I had an entire textbook devoted to nerve cells. The following year I had a single textbook detailing the synaptic transmission between two nerve cells, and another one on ionic channels within nerve cells. The closer we looked at something, the more complex it became. There was never a point in my training that we reached "the basement floor" in which a small structure was completely known and understood. Even with the advent of the electron microscope, we realize that we have only touched the "hem of the garment" in how complex living structures really are. Alone in a lab and "off the record," many of my professors would admit that the complexity we were observing was beyond the realm of cosmological chance. They recognized that the design we were seeing demanded a designer.

If the evidence points toward a designer, then why hasn't everyone embraced Him? Why is there is a new militant atheistic movement taking place in the country? Part of the answer is pride. Another reason has to do with the tremendous job that atheists and evolutionists have done in conning students. The father of a young seventeen-year-old approached me recently concerned that his son was struggling with the very existence of God. Here was a young man reared in the New Testament Church who had "bought into" the secular argument that if you cannot see it, touch it, taste it, smell it, or hear it, then "it" does not exist. However, we know that according to John 4:24, God is a spirit. You can't measure a "spirit" in the lab. We know something exists today, thus something has always existed. We have logical arguments that prove the design we see around us demands a designer. So what about this Being we call Jehovah—what do modern-day individuals need to know about God?

> *Here was a young man reared in the New Testament Church who had "bought into" the secular argument that if you cannot see it, touch it, taste it, smell it, or hear it, then "it" does not exist.*

Not a Problem in the Past

While we do not often think about it, proving the existence of God is a relatively new challenge in the history of mankind. Adam and Eve never wrestled with the question of God's existence because they were privileged to see Him walk through the garden in the cool of the day (Genesis 3:8). Cain heard the voice of the Lord after slaying Abel (Genesis 4:9-10). God spoke directly to Noah and gave him specific directions on how to construct the ark (Genesis 6:14-16). The Lord made a promise to Abraham (Genesis 12:1-3), and spoke to Moses through a burning bush (Exodus 3). He revealed Himself through fleece to Gideon (Judges 6:36-40), and through prophets like Jeremiah, Isaiah, Ezekiel, and Daniel. Those living during the time of Christ could have witnessed first-hand the miracles performed by the Son of God or the Apostles.

A reminder of this was given by the writer of Hebrews, who began his epistle, "God, who at various times and in various ways spoke in time past to the fathers by the prophets, has in these last days spoken to us by His Son, who He has appointed heir of all things, through whom also He made the worlds" (Hebrews 1:1). With the Bible—the inspired Word of God, as we will prove later—completed, God no longer talks to men directly, but rather He speaks to us today through the Bible. This change in dynamics has not changed who God is, or His love for mankind. Many believe that this "hands-off" approach is evidence against a loving God. However, a scholarly examination of Biblical history reveals that mankind today has access to the entire revelation of the scheme of redemption.

Ironically, even though many talked with Him or heard His voice in times past, it did not keep them from straying away or worshipping false gods. In fact, Biblical history records several cycles of men falling away to worship idols. So what makes one God better than other gods?

All Gods or Almighty God

Consider the first four of the Ten Commandments were vertical–dealing with our relationship to God. They were being penned by the finger of God (Exodus 31:18), and emphasized God and worshipping only Him (Exodus 20:1-6). The text reminds us that He is a jealous God (Exodus 20:5). These commands were well warranted. Having just given Moses the two stone tablets "of the Testimony," we find the people commanding Aaron to make a god—eventually bowing down before a golden calf (Exodus 32).

Within the pages of God's Word, we find a multitude of false gods, such as:
Molech (Leviticus 18:21)
Dagon (Judges 16:23; 1 Samuel 5:2-3)
Baal (Judges 2:11-13; 6:20-28)
Ashtoreth (Judges 10:6; 1 Samuel 12:10)
Merodach (Jeremiah 50:1-3)
Zeus (Acts 14:13; Acts 19:35)

"I was reminded of this a few months ago when I saw a survey in the journal *Nature*. It revealed that 40% of American physicists, biologists and mathematicians believe in God–and not just some metaphysical abstraction, but a deity who takes an active interest in our affairs and hears our prayers: the God of Abraham, Isaac and Jacob."

– Jim Holt, "Science Resurrects God," *The Wall Street Journal,* December 24, 1997.

However, when Moses and the children sang a song to Jehovah, they observed, "Who is like You, O Lord, among the gods? Who is like You, glorious in holiness, fearful in praises, doing wonders?" (Exodus 15:11). These false gods paled in comparison to the true holiness of the Almighty.

One might ask, why not embrace a multitude of gods—after all, society often tells us that more is better? **But is it really worth our time, and does a multitude of gods draw us closer in answering the basic questions of life?** In declaring the foolishness of idolatry, the prophet Isaiah recorded, "Who hath formed a god, or molten a graven image that is profitable for nothing?" (Isaiah 44:10, KJV). The inspired psalmist observed, "For the Lord is great and greatly to be praised; He is to be feared above all gods. For all the gods of the peoples are idols, but the Lord made the heavens" (Psalm 96:4-5). **The truth of the matter is that any belief system that requires a multitude of gods does not worship an all-powerful god.** If God can do everything, then why would He need "assistant" gods? How foolish is it that some religions require multiple gods?

The claim has been made that you can indict anything, even a ham sandwich. Likewise, people can fall down and worship anything. History records mankind worshipping everything from animals, plants, and weather to heavenly bodies. The question should arise: Who (or what) was responsible for making the animals, plants, weather, and heavenly bodies in the first place? A true evaluation of the evidence indicates that there must be an eternal source to which everything else owes its very existence. That single entity is the Almighty God. As Jehovah proclaimed: "Before Me there was no God formed, nor shall there be after Me. I, even I, am the Lord, and besides Me there is no savior" (Isaiah 43:10-11).

The Warning Against False Gods

From the time of Adam, Eve, Cain, and Abel, it has been obvious that God expects certain things from His creation. I fear that society as a whole has overlooked or forgotten these expectations. As God was handing down the Mosaic Law, He made sure the people knew they were to "have no other gods before Me" (Exodus 20:3). Like a patient parent, God has warned mankind repeatedly against the error of worshipping false gods.

The book of Deuteronomy holds the distinction of being the last sermons preached by Moses to that second generation, who had been wandering in the wilderness. The word *Deuteronomy* comes from a combination of two Greek words *deuteros* meaning second and *nomas* for law or commandment. Thus, this was the second reading of the Mosaic Law. We learn in the first chapter that these events occurred at the end of the wandering period. "Now it came to pass in the fortieth year, in the eleventh month, on the first day of the month, that Moses spoke to the children of

Israel according to all that the Lord had given him as commandments to them" (Deuteronomy 1:3). It spanned a period of only two months. Moses preached for one month and reminded this second generation all that they needed to know in order to remain faithful in the eyes of the Lord. And then upon the death of Moses, the people mourned for one month (Deuteronomy 34:8). In Deuteronomy, the Israelites were warned: "And there you will serve gods, the work of men's hands, wood and stone, which neither see nor hear nor eat nor smell" (4:28). The warning against idolatry continued in Deuteronomy 29:18: "So that there may not be among you man or woman or family or tribe, whose heart turns away today from the Lord our God, to go and serve the gods of these nations." However, this warning is not limited to the Mosaic Law.

In Acts 20:30 Paul warned elders, "Also from among yourselves men will rise up speaking perverse things, to draw away disciples after themselves." The admonition of knowing truth and rejecting falsehoods is repeated in 1 John 5:21: "Little children, keep yourselves from idols. Amen." However, the whole matter can be summed up in Paul's letter to the church at Ephesus. He declared, "There is one body and one Spirit, just as you were called in one hope of your calling; **one Lord**, one faith, one baptism; **one God** and Father of all, who is above all, and through all, and in you all" (Ephesians 4:4-6, emp. added).

Ah, But I'm a Christian—I Don't Practice Idolatry...

Oftentimes when we consider idolatry, we envision foreign religions such as the Hindus who embrace a multiplicity of gods. We raise our collective noses at such foolishness. After all, we would never practice such idolatry. Or would we?

> *This may sound narrow or intolerant to some, but if the Bible is <u>God's</u> word then it must be a truth statement.*

In Colossians 3:5 Paul wrote, "Therefore put to death your members which are on the earth: fornication, uncleanness, passion, evil desire, and **covetousness, which is idolatry**" (emp. added). Do modern-day Christians have a problem with covetousness? Is it possible that instead of bowing down to Molech or Zeus that we bow down to an automobile in our garage, an expensive entertainment system, a home in the perfect neighborhood, a 401K, or diamonds? Consider the attitude of many in our society when the economy took a dive.

Do we have a problem with covetousness? The phrase "keeping up with the Joneses" has become a familiar motto, as many families tune into the Home and Garden network to see what additions they should be making on their homes to keep up with the neighbors. My generation is so skilled at keeping up with the Joneses that we expected to start our marriages where our parents were when we moved out. Even though it may have taken 35 years for our parents to amass all of their physical possessions, we expected to have it all within six months. So we strapped ourselves with debt; we purchased new homes, new cars, new furniture, and new "toys." Our marriages began to crumble under financial strain. We couldn't give anything back to the Church because we didn't have anything. But we sure could keep up with the Joneses! Maybe it is time for us to refocus our priorities on the One True Living God. While we don't have idols to Baal or Dagon in our homes today, I would encourage you to consider what idols your children see on a regular basis. It may be that we are bowing down to a different list today, such as:

Jewelry • Lexus • Bose • Marble • Sony

Remember, anything that comes in between man and God or takes God's place is considered an idol.

Characteristics of God

We can prove He exists, but who (or what) is He? In teaching future generations about the nature of God, we need to give careful consideration to His attributes and His qualities that are found in the Bible. Sadly, many people who claim to be "believers" have recast God into only a loving, grandfatherly-like figure. Yes, God loves us—we are the pinnacle of His creation (Genesis 1:26-27), and He lovingly sacrificed

His own Son for our sins (John 3:16). But this does not mean that God will overlook sin (Galatians 6:7), or subdue His wrath against disobedience (Ephesians 5:6). In order to love and obey the heavenly Father, we need to fully comprehend His all-powerful nature. Fear of God is the beginning of knowledge (Proverbs 1:8; Psalm 33:8).

James Denney, a Scottish preacher/teacher/theologian, used to warn his students against thinking they could learn all there was to know about God during their university and seminary studies. "Gentlemen," he would tell them, "to study infinity requires eternity." His point is well taken. **It would be impossible to give every characteristic of God in just a few short paragraphs.** However, thanks to His Word, we can acquire a better portrait of who God really is. Consider the following brief survey:

God Is Eternal

God is the only eternal being—He has been called the Alpha and the Omega. If there were a time in which absolutely nothing existed, then we can rest assured nothing would exist today. Moses wrote, "There is no one like the God of Jeshurun, who rides the heavens to help you, and in His Excellency on the clouds. The **eternal** God is your refuge, and underneath are the everlasting arms; He will thrust out the enemy from before you" (Deuteronomy 33:27, emp. added). God literally set time into motion—having been here before time began. One of the hardest concepts for individuals to grasp is that God is eternal.

God Is the Creator

Even though atheism, evolution, and humanism are actively promoted within schools and the media, the complexity of life clearly points to God as Creator. Evolution cannot explain how life allegedly evolved from non-life, or how irreducibly complex systems could have arisen from some cosmological accident. The most logical explanation is that God created the heavens and the earth precisely as it is described in His Word. The inspired psalmist described the creation in the following manner: "By the word of the Lord the heavens were made, and all the host of them by the breath of His mouth.... For He spoke and it was done, He commanded and it stood fast" (Psalm 33:6, 9). We can also read, "Let them praise the name of the Lord, for He commanded and they were created"

(Psalm 148:5). Moses wrote, "For in six days the Lord made the heavens and the earth, the sea, and all that is in them, and rested the seventh day. Therefore the Lord blessed the Sabbath day and hallowed it" (Exodus 20:11). God is the Creator and giver of life (Acts 17:28-29). Indeed, everything around us is a product of His handiwork.

> *Even though atheism, evolution, and humanism are actively promoted within schools and the media, the complexity of life clearly points to God as Creator.*

God Is Alive

During natural disasters or times of crisis, many individuals question the existence of God. Many would argue either that He never existed, or that He is now dead. Inspired Biblical writers confirmed otherwise. "There it shall be said to them, you are the sons of the **living God**" (Hosea 1:10, emp. added). "Beware, brethren, lest there be in any of you an evil heart of unbelief in departing from the **living God**" (Hebrews 3:12, emp. added). Jesus, in responding to the Sadducees, observed: "But concerning the resurrection of the dead, have you not read what was spoken to you by God, saying, 'I am the God of Abraham, the God of Isaac, and the God of Jacob'? God is not the God of the dead, but of the living" (Matthew 22:31-32). Additionally, we know that, unlike human beings who are clothed in a mortal fleshly body, God is a living spirit. "But the hour is coming, and now is, when the true worshipers will worship the Father in spirit and truth; for the Father is seeking such to worship Him. God is Spirit, and those who worship Him must worship Him in spirit and truth" (John 4:23-24). The eternal nature of God demands we are the servants of a living God.

God Is Love

Thanks to God's incredible love (1 John 4:8), humanity has been endowed with free will (see Genesis 2:15-17; Joshua 24:15; Isaiah 7:15; John 5:39-40; 7:17; Revelation 22:17). We read, "Beloved, let us love one another, for love is of God; and everyone who loves is born of God and knows God. He who does not love does not know God, for God is love. In this the love of God was manifested toward us, that God has sent His only begotten Son into the world, that we might live through Him.

In this is love, not that we loved God, but that He loved us and sent His Son to be the propitiation for our sins" (1 John 3:7-10). His love has also provided a means of salvation for all men (John 3:16; Hebrews 5:9). In addition, His love can strengthen and sustain faithful men (Matthew 6:26-33). The love of God has been demonstrated for **all** men. One cannot read the account of the crucifixion without coming to the knowledge of just how much God loves humanity.

God Is Holy

After Isaiah described the Lord and the seraphim surrounding Him, he concluded: "Woe is me, for I am undone! Because I am a man of unclean lips, and I dwell in the midst of a people of unclean lips" (Isaiah 6:5). We know that God is holy (1 Peter 1:16) and that sin separates man from God (Isaiah 59:1-2). The holiness of God is frequently referenced in the Bible. The inspired psalmist observed, "But You are holy, enthroned in the praises of Israel" (22:3). Additionally, we read, "Exalt the Lord our God, and worship at His footstool—He is holy" (Psalm 99:3). The prophet Isaiah noted: "But the Lord of hosts shall be exalted in judgment, and God who is holy shall be hallowed in righteousness" (Isaiah 5:16). He also stated, "Thus says the Lord, your Redeemer, the Holy One of Israel: 'For your sake I will send to Babylon, and bring them all down as fugitives—the Chaldeans, who rejoice in their ships. I am the Lord, your Holy One, the Creator of Israel, your King'" (Isaiah 43:14-15). Moses wrote, "For I am the Lord your God. You shall therefore consecrate yourselves and you shall be holy; for I am holy" (Leviticus 11:44). The acknowledgement of the holiness of God is one of the first keys to obedience.

> *One cannot read the account of the crucifixion without coming to the knowledge of just how much God loves humanity.*

God Is Longsuffering

Thankfully, the Lord is also longsuffering. We read, "And the Lord passed before him [Moses-BH] and proclaimed, 'The Lord, the Lord God, merciful and gracious and long-suffering, and abounding in goodness and truth'" (Exodus 34:6). Moses also recorded: "The Lord is longsuffering and abundant in mercy, forgiving iniquity and transgression"

(Numbers 14:18). This characteristic is reiterated in the New Testament: "The Lord is not slack concerning His promise, as some count slackness, but is longsuffering toward us, not willing that any should perish but that all should come to repentance" (2 Peter 3:9). He truly wants all men to be faithful servants.

God Is Just

Fortunately, God is a righteous judge. Unlike some judges adorning courtroom benches today, God cannot be bought, swayed, or tricked. Revelation 16:7 records: "And I heard another from the altar saying, 'Even so, Lord God Almighty, true and righteous are Your judgments.'" Additionally, God is not a respecter of persons. In Acts 10:34-35 we read, "Then Peter opened his mouth and said: 'In truth I perceive that God shows no partiality.'" It is this just God whom we will stand before on that appointed day (Hebrews 9:27) and face judgment (1 John 4:17). His judgment will be just and final—something that we should all reflect upon daily.

God Is Omniscient (all-knowing)

In accordance with His judgment, we need to fully comprehend that He is all-knowing. The psalmist wrote, "He counts the number of the stars; He calls them all by name. Great is our Lord, and mighty in power. His understanding is infinite" (Psalm 147:4-5). In the New Testament we find that "known to God from eternity are all His works" (Acts 15:18). Nothing is hidden from the eyes of the Lord. The writer of the book of Hebrews observed, "And there is no creature hidden from His sight, but all things are naked and open to the eyes of Him to whom we must give account" (4:13). These words should be extremely sobering to those who do things in secret, thinking they will never have to give an account of evil doings.

God Is Omnipresent (present everywhere)

Additionally, God is everywhere (Jeremiah 23:23-24). Well-known English deist Anthony Collins once asked a man, "Is your God a great or a little God?" The man replied, "He is both, sir." Collins asked, "How can he be both?" To which the young man noted, "He is so great that the heaven of heavens cannot contain Him; and so little that He can dwell in my heart." Collins later declared that this simple answer had more effect on his mind than all the volumes he had ever read about God. The inspired psalmist noted: "Where can I go from Your spirit? Or where can I flee from Your presence? If I ascend to heaven, You are there. If I make my bed in hell (Sheol), behold, You are there. If I take the wings of the morning, and dwell in the uttermost parts of the sea, even there Your hand shall lead me, and Your right hand shall lead me" (Psalm 139:7-10). Indeed, He is everywhere.

God Is Omnipotent (all-powerful)
Toward the end of the book of Job, we find God questioning Job about His creation and His power (see Job chapters 38-41). Afterwards, Job remarks, "I know that You can do everything, and that no purpose of Yours can be withheld from You" (42:2). The only limits on God's power are those things that go against His very nature. Jesus reminded us, "With men this is impossible, but with God all things are possible" (Matthew 19:26). In the New Testament we read, "Alleluia! For the Lord God omnipotent reigns!" (Revelation 19:6). The inspired psalmist inquired, "O Lord God of hosts, Who is mighty like You, O Lord?" (Psalm 89:8). Is anything too hard for God (Jeremiah 32:27)? God alone has the power to conquer sin and death.

> *The promises made to first century Christians are still applicable to Christians living today. For God does not change!*

God Is Immutable (unchanging)
The perfection of God demands that He is unchanging—because all change must be for better or worse, and God is already perfection. There is no need to change. That should be reassuring to those who are obedient to His Word. The promises God has made to us will be kept (Hebrews 6:17-18). In Malachi 3:6 we read, "For I am the Lord, I do not change." James observed, "Every good gift and every perfect gift is from above, and comes down from the Father of lights, **with whom there is no variation or shadow of turning**" (1:17, emp. added). Christians should find comfort in knowing that the God of Moses, Abraham, and Jacob is the same God we worship and praise today. The promises made to first century Christians are still applicable to

Christians living today. For God does not change!

This has not even touched the hem of the garment on the nature of God, but one can rest assured that an accurate portrait of God produces knowledge and obedience.

Why Not God?

So why do intelligent people often abhor the notion of praising and worshipping their Almighty Creator? **The answer in a single word is pride.** Now that's not to say other excuses such as money, fame, rebellion, etc. don't exist. But when you boil it all down, the psalmist was correct: "The fool has said in his heart, 'There is no God.' They are corrupt, they have done abominable works, there is none who does good. The Lord looks down from heaven upon the children of men, to see if there are any who understand, who seek God" (Psalm 14:1-2).

With leaders such as Richard Dawkins, Daniel Dennett, and Christopher Hitchens, the atheistic movement has waged war on Christianity. In his book *God is Not Great*, Christopher Hitchens declared, "Religion spoke its last intelligible or noble or inspiring words a long time ago," (2007, p. 7) and he concluded, "Religion poisons everything" (p. 13). Likewise, Richard Dawkins in his book *The God Delusion* affirmed: "I am attacking God, all gods, anything and everything supernatural, wherever and whenever they have been or will be invented" (2006, p. 36). In his book *Darwin's Dangerous Idea*, Daniel Dennett addressed parents who would teach their children something other than organic evolution: "Those of us who have freedom of speech will feel free to describe your teachings as the spreading of falsehoods, and will attempt to demonstrate this to your children at our earliest opportunity" (1995, p. 519). The pressure to reject God has not slowed down—and if outward appearances are any indicator, things are likely to get worse before they get better.

This behavior is nothing new. For centuries people have been turning their backs on Jehovah. Consider the numerous Biblical examples of the Israelites turning their

"It is an interesting view of atheism, a sort of 'crutch' for those who can't stand the reality of God."

– British playwright
Tom Stoppard

backs on God or worshipping idols. In Deuteronomy we read, "For they are a nation void of counsel, nor is there any understanding in them" (32:28). These were individuals who were "blessed," and yet they turned their backs on their Creator. As such, God continued to lay forth His reasoning as to why Israel would not be spared: "For their vine is of the vine of Sodom and of the fields of Gomorrah. Their grapes are grapes of gall. Their clusters are bitter. Their wine is the poison of serpents, and the cruel venom of cobras. Is this not laid up in store with Me, sealed up among My treasures? Vengeance is Mine, and recompense. **Their foot shall slip in due time, for the day of their calamity is at hand**, and the things to come hasten upon them" (Deuteronomy 32:32-35, emp. added).

God had warned this special group of people in Deuteronomy 18 to avoid wicked customs. In Leviticus 18, we also find Jehovah warning the Israelites against strange customs. God concluded by saying, "Therefore you shall keep My ordinance, so that you do not commit any of these **abominable customs** which were committed before you, and that you do not defile yourselves by them: I am the Lord your God" (Leviticus 18:30, emp. added). Yet, the Israelites continued to forge a pathway to destruction.

> *How long will we allow our pride and rebellion to separate us from our Creator?*

A review of God's Word quickly reveals the specifics of these abominable customs. Listed among these "customs" were practices like idolatry, adultery, killing children, and sexual immorality. In addition, they were warned against using mediums and bad judges. When one turns the mirror of God's Word back upon the United States, it becomes obvious that many individuals are following a similar pattern and committing some of these same abominable customs. How long will we allow our pride and rebellion to separate us from our Creator?

But What About Those Innocent People Who Don't Know About God?

One of the arguments that skeptics and even Christians often pose is "What about the poor innocent Aborigines in Australia?" How can they be held accountable to God if they don't know He exists? Is God really going to send the "poor innocent Aborigine" to Hell—even though they have never heard the Good News of Jesus Christ? Furthermore, is He really going to send millions of innocent people to Hell just because they have not obeyed the Gospel? While I won't judge the motives of the individual asking the questions, I am inclined to believe that this question is often used as a deflection or an escape tactic by those who do not want to humble themselves before Almighty God.

First, I should be clear that I have never met a "poor innocent Aborigine" from Australia or any other country. The key word there is "innocent." Innocence would indicate this person has never sinned and is therefore not in need of the cleansing blood of Jesus Christ. The Bible clearly indicates, "All have sinned and fall short of the glory of God" (Romans 3:23; cf. 1 John 1:8-10). So we can safely know that every person of an accountable age on this planet has at some point sinned—an act that separates us from God (Isaiah 59:2).

Second, the sad fact is that there are people on this planet who have never heard the Gospel. While the Bible indicates that in times past all men heard the Good News (Colossians 1:23; Matthew 24:14), we know today that many generations have passed since that declaration. Sadly, the population has been steadily increasing while the zeal and evangelistic efforts of many Christians have been steadily decreasing.

So what then of the poor "sinful" Aborigine? Do they get a free pass to Heaven? Absolutely not! The inspired Word of God indicates that sin separates us from God, and therefore they too are separated. But what about that word *innocent*? Are they truly innocent? Could ancient tribes of Indians, or children reared in a predominately Hindu culture grow up on this planet and never see evidence of a Supreme Being? In other words, can someone know God exists without being taught? Again, I believe the Bible addresses this as well.

In Romans 1:18-20, Paul is discussing the wrath of God on those who are unrighteous. In verses 19-20, he wrote, "Because what may be known of God is manifest in them, for God has shown it to them. For since the creation of the world His **invisible attributes** are clearly seen, being understood by the things that are made, **even** His eternal power and Godhead, **so that they are without excuse**" (emp. added). Paul was telling those Christians in Rome that God's invisible attributes have been clearly seen since the creation of the world. He then stresses that even His eternal power and Godhead can be understood. But notice the last phrase: "So that they are without excuse."

While many people living in America today are counting on playing the "ignorance" card on the Day of Judgment, Paul tells us that it is not going to work! It's not enough to say to God, "If only I had known. If only You had given me a sign." Paul reveals that those signs have been around literally since creation! Paul, in essence, has stripped away the excuse that millions of people are counting on for that Great Day.

> *Since my children were little, I have taught them that their number one goal in life (above everything else) is to get to Heaven.*

This truth does not give me any pleasure, and it certainly does not rest easy on my mind. In fact, I believe it places a tremendous burden on those of us who know the Truth. Since my children were little, I have taught them that their number one goal in life (above everything else) is to get to Heaven. The second goal in life that I am trying to instill in my children is that we are to take as many people as we can with us to Heaven. **Only when we realize just how many individuals around us are in a lost condition will the importance of this goal be fully comprehended.**

As further evidence that God can be known, the inspired Psalmist observed, "The heavens declare the glory of God; and the firmament shows His handiwork" (Psalm 19:1). The implication is that the existence of God can be known through His creation.

I think it is important that our children recognize that prior to the birth of Jesus, millions of people were guilty of rejecting God—not Christ, because He was not here yet. Thus, several generations of people were judged guilty by God not for rejecting Christ, but for rejecting Him. God expected these people to come to know Him and ultimately obey Him. Where does this judgment leave those "Aborigines" who are also rejecting Him today?

Conclusion

From these simple points, we can know that all humans have sinned and that our iniquities have separated us from God. We can further know that the existence and power of God can be known simply through His creation. Yes, many people (like the militant atheists of today) will suppress that truth, but this does not negate the fact. Now back to the individual living in the backcountry of some third world country, or the millions who have not obeyed the Truth. What is their fate? Is it hopeless for them? Again, we must turn to God's Word. In Deuteronomy 4:29 Moses wrote, "But from there you will seek the Lord your God, and you will find Him if you seek Him with all of your heart and with all of your soul." This proclamation is confirmed in Jeremiah 29:13, "And you will seek Me and find Me, when you search with all your heart." Those who desire to know the Truth will learn the Truth.

Questions:
1. Why is it illogical to assume there are multiple gods?
2. What was the cycle of the Israelites during the period of the kings?
3. What are some practical applications that you can work on to prevent idolatry (covetousness)?
4. Discuss some modern examples of and reasons for people rejecting God.
5. What religions are you aware of that embrace multiple gods? Give two Scriptural examples of why this is incorrect.

Scriptures to Study:
Romans 1:18-20 • Exodus 20:1-11 • Colossians 3:5 • Isaiah 43:10-11

Additional Resources:

McFarland, Alex (2007), *X: The 10 Most Common Objections to Christianity* (Ventura, CA: Regal).

Chesser, Frank (2004), *Portrait of God* (Huntsville, AL: Publishing Designs).

"O my lord, if the Lord is with us,
why then has all this happened to us?"
– **Judges 6:13**

Chapter

The Problem of Evil, Pain, and Suffering

Tyler laid on his bed with tears streaming down his face. He knew life would never be the same. His mind flashed back to the previous day, and all he could think about was, "If only we had spent more time at the gas station." But they hadn't. They had quickly filled up the tank and headed on down the road. It had been less than twenty-four hours since he had jerked the wheel and skidded off the road to avoid a deer standing on the highway. The last thing Tyler remembered was trying to correct the steering wheel and hearing the horrendous crunching sound of metal against a tree. The next few hours were a blur, as emergency vehicles and onlookers surrounded the scene. Eventually, LifeFlight helicopter landed on the highway in an effort to get his lone passenger and best friend Andrew to the hospital quicker. But the damage had already been done. Andrew had been ejected from the car during the wreck and his head hit a tree with deadly force. Tyler walked away with just a few scrapes and cuts. Andrew was pronounced dead upon arrival at the hospital. Three hours ago, doctors had received permission to harvest his organs, and now Andrew's cold, lifeless body was lying in the morgue.

As Tyler sat on his bed, a whole host of emotions ran through his head. He was numb with grief. But he was also mad. Why did this have to happen? He and Andrew were good kids, both growing up in Christian homes. They hadn't been drinking and they weren't speeding. Why didn't God help Andrew when he needed it most? Or why didn't He move that stupid deer off the road before they got to that point in the road? Tyler's tears were mixed with confusion as he thought about Andrew and the fact that he would never graduate, go to college, or get married. Tyler could not even fathom looking Andrew's parents in the eyes ever again. The pain was too raw and too deep. The whole thing just didn't seem fair. Tyler just kept thinking, "How can a loving God allow such a horrible thing to happen to good people? Why did He allow my best friend to suffer and die?"

In hindsight, most individuals begin questioning the little things. Why couldn't they have been stopped by a traffic light, or why couldn't the road have been just a little wider at that particular spot? But these endless questions do very little to stifle the grief and pain that accompany a sudden, horrific tragedy. Few church families have not experienced the devastation of losing teenagers prematurely in automobile accidents. In fact, many congregations have sent their children off on mission trips or retreats only to wake up in a nightmare—receiving a late night call that there had been a tragic wreck. It could be that an oncoming driver fell asleep at the wheel or was intoxicated and unable to control his car. Or it might be that debris was in the roadway, or the streets were slick. No matter what the cause, a common question that rings throughout such tragedies is, "Why me, Lord?"

> *"Where was God, and why did He allow this to happen to these amazing young people?" Did God momentarily turn His back?*

As telephones ring into the night and news crews scramble to provide details about such tragedies, many individuals began to question: "Where was God, and why did He allow this to happen to these amazing young people?" Did God momentarily turn His back? A similar question was echoed thousands of years ago by King David, who desperately asked, "Why do You stand afar off, O Lord, why do You hide in times of trouble?" (Psalm 10:1). During the period of the judges, Gideon questioned, "O my lord, if the Lord is with us, why then has all this happened to us?" (Judges 6:13). During grief and turmoil, questions similar to this are not only asked in front of news cameras, but also whispered through sobs and tears in the dark recesses of private bedroom closets.

I suspect there has never been a bigger weapon in the atheists' arsenal than the problem of evil, pain, and suffering. Wielding it like a club, men like Richard Dawkins,

Christopher Hitchens, and Daniel Dennett ridicule Christians—pointing out examples of suffering all over the world. These attacks have taken their toll, as many Christians question God's existence during times of trial. Rather than leaning on Him during times of sorrow, they abandon Him and become bitter.

The appeal is simple enough to understand: "If there really is a God, then why do so many congregations experience these horrendous nightmares?" Evolutionists often phrase it this way: "If God is a loving God, then why do bad things happen to good people?" This simple question frequently becomes a stumbling block for some individuals— who end up making a conscientious decision not to believe in God. Unfortunately, all too often it is during pain and suffering that we forget that God is in the same place now that He was when His own Son was being maliciously nailed to an old rugged cross almost two thousand years ago. How thankful we should be that on **that** grim day, God **did** remain in Heaven as the sin of all humanity was placed on His Son's back and nailed to that cross! Had Christ not died for our sins, we would have no hope of inheriting Heaven (1 Corinthians 15). We must remember that while we may not understand every facet of human suffering in the here and now, we can explain enough to negate the charge that misery is incompatible with the existence of God.

Without a Doubt, Suffering Is Real

While postmodernists assure us that "we can't know" and that there are "no absolutes," none would argue that pain and suffering do not exist. Anyone who has spent more than a decade on the earth has experienced some form of pain and suffering. Oftentimes it appears that some families receive more than their "fair" share, as they are hit with one tragedy after another. Fathers who are the sole providers for their home wake up one day to find their jobs have been downsized. Parents whose child suffered a "bruise that wouldn't go away" listen as a doctor delivers that terrifying word—cancer. A child enjoying the state fair with his family suddenly finds his way in the back of a stranger's van. A creek that one time provided enjoyment and beauty swells and rages through a house taking with it a lifetime of memories. It's also because of this suffering that many Christians end up blaming God for the hurt they feel in their lives. So why do evil, pain, and suffering exist?

Evil, pain, and suffering are real. Because of this fact, atheists love to ridicule the notion of a loving God.

Two important points must be made before answering the question of why suffering exists. (1) God created man with free will. Could God have created mankind as "automatrons" that had to worship Him in a certain fashion? Absolutely. But God loves mankind (John 3:16), and thanks to His incredible love (1 John 4:8), humanity was endowed with free will (see Genesis 2:16-17; Joshua 24:15; Isaiah 7:15; John 5:39-40; 7:17; Revelation 22:17). As such, each morning every person on the planet has the opportunity to do good or evil. We have the opportunity to serve God or Satan. God will never force mankind to worship or serve Him. We can wake up hating the world around us or embracing it in love. The choice is ours to make. (2) God is not a respecter of persons (Acts 10:34). We know He makes the rain to fall on the fields of the just and unjust (Matthew 5:45). With these two facts in mind, we are now able to examine why God allows evil, pain, and suffering.

Why Does God Allow Suffering?

Some of the Suffering Comes from Past Generations

Much of the suffering present in the world today is a direct result of the misuse of the freedom of choice by past generations. Aside from Adam and Eve, we are currently living with decisions our forefathers made that have greatly impacted our lives. Who knew fifty years ago that filling our schools with asbestos and painting our homes with lead paint would cause cancer? Who knew that spraying our troops in Vietnam with Agent Orange (in an effort to kill the foliage) would have mutagenic effects? Who knew that treating pregnant women with thalidomide would produce infants with gross deformities? Past generations have carried out actions that result in suffering, even today. The ultimate example of this would be Adam and Eve. Because of their decision to sin, they brought death into the world. A modern-day example would be the pharmaceutical

"In a universe of blind physical
forces and genetic replication, some
people are going to get hurt, and other
people are going to get lucky; and you won't
find any rhyme or reason to it, nor any justice.
The universe we observe has precisely the
properties we should expect if there is at the
bottom, no design, no purpose, no evil and
no good. Nothing but blind pitiless indifference.
DNA neither knows nor cares. DNA just is,
and we dance to its music."

– **Richard Dawkins**, 1996,
River Out of Eden, p. 133.

companies, who for years produce a drug that is meant to cure a
specific ailment. Only decades later—after thousands have taken
that particular drug—do we discover that in addition to curing
the ailment, it also causes additional health problems. How many
food preservatives are being used today that will be determined
harmful later in the lives of our children or grandchildren? This
does not mean we should blame people of the past or toss up our
hands and "give up." Rather, it simply explains why we see **some** of
the evil, pain, and suffering around us today.

Some Suffering Results from Our Own Mistakes
Do not think that all the pain and suffering in this world can be blamed on past
generations. Each one of us makes wrong decisions and incorrect judgments,
and in doing so, we frequently inflict pain and suffering upon ourselves and
upon others. As mentioned above, God loves us enough to allow us freedom of

choice. However, consider the young man who decides to "sow his wild oats," who eventually will learn that every person reaps what he sows (Galatians 6:7). Many destitute people have awakened in a gutter because they freely chose to get drunk the night before. And many drunk drivers have killed themselves, their passengers, and innocent victims, because they chose not to relinquish the keys. All of us must understand that actions have consequences! Young teens who engage in sexual activity before marriage will carry the burden, both physically and emotionally, of their decision. What we do today can (and often does) determine what our life will be like tomorrow. God will allow us to be forgiven of our sins, but He will not always remove the painful consequences of our actions. Let's face it: much of the pain and suffering that we experience in this world is our own fault!

Some Suffering Comes from Our Own Selfishness
There is a generation living today who can recall a time when things were much simpler. This generation grew up before the advent of television (and commercials). They can recall making all of their purchases from a single "department store" such as Woolworth's. Many from this older generation can even remember paging through the Sears catalog in search of Christmas gifts or home furnishings. (In fact, some can even recall using catalogs for "other" purposes in outhouses.) While abundant material goods did exist in the past, they did not inundate every aspect of life as they do today.

Yet today, my generation has perfected the art of "keeping up with the Joneses." We want to be surrounded in luxury. We are constantly bombarded with products to make our yards greener, children smarter, houses cleaner, television signals stronger, or food taste better. We constantly see the products in magazines and on television—and we covet them all as our children watch. Our children are growing up in an age in which "work ethic" is a bygone concept. They simply see all our "stuff" and they desire even more. As a result, many are withholding what is already God's when it comes to giving. The latest research indicates Christians are actually only giving 3-4% of their incomes. Consider how much pain and suffering could be alleviated in this world if Christians would actually give 10-15% of their incomes! How many hungry children could be fed? How many naked could be clothed? And how many homeless could have shelter?

> *Consider how much pain and suffering could* *be alleviated in this world if Christians would actually give 10-15% of their incomes!*

This is one reason that may be distasteful to our own palate—however it still exists. The truth is many people who profess Christianity are still clinging to the things of this world. Sure, we give to the Church, but it's usually a pittance. It may be we even budget and give God from our "firsts," but is our giving tight-fisted? Consider how much good could come to those who hunger, those who are naked, and those who are sick if **every** Christian set 10% of their income as the minimal starting point of giving back to God. Caring for those in poverty-stricken areas or those who are suffering from the natural laws of a hurricane would be much easier if Christians put their priorities in things above. We are told that pure, undefiled religion is caring for the widows and orphans (James 1:27), and yet far too often we only do this "on the surface."

Paul warned the Christians in Colosse that covetousness was a form of idolatry (Colossians 3:5). We must instill in our hearts, and the hearts of our posterity, Jesus' admonition: "Take heed and beware of covetousness, for one's life does not consist in the abundance of the things he possesses" (Luke 12:15). Consider the real difference we would see in our nation if our families recognized what holds **real value** and took to heart Paul's words to Timothy:

> Now godliness with contentment is great gain. For we brought nothing into this world, and it is certain we can carry nothing out. And having food and clothing, with these shall we be content. But those who desire to be rich fall into temptation and a snare, and into many foolish and harmful lusts which drown men in destruction and perdition. For the love of money is the root of all kinds of

evil, for which some have strayed from the faith in their greediness, and pierced themselves through with many sorrows (1 Timothy 6:6-10).

So yes, some of the suffering around us is due to our own selfishness.

Some Suffering Comes from Violating Natural Laws

Evolutionists are quick to ask, "Why, then, didn't God reach down and save the Christian teenagers on their way home from a mission trip? Why didn't He just stretch out His almighty arm and cradle those faithful believers in the palm of His hand?" As odd as it may sound at first, God did not act in such a fashion because He loves us! We live in a world regulated by **natural laws that were established at the creation of this world.** For example, the laws of gravity and motion behave consistently. Thus, if you step off the roof of a fifteen-story building, gravity will pull you to the pavement beneath and you will die. If you step in front of a moving bus, the laws of momentum will keep that bus in motion, even though it will result in your death. Does this mean God doesn't love us? Absolutely not. It simply means God has put into place physical laws that we can count on, and those laws are in effect, and may have even resulted in the death of a loved one. But individuals still ask, "Why?" Why couldn't God intervene to prevent such disasters? Think for just a moment what sort of world would this be if God directly intervened, suspending His natural laws, every time a human encountered a life-threatening situation. For instance, imagine working in a bookstore. As you are busy arranging books, some-one in China falls from a high place. So God suspends the law of gravity in order to set them on the ground safely. All of the books would come flying off the shelf, and you would spend the next hour picking them up. Then 45 minutes later, someone in India falls from a high place, and once again the law of gravity is suspended. **Remember, God is not a respecter of persons**, so if He saves one individual from falling from a high place, He would have to likewise save everyone that falls from high places. This would cause indescribable chaos and confusion all over our planet. This chaotic, haphazard system would argue more for atheism than it would for theism!

If you step in front of a moving bus, the laws of momentum will keep that bus in motion, even though it will result in your death. Does this mean God doesn't love us?

In Luke 13:2-5, Jesus told the story of eighteen people who died when the tower of Siloam fell on them. Did they die because they were wicked or more deserving of death than others around them? No, they died because of natural laws that were in effect. We know that God is "no respecter of persons" (Acts 10:34). Fortunately, natural laws are constant so that we can study them and benefit from them. We are not left to sort out some kind of random system that works one day but not the next. Once a car crosses the centerline, laws of nature take over—and often-times death is the result. Is it tragic and painful? For sure. But does it change God's love for mankind? Not in the least. So, some of the suffering we experience comes from natural laws that have been in effect since creation.

Some Suffering May Be Beneficial

Furthermore, there are times when suffering is beneficial. Think of the man whose chest and arm begin to throb and tighten, or the woman whose side starts to ache at the onset of appendicitis. While the pain is not pleasant, it alerts us that there may be something more serious going on. Pain in the chest, if caught early, can help someone seek treatment and stave off a heart attack by the use of drugs or stints. Consider children who are born with no pain receptors in their skin. While this may sound like a good thing, realize that the only way they have to know bath water is too hot is if they see their skin turning red. The only way they know the stove is hot is if they smell their own flesh burning. Physical pain can act as a warning, often sending us to the doctor for prevention or cure before things get too bad.

Without that pain, individuals with chest pain or infections would never have their ailments tended to. Suffering and tragedy can also help humans develop some of the most treasured traits known to mankind—bravery, heroism, and self-sacrifice—all of which flourish in less-than-perfect circumstances. The writer of the book of James admonishes, "My brethren, count it all joy when you fall into various trials, knowing that the testing of your faith produces patience. But let patience have its perfect work, that you may be perfect and complete, lacking nothing" (James 1:2-4).

A dear friend once told me that she welcomed the pain and suffering in her life, because without it she would not be able to recognize the good. Her point was that if we spend all of our time on the "mountaintop" we never truly appreciate the view. It's only when we've spent some time in the valleys that we come to appreciate the view from the mountaintop.

> *"My brethren, count it all joy when you fall into various trials, knowing that the testing of your faith produces patience."*

There Are Times When Suffering Seems Illogical

But sometimes there seems to be no logical explanation for the immense suffering that a person is experiencing. As mere humans, we often forget that we cannot see the "big picture," and so therefore what may seem unfair or horrible at one moment may be a part of a bigger plan. Take the Old Testament character of Job as an example. He lost ten children and all of his wealth in a few short hours. Yet the Bible described him as upright and righteous. We know the end result of what happened in Job's life, and that his loss was restored two-fold. But remember, Job did not have the pleasure of turning to the "back of the book" to see how his life would turn out. Why would God allow such a man to suffer? James 1:2-3 helps us see the answer: "My brethren, count it all joy when you fall into various trials, knowing that the testing of your faith produces patience."

From a personal level, I experienced this when I was much younger. My oldest brother Calvin died in his early twenties. At the time of his death, my family was rocked to the core. We could not envision anything good that could have come from such a senseless loss. Now, almost twenty years later, I can see more of the bigger picture. Calvin's death actually put me on the pathway to teaching Christian evidences. Following his death, I decided to pursue a career in neurology. I wanted to know all I could about the brain and spinal cord and disorders of the nervous system. During my training, I was approached about a different career

"I thank God
for my handicaps, for
through them I have
found myself, my work,
and my God."
– Helen Keller

path—using my scientific training. It seemed as though I was in the right place at the right time "for such a time as this" (Esther 4:14). I can see more of the "big picture" today. While we still miss my brother and holidays are bittersweet, his death does not seem as senseless today. Bear in mind God can see the Big Picture.

Conclusion

Atheists are not afraid to pour salt into your wounds or kick you when you are down in an effort to discredit the existence of God. They position their poison pens and smirk at every human tragedy as proof that there is no God. However, the existence of evil, pain, and suffering does not discount God's existence. We have already proven that there must be a Creator, and the presence of evil or suffering does not negate this fact. When humans experience pain and loss, we must not lose focus on what is truly important. We can't allow the evil, pain, and suffering in this world to become a wedge between ourselves and Jehovah God. Never forget that God's love for mankind led to a scheme of redemption that resulted in the brutal death of His own Son. Jesus Christ was the only truly innocent individual ever to live, yet even He suffered immensely.

Instead of blaming God for pain, or denying His existence, we should be looking to Him for strength and let tragedies remind us that this world never was intended to be our final home (read Hebrews 11:13-16). James 4:14 instructs us that our time on this earth is extremely brief. The fact that even the Son of God was subjected to incredible evil, pain, and suffering (Hebrews 5:8; 1 Peter 2:21ff.) proves that God does love and care for His creation. He could have abandoned us to our own sinful devices, but instead "God demonstrates His own love toward us, in that while we were still sinners, Christ died for us" (Romans 5:8). Maybe instead of screaming, "Why me, God?" and being angry when tragedy strikes, we should take a moment to reflect on what Jesus endured during His scourging and crucifixion on our behalf. Then we are more prepared to humbly and quietly ask, "Why me, God? Why did You allow Your Son to go through all of that for me?"

Questions:
1. Why is the problem of evil, pain, and suffering such an effective tool for atheists?
2. Give an example (aside from the death of Christ) of suffering in the Old Testament and New Testament.

3. What can parents do to help prepare their children for the problem of evil, pain, and suffering?
4. Why do Christians sometimes feel we should get a "free pass" from bad things or suffering?

Scriptures to Study
James 1:2-4 • Luke 6:26 • 1 Peter 4:14 • Job 1

Additional Resources

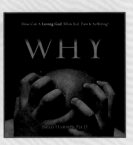

Harrub, Brad (2008), *Why* (DVD), (Brentwood, TN: Focus Press).

Ham, Ken (2000), *Why is There Death and Suffering?* (DVD), (Answers in Genesis).

Ham, Ken (2006), *How could a Loving God…?* (Answers in Genesis).

"All Scripture is given by inspiration of God, and is profitable for doctrine, for reproof, for correction, for instruction in righteousness, that the man of God may be complete, thoroughly equipped for every good work."

– 2 Timothy 3:16-17

THE FIRST BO

CAL

GEN

CHAP. 1.

1 *The creation of heaven and earth, 3 of th light, 6 of the firmament, 9 of the earth sep rated from the waters, 11 and made fruitf 14 of the sun, moon, and stars, 20 of fish a fowl, 24 of beasts and cattle, 26 of man in image of God. 29 Also the appointment food.*

IN the beginning God created the hea and the earth.

2 And the earth was without form, void; and darkness *was* upon the face o deep: and the Spirit of God moved the face of the waters.

3 And God said, Let there be light there was light.

4 And God saw the light, that *it was* and God divided the light from the dar

Chapter

Does God Speak to Us Today?
The Inspired Word of God

If there really is a God, wouldn't it be easier if He just made Himself known? Think of how many fewer arguments there would be if Jehovah God spoke directly to man. It would end the quarrel regarding His existence forever. Or would it? Straying away from God has been an ongoing reality since the days of Adam and Eve. Consider for a moment that Adam and Eve were in a covenant relationship with God, having watched Him walk through the midst of the garden, and yet they disobeyed. God spoke directly to Abraham, making a covenant with him and promising to multiply his seed. But still Abraham and Sarah questioned His ability to give them a child in their old age. The Israelites watched the Red Sea parting before their eyes and feasted every day on quail and manna, and yet they turned away in rebellion. During the period of the judges and kings, God revealed Himself through prophets and yet many turned away, choosing instead to worship false gods such as Baal. Many individuals who clamor to hear the Almighty Creator have lost sight of the fact that He does speak to us today—and thankfully, unlike those men of faith in the past, we have His complete Word. God, through His infinite wisdom, has laid before all men His inspired Word. Whether we take the time to listen and obey is another story.

Just as a frog does not realize incremental changes in temperature as he sits in a pot of water, Christians, too, have remained complacent—only to suddenly realize that the water is boiling all around us. The attacks on God and His Word are coming from many different directions and many different groups. But they all have one thing in common. They want, more than anything in the world, to excise God (and all references to Him) from our society. In discussing the agenda of abolishing God, geneticist Richard Lewontin noted:

> Our willingness to accept scientific claims against common sense is the key to an understanding of the real struggle between science and the supernatural. We take the side of science **in spite** of the patent absurdity of some of its constructs, **in spite** of its failure to fulfill many of its extravagant promises of health and life, **in spite** of the tolerance of the scientific community for unsubstantiated just-so stories, because we have a prior commitment, a commitment to naturalism…. **We are forced to our adherence to materialism…**no matter how counter-intuitive, no matter how mystifying to the uninitiated. Moreover, **that material-ism is absolute, for we cannot allow a Divine Foot in the door** ("Billions and Billions of Demons," *The New York Review*, January 9, 1997, p. 31, emp. in orig. except for last two sentences.).

> *Atheists have "taken aim" at God, religion, the supernatural, and the Gospel message and intend to "shoot to kill."*

That mantra—that we cannot allow a Divine Foot in the door—is being stridently echoed in the halls of academia and among the news media. Atheists have "taken aim" at God, religion, the supernatural, and the Gospel message and intend to "shoot to kill." Consider, for example, this statement from Kai Nielsen, humanist philosopher and former editor of *The Humanist* magazine.

> In cultures such as ours, religion is very often an alien form of life to intellectu-als. Living as we do in a post-enlightenment era, it is difficult for us to take reli-gion seriously. The very concept seems fantastic to us…. That people in our age can believe that they have had a personal encounter with God, that they could believe that they have experienced conversion through a "mystical experience of God" so that they are born again in the Holy Spirit, is something that attests to human irrationality and a lack of sense of reality (1977, p. 46).

French
infidel Voltaire
noted that within 100
years of his time, Christianity
would be swept away from existence and the Bible would pass into
the obscurity of history.

Yet 50 years after his death, the
Geneva Bible Society used his
house and printing press to
produce stacks
of Bibles.

The message is clear. Those people who accept God, His Son, His Word, and His salvation are "out of touch with reality," "irrational," and "unreasonable." There is no misunderstanding what the new humanistic/atheistic message is, what it teaches, or what it hopes to accomplish. *The Humanist Manifesto II* is quite specific on a number of important points. Consider, for example, their comments on religion:

We believe, however, that traditional or dogmatic or authoritarian religions **that place revelation, God, ritual, or creed above human needs and experience do a disservice to the human species.** Any account of nature should pass the tests of scientific evidence; in our judgment, the dogmas and myths of traditional religions do not do so.... We find insufficient evidence for belief in the existence of a supernatural; it is either meaningless or irrelevant to the question of the survival and fulfillment of the human race.... Promises of salvation or fear of eternal damnation are both illusory and harmful. They distract humans from present concerns, from self-actualization, and from rectifying social injustices. Modern science discredits such historic concepts as the "ghost in the machine" and the "separable soul." Rather, science affirms that the human species is an emergence from natural evolutionary forces. As far as we know, the total personality is a function of the biological organism transacting in a social and cultural context. There is no credible evidence that life survives the death of the body (1973, p. 15- 17, emp. added).

The message is unmistakable: Religion is useless, and we should be tolerant of everything.

Is It Just a Good Book?

Some vehemently oppose its teachings and routinely pull verses out of context to paint a wretched picture of religion. Others are willing to concede it has some

historical significance and will at least give it a bit of credibility from a historical perspective. The large majority would even go the next step and describe it as a "good book" containing "good principles." But is that enough? The Bible claims to be inspired. [Consider the following passages: Acts 10:36; 2 Timothy 3:16-17; John 17:17; 8:32.] It can't be considered a "good book" and yet lie about being inspired. How many individuals are willing to cast aside the label of just a "good book" and take that final step of defending the Bible as the Word of God?

Whether individuals are standing around the office cooler, door-knocking in foreign lands, or debating devout atheists on television, the validity of the Bible will ultimately come up. If you really stop and consider it for a moment, everything (and I do mean **everything**) hinges on this one topic. If the Bible is not real, then how can one know of his/her salvation? If the Bible is not the Word of God, then there can be no absolutes. How do we know how to worship or how to conduct ourselves? If the Bible is not inspired, then people are allowed to pick and choose whatever suits them as they pursue the pleasures of this life—in essence, they can enjoy a "buffet attitude" towards religion. This "buffet" approach to religion has critically infected the 20 somethings. If the Bible is not God's method of communicating with mankind, then where does that leave the plan of redemption and the New Testament description of salvation?

Consider the dilemma: The majority of people would much rather paint the world "gray" and be allowed the flexibility of their own judgment rather than to humble themselves and be obedient servants to Him. Thus, they embrace the idea of the Bible being just a good book—an attitude that allows them to do as they please. Whereas if the book is God's Word, then suddenly it is no longer a question of an individual's likes or dislikes, but rather everything revolves around the Author of that book—God. Man is no longer able to do what is right is his own eyes, but rather he must acknowledge that Almighty God has bestowed upon mankind divine edicts that we are to follow—or pay the consequences. We have examined the evidence for God–in this chapter we will examine how He communicates with man today.

> *The majority of people would much rather paint the world "gray" and be allowed the flexibility of their own judgment rather than to humble themselves and be obedient servants to Him.*

So the question becomes: How do we teach the lost that the Bible is more than just a good book? Critics and skeptics love to belittle anyone who views the Bible as the literal Word of God. They are quick to ridicule those who quote Scripture when asked questions about science or nature. They love to spotlight films calling the authenticity of the Bible into question—such as the current debate about the alleged ossuary of Jesus. Add to this that the majority of the world would like to simply live in a "gray" world where they get to discern right from wrong using situation ethics. So how do we effectively teach that God has established clear black and white boundaries?

We Must Establish the Bible As "God-Breathed"

Before we can teach people about God and the Gospel, we must be able to demonstrate to them the authenticity and accuracy of the Bible. It is one thing to say, "It's in the Bible." It's a totally different thing to say those words, having already established that the Bible is inspired and thus is the only book to which we should heed in obedience.

So what do we tell them? How do we move from simply stating opinions to convincing them to accept the Truth? What are some tools the average person can utilize in order to teach our friends, family, and neighbors about the accuracy of God's Word? There are many methods of demonstrating the inspiration of the Bible. For instance:

Unity of the Bible—Unlike modern allegedly inspired books, this one was written by more than 40 authors over a period of 1,600 years, and yet the authors maintained a consistent theme. (Just as a way of comparison, The Book of Mormon and Quran were penned each by a single man in a short period of time.)

Miracles of the Bible—Unlike modern-day alleged miracles, these were truly signs that pointed to the existence of a Creator. The word *miracle* has been so overused (and misused) that we no longer consider what it was like to raise someone from the dead or walk on water. The story is told of a Pentecostal congregation who was going to raise someone from the dead. They took out a full-page newspaper ad and invited the community. At the designated hour, they allowed individuals to walk by the casket and view this "dead" man. Everything went well right up to the point in which a member of the Church took out his pocket knife and stabbed it into the thigh of the dead man—who then came to life very quickly. Biblical miracles are not like this.

Have you ever considered the statistical odds of one man—Jesus Christ—fulfilling every single Messianic prophecy?

Prophecy of the Bible—Have you ever considered the statistical odds of one man—Jesus Christ—fulfilling every single Messianic prophecy? To be born in the right city is one thing. But to be born of the right family lineage, under the right conditions, and fulfilling every single prophecy is another. In order for a prophecy to be valid, it must meet certain criteria. First, it must be a specific, detailed statement—not something that is vague or general in nature. Second, there must be enough time between the prophetic statement and its fulfillment so that there is no chance whatsoever of the prophet having the ability to influence the outcome. Third, the prophecy must be stated in clear, understandable terms. Fourth, the prophecy must not have historical overtones. In other words, true prophecy should not be based on past (or current) societal or economic conditions. Fifth, a clear, understandable, exact prophecy must have a clear, understandable, exact fulfillment. It is not enough to suggest that a certain event came true with a "high degree of probability." The fulfillment must be unmistakable and must match the prophecy in every detail.

Factual Accuracy of the Bible—Without a doubt the Bible claims inspiration. This being the case, it should be that any time facts are given in the Bible they should withstand scrutiny. For instance, countries or cities referenced should be checkable—and should correspond to the geographical location given in the Bible. Without fail, every time the Bible mentions something that is "checkable," the Bible is always correct. One of the best examples is the conversion of Sir William Ramsey. Ramsey was an archaeologist who set out to disprove the validity of God's Word. He decided to use Luke's recorded events in an effort to disprove the factual accuracy of the Bible. However, every time he turned over his spade, he was confronted with the historical accuracy of Luke's account. Every city he uncovered matched precisely to the information given hundreds of years earlier by Luke.

"We account the Scriptures of God to be the most sublime philosophy. I find more sure marks of authenticity in the Bible than in any profane history whatsoever."

– Sir Isaac Newton,
as quoted in Henry H. Morris',
Men of Science-Men of God,
1988.

Scientific Accuracy of the Bible—One of the best tools to demonstrate the inspiration of the Bible is the scientific accuracy found within God's Word. While space will not permit a full review of every incidence of scientific foreknowledge contained in the Bible, the following examples provide strong evidence for the inspiration of God's Word. Press upon those you study with that these statements were written thousands of years ago, long before man was able to truly discern the validity of these Scriptures. The only way these scientific accuracies could have found their way into God's Word is via inspiration.

Medicine

- Numbers 19:16-18 gives a recipe for antibacterial soap. Most know that making lye soap involves ashes from the fat of an animal, but God also specifies the delivery mechanism—the hyssop plant—which we know today has antifungal properties. These instructions were given to cleanse a person and their possessions after touching a dead person—long before we knew about bacteria and viruses.

- Leviticus 17:15 teaches that an animal that has died naturally—an animal in which bacteria are already growing unchecked by the body's immune system—is not to be eaten. We know that today it is against local, state, and federal public health procedures to take an animal that has died naturally to a slaughterhouse. What if the animal had died from rabies, anthrax, brucellosis? Yet how did the Israelites know this?

- Leviticus 11 gives restrictions regarding safe foods. Verse 7 specifically points out that the Israelites were not to eat pork. We know today that these scavengers often ingest parasites such as *Trichinella spiralis*, the organism that causes trichinosis.

- Deuteronomy 23:12-14 instructed the Israelites to bury human waste. Today we know this is good hygiene. However, during the Middle Ages many Europeans threw human waste into back alleys, which allowed microorganisms to flourish. Those microorganisms infected fleas, which would travel into individual homes on rats, allowing the fleas to then bite and infect millions of people. The Black Plague resulted from this carelessness and killed more than 13 million people.

- In Genesis 17:12, God commanded Abraham to circumcise newborn males on the eighth day. But why not day 2 or day 12? After centuries of experiments on blood-clotting, we have learned that blood clotting is dependent on three factors: platelets, prothrombin, and Vitamin K. We know today after years of scientific study that it is on the eighth day that blood-clotting factors (such as prothrombin) are present in their highest amounts. Yet we have this information recorded literally thousands of years earlier.

Physics
• In Genesis 2:1 Moses described God's creative activities using the past definite tense for the verb "finished," indicating an action done in the past, never to occur again. This is exactly what the First Law of Thermodynamics states—that neither matter nor energy can be created or destroyed. We know this to be true today, and yet the Bible had recorded it years earlier.

• In at least three places in the Bible (Hebrews 1:11; Isaiah 51:6; Psalm 102:26), the indication is given that the earth, like a garment, is wearing out. This is exactly what the Second Law of Thermodynamics states—that as time progresses, entropy (or disorder) increases. Where does this leave the Big Bang theory—a theory that speaks of an ordered universe resulting from a cosmic explosion?

Where does this leave the Big Bang theory—a theory that speaks of an ordered universe resulting from a cosmic explosion?

Oceanography
• Psalm 8:8 details that the seas have paths in them. Matthew Maury set out to chart the paths upon hearing this Scripture. There is a statue of Matthew Maury at the U.S. Naval Academy in appreciation for his discovering something that was already described in God's Word.

• Ecclesiastes 1:7 tells us that all rivers run into the sea, yet the sea is not full. This statement, considered by itself, may not appear all that significant. Yet it was made long before satellite images were available to show the distributions of the rivers. Also, when we consider Ecclesiastes 11:3 and Amos 9:6, we realize that the Bible discusses the water cycle long before it was discovered by scientists in Europe.

- In Job 38:16, God mentioned to Job the springs or recesses (trenches) in the sea. Yet it wasn't until the late 1800s that we possessed sufficient technology to discover these freshwater springs and deep trenches.

- Genesis 6:15 describes Noah being given specific directions regarding the dimensions of the ark. That same ratio of 30 to 5 to 3 has been used countless times by shipbuilders to make vessels seaworthy—in fact, the U.S. built an entire fleet of boats with those exact proportions. One remaining ship, the U.S.S. *Jeremiah O'Brien* that was used in World War II, is currently docked in San Francisco, CA.

Astronomy

- Isaiah 40:22 describes the circle of the earth—even though many ancient people, up through the days of Christopher Columbus, believed the earth was flat (see also Job 26:10).

- Psalm 19:4-6 indicates the sun has an orbit—a fact that we did not verify until June 1, 1999.

- In Job 38:19 the Lord describes light traveling in a "way"—a fact discovered by Sir Isaac Newton in the seventeenth century. So how did the writer of Job know about this?

- In Job 38:24 God asks by what way is light parted? We know today that light can be parted. Sir Isaac Newton discovered this by passing sunlight through a prism and separating light into seven individual bands of color as they appear in the spectrum thousands of years after this verse was written (Remember ROY G. BIV?).

Biology

- In Genesis 1:11, 12, 21, 24 Moses wrote that things reproduce "after their kind." We know this to be true today. We have discovered the laws of genetics and heredity, which ensure that things do indeed reproduce "after their kind." If a farmer plants tomato seeds, he knows full well that he will not be harvesting corn. We recognize this evident truth. But how did Moses know—long before the science of genetics was discovered?

• Acts 17:25 describes God as the "giver of life." For centuries, men have been trying to "create life" through processes of spontaneous generation. The example most often cited is the Miller/Urey experiment performed in the 1950s. Even though men like Spallanzani, Redi, Pasteur, and hundreds of others have proven time and again that spontaneous generation is impossible, evolutionists still keep on trying. But the fact still remains—man has never created living material from non-living material. Paul knew long ago that it was God who gives life. This fact has not changed!

• In 1 Corinthians 15:39, Paul also stated that there are four fleshes—those of men, beasts, birds, and fishes. Today, even evolutionists accept this fact of science. These fleshes are indeed different in their biochemical make-up. But how did Paul living in the first century A.D. know this truth?

Conclusion

Not long ago, I had a conversation with someone who made the comment: "I just wish I could have been around when God spoke to men directly. Think about how powerful that would be to have been Moses or Abraham and heard from God directly." Have we forgotten that the Bible is God's Word? It is His way of speaking directly to us today. We have the complete Word of God.

Consider your own personal approach to the Bible. Is it simply just a good book or is it God-breathed? On a scale of 1 to 10, how important a role does the Bible play in your everyday life? What would your coworkers' or children's response be if you spread a copy of the Bible, the Quran, the Book of Mormon, the New World Translation, the works of Shakespeare, and the latest New York Times best seller on a table? How do we know that one of those books stands out above the rest? Can our children discern the difference between a "good book" and an inspired book, or have they bought into the notion that all religions are equal? Does it really make any difference at all whether you adhere to Biblical principles, good morals, or simply follow the dictates of your heart?

Science textbooks are telling your children and grandchildren they have "proof," "facts," and "evidence." It is high time we give our children and grandchildren the proof, facts, and evidence *that God's Word is more than just a good book. It is truly the only God-breathed book in existence, and it is filled with examples that support its accuracy and authenticity— examples that demonstrate the power and authority of Almighty God. The only question is will you heed what this inspired Book records?*

Questions:
1. What difference does it make whether or not the Bible is inspired?
2. What other books claim inspiration?
3. Why is inspiration such a valuable key when teaching the lost?
4. What are some other ways of proving inspiration?

Scriptures to Study:
2 Timothy 3:16-17 • 2 Peter 1:20-21 • 1 Corinthians 2:12-13

Additional Resources:

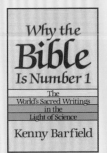

Barfield, Kenny (1997), *Why the Bible is Number 1* (Eugene, OR: Wipf and Stock Publishers).

Jackson, Wayne (2009), *The Bible on Trial* (Stockton, CA: Christian Courier)

McDowell, Josh (1999), *The New Evidence that Demands a Verdict* (Nashville, TN: Thomas Nelson).

"*The grass withers, the flower fades,*
but the word of our God stands forever."
– Isaiah 40:8

Chapter

A Book of Mistakes Collected by Fallible Men?

What started out as a simple research project turned into a nightmare with eternal consequences. While doing some online research for a literature class paper, a Christian teen stumbled across a Web site that alleged the Bible is full of contradictions. The teen had never heard of this and suddenly became fascinated in what the author of the Web site was promoting. This particular site listed 101 alleged Bible contradictions that looked legitimate from this teen's perspective. She found herself clicking on the various passages, digesting each Scripture and sinking deeper and deeper into a cloud of doubt and confusion. Three hours and two Web sites later, this young girl found herself unable to believe anything in God's Word. Not only did she buy into the alleged contradictions, but she also found a Web site that informed her that the Bible was not really inspired by God, but rather was a product of the Roman Catholic Church. With mouse in hand, she slowly replaced her religious faith with skepticism and disbelief.

The charge has been made that contradictions prove the Bible is not inspired. For instance 1992, Jim Meritt wrote a list of Bible contradictions that has been posted to the "infidels" Web site. Dennis McKinsey wrote *The Encyclopedia of Biblical Errancy*, in which he claimed:

Every analyst of the Bible should realize that the Book is a veritable miasma of contradictions, inconsistencies, inaccuracies, poor science, bad math, inaccurate geography, immoralities, degenerate heroes, false prophecies, boring repetitions, childish superstitions, silly miracles, and dry-as-dust discourse. But contradictions remain the most obvious, the most potent, the most easily proven, and the most common problem to plague the Book (1995, p. 71).

Oh what a difference 100 years makes in the conveyance and acceptance of such skepticism! In times past, questions regarding specific passages were passed along by individuals **who had actually read** God's Word and then seriously posed questions about what seemed to be conflicting passages. These questions were either passed along verbally or written in book form. Oftentimes these alleged discrepancies never made it past tight theological circles, as men of the Word studied and found logical, cogent answers to the proposed dilemma.

Men like John W. Haley and George Dehoff penned landmark books that thoroughly refute alleged Bible contradictions (both are still available online at sources like www.amazon.com). Both of these men wrote their classic books before "Web site" became common words. But with the advent of the Internet, these alleged Bible contradictions garnered a new spotlight—a spotlight oftentimes wielded **by skeptics who have never read the text** but instead are simply parroting contradictions they have viewed on other Web pages. How about some knowledge, reason, and common sense?!

Do Meritt's charges against God's Word have any validity? Meritt's initial question deals with the goodness of God. He questions, "Is God good to all, or just a few?" Meritt then cites two Scriptures, which he alleges contradict one another. Psalm 145:9 reads, "The Lord is good to all: and His tender mercies are over all His works." Jeremiah 13:14 says, "'And I will dash them one against another, even the fathers and the sons together,' says the Lord. 'I will not pity nor spare nor have mercy, but will destroy them.'"

One doesn't have to be a "Bible scholar" to see the flawed rationale in Meritt's logic. Using the passage in Psalms, Meritt constructs a straw man that God is **only** a God of love and goodness. He then reaches into a totally different passage (written by a different writer) dealing with a different time-frame and a different issue that underscores God's anger over the pride and sinfulness of Judah.

Obviously, Jim Meritt never had children—or at least his argument does not demonstrate his understanding of parenthood. Christian parents love and want what is good for their children. They have loved them from the very beginning of their existence. They show concern and mercy for their sons and daughters. However, this does not negate the fact that parents can get extremely riled up when a child disobeys or does something stupid. Those same loving parents can yield a rod of correction in an effort to discipline an unruly child. Yes, God is good to mankind—all men. But He will not, and does not, stand for sin.

The passage under consideration in the book of Jeremiah is contained in one of the prophet's sermons to Judah. By this time in history, Judah and Israel had become divided nations. Both had elected many evil kings who had led them away from the One True God, and instead they began worshipping false gods like Baal. Jeremiah had been on good terms with Josiah—a king who tried to bring about a spiritual reformation to Judah. But following Josiah's death, the southern nation of Judah began sliding down the slope toward immorality and paganism. Eventually God gave them over to the Babylonians. The passage in question here comes from one of Jeremiah's warnings to the people of Judah, pleading with them to return to God.

> *These alleged contradictions are now a source of confusion in this information generation—for both young and old alike.*

Meritt's argument does not take into consideration the full portrait of God—something many are guilty of today. He tries to convey that God could not both be good and also angry toward mankind. When one takes the time to reflect on all of the characteristics of Jehovah God, one can see that these passages do not represent any type of contradiction.

While it is not my intent to rewrite the classics authored by Haley and Dehoff, I would like to offer a few examples to demonstrate the allegations and a rational argument for such charges.

Death of Judas
One of the favorite alleged contradictions that skeptics like to use is the method of death

for Judas. In Matthew 27:5 we read, "He [Judas] threw down the pieces of silver in the temple and departed, and **went and hanged himself**" (Matthew 27:5, emp. added). However, in speaking of Judas, Acts 1:18 records, "Now this man purchased a field with the wages of iniquity; and falling headlong, he **burst open in the middle and all his entrails gushed out**" (Acts 1:18). So which was it? Did Judas hang himself as Matthew indicated, or did he fall headlong and burst in the middle? Atheists are quick to point out these two different scenarios and boldly proclaim that the Bible is not inspired. However, a more scholarly investigation reveals that both instances could (and did) occur.

> *Did Judas hang himself? Yes. Did his body burst after hitting the ground? Definitely. Are these two different accounts contradictory, leaving the inspiration of the Bible in question? Absolutely not!*

When the body dies, bacteria that are normally kept in check inside the body begin to immediately multiply and produce gases, which cause the body to swell up. [Today we don't worry about this much thanks to preparations made at funeral homes.] A quick look at animals killed on the side of the road will attest to this truth, as their bodies can oftentimes be seen swollen and bloated. When Judas hung himself, his body experienced this same phenomenon, with bacteria producing gases as his body was suspended in the sun. While we are not told how he was brought down, two very good possibilities exist: either (1) he was cut down prior to the observance of special religious days (e.g., Sabbath); or (2) the rope he used eventually broke due to the weight. In either case, we can see how his body would fall—headfirst, as the torso is heavier than the legs—and then the bloated body burst open to reveal his entrails. Did Judas hang himself? Yes. Did his body burst after hitting the ground? Definitely. Are these two different accounts contradictory, leaving the inspiration of the Bible in question? Absolutely not! Rather than focusing on this alleged contradiction, skeptics would do better to realize the result of a man who walked with Jesus Christ and eventually sold out, giving in to temptation.

Burial of Judas
Another question regarding the death of Judas deals with the field that was purchased with the money he was given for betraying Jesus. The passage quoted above

"We must not build on the sands of an uncertain and everchanging science...but upon the rock of inspired Scriptures."

– Sir Ambrose Flemming,
British electrical engineer and inventor,
1849-1945

(Acts 1:18) indicates that Judas purchased a field with the wages of iniquity. Yet, Matthew 27:6-7 indicates, "But **the chief priests** took the silver pieces...consulted together and bought with them the potter's field, to bury strangers in" (emp. added). So who actually purchased this field? The answer is easily explained as an example of someone acting through another. The priests physically purchased the field, using money they had been given by Judas. We can find other examples of people acting through others in God's Word (see the scourging of Jesus in John 19:1, or the baptisms recorded in John 4:1-2). A modern example would be if someone at my office gave me money to go buy him a cup of coffee. Could I honestly tell individuals that I bought a cup of coffee? Sure. Could he not as well tell someone he had bought coffee that day? Absolutely. I was simply acting through them in order to carry out his wishes. No contradictions there.

When one looks at such alleged contradictions, we are left to wonder if these skeptics are intellectually honest and truly searching, or if they are merely tossing out anything they can to put doubt and skepticism in the hearts of young and old alike. How much time do they actually spend researching and trying to resolve the issues they put forth?

Tomb of Jesus

For example, Meritt asks the question: Who was at the tomb? In asking this question, he cites three Scripture references:

- Matthew 28:1—"In the end of the Sabbath, as it began to dawn toward the first day of the week, came Mary Magdalene and the other Mary to see the sepulchre."

- Mark 16:1—"And when the Sabbath was past, Mary Magdalene, and Mary the mother of James, and Salome, had bought sweet spices, that they might come and anoint Him."

- John 20:1—"The first day of the week cometh Mary Magdalene early, when it was yet dark, unto the sepulchre, and seeth the stone taken away from the sepulchre."

While these three different accounts may appear, at first glance, to be contradictory, a closer examination reveals that they are not. Could not all three be correct? While different authors give specifics and may add additional information, none contradicts the other. **There is a vast difference between one author supplementing additional information versus truly contradicting another.**

Let's start with Meritt's charge. In order for this to be a contradiction, one of two things must have occurred: (1) one author specified someone was present and another author declare that the same person was not present; or (2) the authors specified that "only" a certain individual was present, and then another author added other people to this account. Neither of these situations occurred.

> *"But these are written that you may believe that Jesus is the Christ, the Son of God, and that by believing you may have life in His name."*

Second, we need to consider the audience and purpose of each book. The book of Matthew has numerous passages detailing the fulfillment of Messianic prophecies, indicating this book was written primarily for a Jewish audience. It has been said this was a book written by a Jew for Jews about a Jew. Matthew focuses much of his attention on teaching his countrymen that Jesus is the King of the Jews. The Gospel of Mark emphasizes the servanthood of Jesus. It also spends a great deal of time detailing the last week of Jesus Christ. A good body of evidence indicates that Mark was probably writing to an audience of non-Jews—people who would seek additional information. The reasoning for this is the use of the Greek and the frequent explanation of Jewish customs. While scholars debate who the audience was for the book of John, the writer is crystal clear on the purpose of his writing as he records in 20:31, "But these are written that you may believe that Jesus is the Christ, the Son of God, and that by believing you may have life in His name." Three different writers writing to different audiences for different purposes. Logic would demand that one author might detail certain events while another might supplement additional information. Should this cause Christians to question or doubt the validity of God's Word or to wonder what really transpired at the tomb of Jesus? Absolutely not! Clearly Mary Magdalene, Mary the mother of James, and Salome were all present on that incredible occasion. (Another example of this can be found in the Gospel accounts of the arrest of Jesus, where we are given various pieces of information about the servant of the high priest whose ear was cut off.)

Most people readily understand that a message is often changed according to the audience. For instance, I routinely alter my weekend seminars depending on the age and education level of my audience. The same basic message is there, but I might use different analogies or different examples. Likewise, if four eyewitnesses to a car wreck were asked to give their testimony, they would all probably add different details while explaining the same incident. As we come across passages like the ones above, we must remember that the writers were writing to different groups of people, and they stressed different items. This by no means substantiates the Bible as unreliable.

The final contradiction that I would point out calls into question the lineage of Jesus Christ. Consider the following two Scriptures:

Matthew 1:16—"And **Jacob begat Joseph** the husband of Mary, of whom was born Jesus, who is called Christ."

Luke 3:23—"And Jesus himself began to be about thirty years of age, being (as was supposed) the son of **Joseph, which was the son of Heli.**"

While many skeptics are quick to point out this seemingly problematic discrepancy, few have actually given much thought as to a logical and cogent explanation. These two different accounts reflect both the paternal and maternal lines of Jesus. Most scholars agree Matthew's account is outlining the genealogy of Joseph, while Luke records that of Mary. Matthew's lineage follows Joseph's family establishing His royal ancestry through the royal line of the kings of Israel, whereas Mary's family lineage traces Christ as a literal descendant of David. But why did Luke's account list Heli as the father of Joseph? A. Torrey revealed one possible explanation when he stated, "Joseph's name is introduced into this place in place of Mary's, he being Mary's husband. Heli was Joseph's father-in-law; and so Joseph was called 'the son of Heli.' While Joseph was son-in-law of Heli, he was, according to the flesh, actually the son of Jacob." Again, no contradictions here.

How Did We Get the Bible?

Many skeptics claim that the Bible is a relatively recent document, as mankind did not possess the capability for written language until just a few thousand years ago. However, archeological evidence proves that writing was well established long before the beginning of the Hebrew nation. In fact, inscriptions found in ancient Babylon date back more than four thousand years. The importance of this should not be overlooked. Some would like to claim writing was not around when Moses walked the earth, yet evidence proves otherwise. Ancient people used many kinds of material for writing purposes—the Bible actually makes mention of a number of these materials:

- Stone
- Clay
- Leather
- Papyrus
- Vellum or Parchment

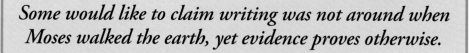

Some would like to claim writing was not around when Moses walked the earth, yet evidence proves otherwise.

Stone is the substance upon which the earliest writing in the Bible is found. Biblical examples of writing on stone can be found in Exodus 31:18; 34:1, 28; Deuteronomy 27:2-3; and Joshua 8:30-32. **Clay** was the predominant material for writing in Assyria and Babylonia. This type of preservation of writing is what is referred to in Ezekiel 4:1: "You also, son of man, take a clay tablet and lay it before you, and portray on it a city, Jerusalem." **Leather** is not mentioned specifically in the Bible, though it was undoubtedly the material used for writing by the Hebrews. A scribe's knife, used for the purpose of erasures, is mentioned in Jeremiah 36:23. The Jewish Talmud, a code of traditional laws, explicitly called for the Scriptures to be copied on animal skins. **Papyrus** was the most widely used material for writing in the Grecian/Roman culture, though the Egyptians used it as far back as 2500 B.C. **Vellum or parchment** came into prominence as a writing material due to the desire to build a worldwide library. No doubt, this was the material Paul requested Timothy to bring him in 2 Timothy 4:13. This material—made from the skins of animals but not tanned into leather—became the material upon which copies of the New Testament were made for about 1,000 years.

Remember the Bible was not written on a single occasion by a single author, but rather by a multitude of men over 1,600 years through gradual stages of growth.

Initially God's communication with man was oral. However, the time came when it was necessary for the divine will of God to be put in a permanent form. The Bible was written originally in three languages: Hebrew, Aramaic, and Greek. Scholars agree that almost all of the 39 Old Testament books were written in Hebrew (written backwards, right to left). Aramaic is a kindred language to Hebrew. (Nehemiah 8:8 suggests that the returned exiles did not understand pure Hebrew). The books comprising the New Testament were written in Greek—a "worldwide" language.

> *Remember the Bible was not written on a single occasion by a single author, but rather by a multitude of men over 1,600 years through gradual stages of growth.*

Until the invention of printing press around 1450, the Bible had to be hand copied, word-for-word by scribes. These men took their jobs very seriously, counting letters and rows and destroying any copy that was deemed incorrect. Between the 7th and 11th century, groups of Jewish scribes known as Masoretes began to copy the Old Testament texts according to strict guidelines. The Masoretes maintained nearly perfect accuracy in their copies. It was the Masoretic manuscripts from which many versions of the Bible were translated.

Still, none of the original New Testament documents is in existence. We only have copies of copies of copies. This circumstance has led skeptics to claim that we cannot know whether we have the original Bible. For instance, in his book *Misquoting Jesus: The Story Behind Who Changed the Bible and Why*, Bart Ehrman remarked:

> Not only do we not have the originals [of the Biblical manuscripts], we don't have the first copies of the originals. We have only error-ridden copies, and the vast majority of these are centuries removed from the originals and different from them in thousands of ways. Mistakes multiply and get repeated; sometimes they get corrected and sometimes they get compounded (2005, p. 10-11).

Ehrman continued: "And so it goes. For centuries. In some places, we simply cannot be sure that we have reconstructed the text accurately. It's a bit hard to know what the words of the Bible mean if we don't even know what the words are" (p. 57).

A God that can create the world can surely communicate His Will to His creation. God knew that His Word would be preserved throughout history. Jesus declared, "Heaven and earth will pass away, but My Words will by no means pass away" (Matthew 24:35, see also Luke 21:33). The prophet Isaiah maintained, "The grass withers, the flower fades, But the Word of our God stands forever" (40:8). One can rest assured that the transmission and translation procedure is sufficiently stable for God's Word to be passed down to future generations by uninspired, imperfect translators. But how can we be sure what we read today is what the original writers penned?

We know how the original New Testament documents read because we have three surviving classes **of evidence** with which to reconstruct the original New Testament:

Greek manuscripts • Ancient versions • Patristic citations

The current number of Greek manuscript copies containing all or part of the New Testament is **5,745**. The official listing (as of 2007) of the several important categories of Greek New Testament manuscripts was put together by Bruce M. Metzger and can be summarized as follows:

Papyri...	118
Majuscule MSS...	317
Minuscule MSS...	2,877
Lectionary MSS...	2,433
Total...	5,745

Manuscript Type	Year				
	1962	1980	1989	2003	2005
Papyri	76	86	96	116	118
Majuscules	297	274	299	310	317
Minuscules	2674	2795	2812	2877	2877
Lectionaries	1997	2209	2281	2432	2433
Total	**5044**	**5364**	**5488**	**5735**	**5745**

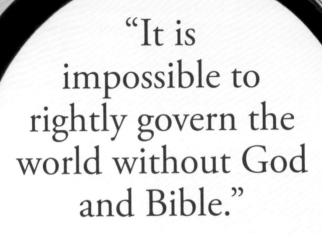

"It is impossible to rightly govern the world without God and Bible."

–George Washington, first U.S. President

Papyrus = writing material made from reed plants, in this case MSS that survive in fragments, but significant ones.

Majuscule (or uncials) = Greek MSS written in capital letters.

Minuscule = Greek MSS written in cursive.

Lectionary MSS = a handwritten copy of a lectionary, or book of New Testament Bible readings. Lectionaries may be written in uncial or minuscule Greek letters.

Given that we have only a scant few manuscripts for other well-known books, and their authenticity is not questioned, one wonders why the authenticity of the Bible—which boasts more than 5,000 manuscripts—is often questioned.

Others maintain that the books in the Bible were not chosen through the will of God but rather by the Catholic Church at the Synods of Hippo, in 393 A.D., or later in Carthage at 397 A.D. **Yet, the books included in God's Word were accepted long before the Catholic church made any official declaration.** For instance, years earlier in 367 A.D., Athanasius wrote his annual pastoral letter to the Egyptian churches under his jurisdiction, and in it he listed our twenty-seven New Testament books, excluding all others. Even before this date, there was widespread agreement among Christians from the first century onward about which writings were authoritative. Additional evidence can be found in the sermons of the third-century theologian Origen of Alexandria in which he clearly recognized the authority of the New Testament writings.

The canon—coming from the Greek *kanon* meaning "a reed or measuring stick; something serving to determine, rule, or measure"—contains the definitive list of the books, which are considered to be the inspired Word of God including the 27 books of the New Testament. The standard for deciding which books were authoritative emerged long before the fourth century—and the standard wasn't the word of a powerful bishop. Hints of this standard can, in fact, be found in Christian writings of the first century A.D. The basic idea was this: Eyewitness testimony from those who had seen the risen Savior was uniquely authoritative among early Christians.

Verification in the Dead Sea

In 1948, an Arab boy named Muhammad edh-Dhib was looking for a lost goat amid the limestone cliffs near Khirbet Qumran. Along the way, this young boy entertained himself by throwing rocks as he walked. He threw one of those rocks into a small cave and heard the sound of pottery breaking. Scampering up the hill and into the cave, the boy found some leather scrolls with ancient writing on them. Amazingly, the cave contained hundreds of clay pots, each containing scrolls, most likely written by a group of people known as the Essenes. They had been placed there by a community years earlier for protection from the Roman army's advance. The scrolls were wrapped in linen cloths and placed inside clay pots in hopes that one day these people could return and uncover the hidden Scriptures. Since that initial find, additional discoveries have been made in surrounding caves.

> *One scroll found in the Dead Sea caves was of particular importance. It was a 24-foot-long parchment that contained practically the entire book of Isaiah!*

Among the important discoveries from the caves were copies of the Old Testament books. These copies were produced from about 200 B.C. to 100 A.D., making them al-most **900 years older than the oldest available copies of Old Testament books.** (Keep in mind the Dead Sea scrolls were found in 1948, and the King James Bible was trans-lated into English in 1611.) One scroll found in the Dead Sea caves was of particular importance. It was a 24-foot-long parchment that contained practically the entire book of Isaiah! What was amazing about this scroll was that, when it was compared to the text of Isaiah produced 900 years after it, the two matched almost word for word!

In addition, this cave also contained portions of the book of Daniel (on three small pieces of leather), and the Habakkuk commentary that contained the first two chap-ters of Habakkuk's prophecy. In 1952, Cave 2 yielded portions of Exodus, Leviticus, Numbers, Deuteronomy, Ruth, Psalms, and Jeremiah. Cave 4 was a sensational find—with 330 manuscripts, of which about 90 were Biblical books. All the books of the Old Testament are represented with the sole exception of Esther. This discov-ery contained five manuscripts of books of the Pentateuch, ten of Psalms, and twelve of Isaiah, along with fragments of Ecclesiastes. As more and more discoveries were made, one fact became clear—the text we are reading in our Bibles today is exactly the same as text found on the ancient parchments of the Dead Sea scrolls. Thus, we can be **confident** that the inspired Bible we hold in our hands today is worded exactly as the original writers wrote it (see Matthew 5:18).

Questions
1. What are some books that claim inspiration?
2. Is it logical to conclude that an all-powerful God can use providence to guide His written Word to men today? Why or why not?
3. Give Scriptural examples of alleged Bible contradictions and the resolution of these passages.
4. What did the Dead Sea Scroll discovery do in regards to the accuracy of the Bible?

Scriptures to Study:
Acts 10:36 • 2 Timothy 3:16-17 • 1 Corinthians 2:12-13 • 2 Peter 1:20-21

Additional Resources:

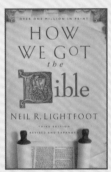

Barfield, Kenny (1997), *Why the Bible is Number 1* (Eugene, OR: Wipf and Stock Publishers).

DeHoff, George W. (1982), *Alleged Bible Contradictions Explained by DeHoff* (DeHoff Publications).

Geisler, Norman, and William Nix (1986), *A General Introduction to the Bible* (Chicago, IL: Moody Publishers).

Haley, John (1996), *Alleged Discrepancies of the Bible* (New Kensington, PA: Whitaker House).

Lightfoot, Neil (2003), *How We Got the Bible* (Ada, MI: Baker Books).

References
Ehrman, Bart (2005), *Misquoting Jesus: The Story Behind Who Changed the Bible and Why* (New York's Harper Collins).

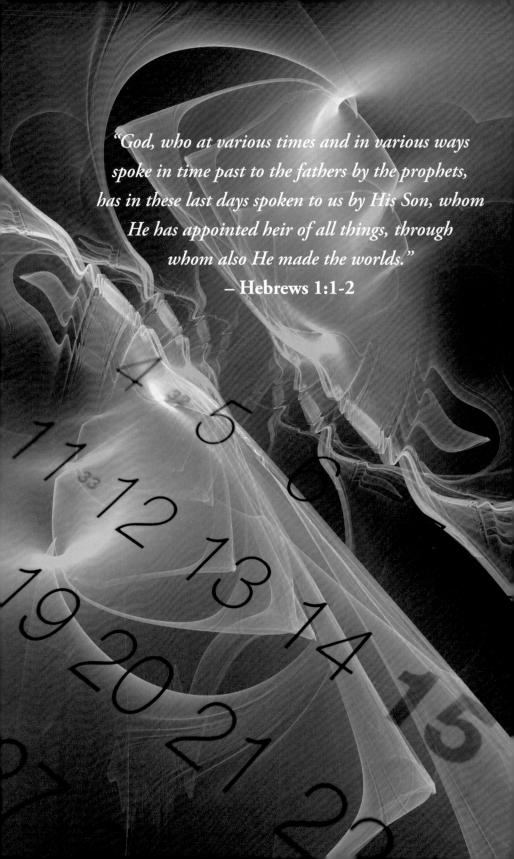

"God, who at various times and in various ways spoke in time past to the fathers by the prophets, has in these last days spoken to us by His Son, whom He has appointed heir of all things, through whom also He made the worlds."
– Hebrews 1:1-2

Chapter

Fitting It All In: A Summary of World History and Biblical History

"Historic continuity with the past is not a duty, it is only a necessity."
– Oliver Wendell Holmes, Jr.

Most of us can recall sitting through high school learning world history. However, stop for a moment and consider what you learned and how you learned it. If you are like most individuals, you went to church on Sunday and Wednesday night and you learned "Bible." Then through the week at school you learned "history." But the two never met. If God's inspired Word is true, then we should be able to mesh Biblical history with secular world history. For example, most of us can remember sitting through a history or science class hearing the teacher describe a landbridge that connected Asia with North America. Images of creatures like the woolly mammoth paint a picture in our minds of what we identify as the Ice Age. But was it real? Did the Ice Age really happen? And if so, when? Or how about the Egyptian pyramids? Did Moses have the opportunity to see them? And how does the construction of the Great Wall of China fit into Biblical history?

A Biblical worldview demands a Biblical timeline. If someone were to ask us the age of the earth, our answer should start with God's Word and then move into God's world. Ultimately, what we see in God's world will correspond to what we read in His Word. [While the media wants the general public to view it as science vs. the Bible, remember that God is the author of science and the two go hand-in-glove.] **So how old is the earth? Here are seven verses to help answer that question:**

1. Genesis 1:1–"In the beginning God created the heavens and the earth."
2. Psalm 33:6, 9–"By the word of the Lord the heavens were made, and all the host of them by the breath of His mouth. For He spoke and it was done. He commanded and it stood fast."
3. Colossians 1:16–"For by Him all things were created that are in heaven and that are on earth…"
4. Matthew 19:4–"And He answered and said to them, 'Have you not read that He who made them at the beginning made them male and female?'"
5. Mark 10:6–"But from the beginning of creation God made them male and female."
6. 1 Corinthians 15:45–"And so it is written, 'The first man Adam became a living being.' The last Adam became a life-giving spirit."
7. Genesis 3:20–"And Adam called his wife's name Eve, because she was the mother of all living."

From these seven verses we learn:
- The earth was created in the beginning.
- It was a fast event.
- He created all things (not an evolutionary process).
- Males and females were here from the beginning.
- Adam was the first male (here from the beginning of creation).
- The entire linage of humanity would come through Adam's wife, Eve.

Evolution teaches that the earth is billions of years old, and man evolved only 3 million years ago. However, this man-made theory is diametrically opposed to the words of Jesus Christ Who stated that man had been here from the beginning of creation. With that in mind, we can look at the family lineage of Adam in Genesis 5 and begin to access the age of the earth. Using the father's age at which he has children, we can build a timeline:

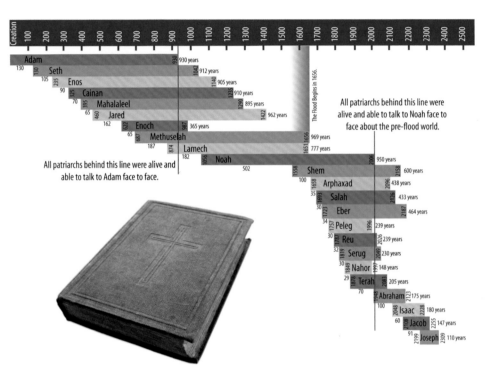

By continuing on through Genesis 5, we begin to get an accurate picture for the age of the earth (see also Genesis 11 and Luke 3). This timeline demonstrates that Adam could have spoken to Methuselah. Methuselah likewise could have spoken to Shem, who lived contemporarily with Abraham and Isaac!

The temptation is to assume there are gaps in the genealogies that might allow additional time. However, the inspired New Testament book of Jude (verse 14) records that Enoch was the seventh from Adam—a fact supported in Genesis 5. So if you are going to argue for missing genealogies, they are going to have to come after Enoch—and there aren't enough gaps in the world to fit in evolutionary time of billions of years!

Genealogy vs. Chronology

"In the beginning was matter, which begat the amoeba, which begat the worm, which begat the fish, which begat the amphibian, which begat the reptile, which begat the lower mammal, which begat the lemur, which begat the monkey, which begat man, who imagined God" (1928, p. 15). This, according to atheist Charles Smith, is the genealogy of man. Sadly, he is far from being alone in his views of man's origin. In fact, a vast majority of modern-day scientists cling vehemently to—and teach—this Darwinist view of origins as "gospel" on the matter. It has become the light under which all new data are examined. It has become their religion—one for which they will fight in order to secure its place in academia. And it appears that they are winning, as this is the only theory for the origin of mankind that can legally be taught in the public school classroom.

The above genealogy is vastly different from the Bible's account, in which man was created in the image and likeness of God (Genesis 1:26-27) and then brought death into the world through sin. Adam was listed as the first man (Genesis 2:19-20; 1 Corinthians 15:45), and the inspired writers then provide the genealogy of man from Adam to Christ (Luke 3). The Bible gives the family lineage of Jesus through Joseph's family line (Matthew 1:1-17) and Mary's family line (Luke 3:23-38). The importance of these genealogies should not be missed—as the Holy Spirit would never provide mankind with irrelevant information. The Bible provides the genealogy from Adam to Christ!

In his handbook for New Age religion titled _A New Earth_, Eckhart Tolle gives what he believes to be the diagnosis of mankind:

> If the history of humanity were the clinical case history of a single human being, the diagnosis would have to be: chronic paranoid delusions, a pathological propensity to commit murder and acts of extreme violence and cruelty against his perceived "enemies"—his own unconsciousness projected outward. Criminally insane, with a few brief lucid intervals (2005, p. 12).

Criminally insane? **Does this sound like the creature that was created last—at the pinnacle of God's creation—and made in His image and likeness?**

> _Does this sound like the creature that was created last —at the pinnacle of God's creation—and made in His image and likeness?_

> "In every conceivable manner, the family is link to our past, bridge to our future."
>
> – Alex Haley

Some have tried to downplay or criticize the genealogies, using the work of nineteenth-century author William H. Green (1890). Green's work was widely accepted and unfortunately not carefully scrutinized. His basic tenet was that there were gaps in the genealogies, and yet as Dr. Arthur Custance pointed out:

> We are told again and again that some of these genealogies contain gaps: but what is never pointed out by those who lay the emphasis on these gaps, is that they only know of the existence of these gaps because the Bible elsewhere fills them in. How otherwise could one know of them? But if they are filled in, they are not gaps at all! Thus, in the final analysis the argument is completely without foundation (1967, p. 3).

Custance should know. He spent his entire life trying to harmonize the genealogies to fit an old earth scenario. Yet after years of trying, he finally recognized that arguments alleging that the genealogies contain sizable gaps are unfounded.

Another point that should not be missed is this: Even if there were a few gaps in the genealogies, it does not affect the **chronologies** recorded in Genesis 5 and Genesis 11. Chronology is a record of time, while genealogy is a record of offspring. Recall that in these chapters the age of the father at the birth of his son is recorded, along with his age when he dies. That's not just genealogy—that's chronology! Using this information we can deduce an accurate age of historical events, including the age of the earth.

For instance, not too many individuals would argue that the time from present back to Jesus is (in round numbers) roughly 2,000 years. Ironically, the old B.C. /A.D. dating system, which most are familiar with, is even under attack. This dating system, which used the designation B.C. to stand for "before Christ" and A.D. for *anno domini* ("in the year of our Lord"), is being phased out. Rather than using the familiar B.C. /A.D. system in textbooks today, which uses Christ's appearance on earth as the central framework, humanists have been successful in employing B.C.E. and C.E. (which stands for "before the common era" and "common era"). However, a careful observation still recognizes that the central starting point for all of these designations revolves around the life of Christ!

We can also use archaeological data to determine that the time from Jesus to Abraham was also roughly 2,000 years. Thus, roughly 4,000 years have passed between man today and Abraham. The Bible also records 20 generations listed from Abraham back to Adam (cf. Luke 3). Since Genesis chapters 5 and 11 provide the ages of the fathers at the time of the births of the sons between Abraham and Adam (thus providing chronological data), one can calculate in round figures that the time expired between Abraham and Adam is also roughly 2,000 years.

While it may be true on the one hand to say an **exact** age of the earth is unobtainable from the information contained within the genealogies, at the same time it is important to note that—using the best information available to us from Scripture—the genealogies hardly can be extended to anything much beyond 10,000 years. For someone to suggest that the genealogies do not contain legitimate chronological information or that the genealogies somehow are so full of gaps as to render them useless, is to misrepresent the case, ignore the inspiration of the Bible, and distort the facts.

The Big Picture

The chart here shows a timeline that flows from Jesus back to creation with several major events marked on it (adapted from Dr. Floyd Jones). Keep in mind no one presently living was physically around during that time, so these are all approximate dates that take the creation of the world back to **approximately** 4004 B.C.

An easy way to remember it (in round numbers):

Present to Christ ~ 2,000 years
Christ to Abraham ~ 2,000 years
Abraham to Adam ~ 2,000 years

Thus we can be assured that according to the Bible the earth is less than 10,000 years old.

The dates provided allow one to build a timeline in which to place important events such as the Ice Age, the death of Christ, the construction of the Egyptian pyramids, crossing of the Red Sea, the building of the Great Wall of China, the Global Flood, etc.

CREATION to JESUS CHRIST

AM	BC	Event
4000 AM	4 BC	JESUS born - Spring - Herod died
3418 AM	586 BC	Final (3rd) *FALL OF JUDAH* - Babylon
3283 AM	721 BC	*ASSYRIAN* Captivity - ISRAEL
3029 AM	975 BC	Kingdom *DIVIDED* (586=390 of EZK 4:4-5 <u>inclusive</u> years)
	+40	
2989 AM	1015 BC	*SOLOMON* begins reign - 40 years - (1 KG 11:42)
	-3	In his 4th year Solomon begins the *TEMPLE*
2992 AM	1012 BC	on the 2nd day 2nd Mo. (1 KG 6:1, 37-38; 2 CHR 3:1-2, 5:1-5)
	+480	Years to the EXODUS - (1 KG 6:1) <u>in</u> the 480th year = 479+
2513 AM	1491 BC	the *year* of the EXODUS - Moses
	+430	From COVENANT with Abraham to Exodus
2083 AM	1921 BC	Begins SOJOURN (GEN 12:4, EXO 12:40, GAL 3:17)
	+427	number of years from *FLOOD* to *COVENANT* with Abraham
1656 AM	2348 BC	the year of the FLOOD
	+1656	GEN 5 - FLOOD to CREATION
0 AM	4004 BC	year of CREATION

AM = ANNO MUNDI = in the year of the world

– Adapted from Dr. Floyd Jones

Major Dates (approximates) to Keep in Mind:

Global Flood	2400 B.C.
Ice Age	2401 B.C.
Construction of Egyptian pyramids	2300 B.C.
Exodus and crossing of the Red Sea	1500 B.C.
Interbiblical period (beginning of synagogues)	300 B.C.

Building of the Great Wall of China	220-200 B.C.
Death of Christ	30 (or 33) A.D.
Us today	2009 A.D.

> *Thus we can be assured that according to the Bible the earth is less than 10,000 years old.*

Twelve Periods of History

In order to get a better understanding of how everything fits in, it is useful to view God's Word in twelve different periods of history (adapted from Wayne Jackson). An understanding of these separate pieces will aid a reader in knowing where the Biblical event fits in the overall timeline of world history. The twelve periods are:

1. Creation and a Period of New Beginnings
2. Patriarchal Age
3. Israelite Bondage
4. 40 Years of Wandering
5. Canaan—the Land of Milk and Honey
6. United Kingdom
7. Divided Kingdom
8. Babylonian and Assyrian Captivity
9. The Dark or Silent Years
10. Christ on Earth
11. Formation of the New Church and Expansion of Christianity
12. Admonition to Established Churches

Brief Summary of the 12 Periods:

Creation and the Patriarchal Age—This period covers the creation account and the initial history of mankind. It includes the accounts of Adam and Eve through the dispersion of people at the Tower of Babel (the first eleven chapters of Genesis). Major events during this period would include the creation (Genesis 1), the fall of man (Genesis 3), the Noahic Flood (Genesis 6-9), and the confusion of languages and dispersion of people (Genesis 11).

Covenant and Establishment of the Chosen People—This period primarily deals with Abram (later changed to Abraham), Isaac, Jacob, and Joseph. In Genesis 12 God makes a promise to Abraham—preparing the way for His Son. Major events during this period would include the life of Abraham and his wife Sarah (Genesis 12-18), God's covenant with Abram (Genesis 15), the destruction of Sodom and Gomorrah (Genesis 19), birth of Isaac (Genesis 21), Sarah's death (Genesis 23), Abraham's death (Genesis 25), birth of Jacob and Esau (Genesis 25), Isaac blessing Jacob (Genesis 27), Jacob marrying Rachel (Genesis 29), Joseph being born (Genesis 30), Joseph mistreated by his brothers and sold into slavery (Genesis 37), Joseph's rise to power (Genesis 41), Jacob journey's to Egypt (46), and the death of Joseph (Genesis 50).

Israelite Bondage—This period encompasses the period when the Israelites were under Egyptian bondage from a new king "who did not know Joseph" (Exodus 1:8). In Exodus 12:40 we learn that this bondage period lasted 430 years. However, there is some controversy as to whether this time period included the patriarchs' sojourn in Canaan (as included in the Septuagint and the Samaritan Pentateuch). Wayne Jackson pointed out that some contend the bondage period was only 215 years based upon Paul's statement in Galatians 3:16-17 that from the "promise" to the "law" was 430 years. Major events during this period are the birth of Moses (Exodus 2), Moses at the burning bush (Exodus 3), Moses confronting the Pharaoh (Exodus 5), and the twelve plagues (Exodus 7-11).

Wilderness and 40 Years of Wandering—This is the "waiting period" for the second generation of Israelites who will eventually enter the Promised Land. It was during this period that the people fell under the Mosaic Law. Having spied out the land of Canaan, the Israelites were scared and refused to enter. God punished them and noted: "According to the number of days in which you spied out the land, forty days, for each day you shall bear your guilt one year, namely forty years, and you shall know My rejection" (Numbers 14:34). Estimates put the

Israelites during this time at more than two million people. Major events during this period are crossing of the Red Sea (Exodus 14), Law of Moses handed down (Exodus 19-31), incident with the golden calf (Exodus 32), covenant renewed (Exodus 34), formation of the tabernacle (Exodus 35-40), spies sent to Canaan (Numbers 13), Israel refusing to enter Canaan (Numbers 14), and the death sentence delivered to rebellious generation (Numbers 14).

Canaan—the Land of Milk and Honey—The book of Deuteronomy was primarily a series of sermons from Moses to the Israelites prior to their entering the Promised Land. The twelve tribes were given the Promised Land, and they were asked to conquer those currently inhabiting Canaan. It would be during this period that they experience a spiritual renewal, as circumcision was reinstituted and Passover was observed. During this period the people divided the land according to tribes and were ruled by judges. Wayne Jackson recorded, "This period of history, of more than three and one half centuries (cf., 1 Kings 6:1), was characterized by four cycles: (a) The people would rebel against Jehovah; (b) The Lord would send an oppressor to punish them; (c) Israel would cry out for deliverance; and (d) God would raise up a judge to overthrow the enemy and free His people." Major events during this period are the entering of Canaan (Joshua 1), destruction of Jericho (Joshua 6), day lengthened for Joshua (Joshua 10), land divided among the tribes (Joshua 13-21), death of Joshua (Judges 2), Gideon called by God (Judges 6), succession of judges (Judges 9-12), birth of Samson (Judges 13), Samson's defeat of the Philistines (Judges 15), Samson and Delilah (Judges 16), and the death of Samson (Judges 16).

> *The book of Deuteronomy was primarily a series of sermons from Moses to the Israelites prior to their entering the Promised Land.*

United Kingdom—This period in history represents a time of peace that would end in turmoil, as the Israelites sought for a king that they might be "like all the nations" (1 Samuel 8:5). The last judge was Samuel. He was followed in succession by kings Saul, David, and Solomon. Solomon's multiple wives would play a role in the division of the Kingdom. Major events during this period were the birth of Samuel (1 Samuel 1), Israel's demand for a king (1 Samuel 8), Saul chosen to be king (1 Samuel 9), Saul anointed king (1 Samuel 10), Saul rejected as king (1 Samuel 15), David anointed king (1 Samuel 16), David's defeat of Goliath (1 Samuel 17), David sparing Saul the first time (1 Samuel 24), death of Samuel (1 Samuel 25), David sparing Saul a second time (1 Samuel 26), Saul's death (1 Samuel 31), God's covenant with David (2 Samuel 7), David and Bathsheba (2 Samuel 11), death of David's son (2 Samuel 12), Solomon's birth (2 Solomon 12), David naming Solomon king (1 Kings 1), death of David (1 Kings 2), Solomon requesting wisdom (1 Kings 3), Solomon building the temple (1 Kings 6), Ark of Covenant brought into temple (1 Kings 8), Solomon's heart turning from the Lord (1 Kings 11), and the death of Solomon (1 Kings 11).

Divided Kingdom—The split of the United Kingdom occurred under the reign of Rehoboam, the son of Solomon. The ten northern tribes became known as Israel. They had 19 kings, all of which God considered evil. Prophets such as Elijah, Elisha, Amos, and Hosea tried to bring this rebellious group back. They persisted in their evil ways, and in 722 B.C., God gave them up to the Assyrians (after only 213 years). The tribes of Benjamin and Judah became known collectively as the southern kingdom of Judah. They had twenty kings of which only two would be considered good; the rest committed abominable acts. Prophets like Jeremiah, Ezekiel, and Daniel tried to call them to repentance. Ultimately God gave them up to Babylonian captivity in 606 B.C. (after only 349 years).

Babylonian and Assyrian Captivity—It was during this period that people were exiled, the temple destroyed, and the city of Jerusalem burned. Wayne Jackson recorded that this occurred during three deportations: (1) There was the "princely" exile in 606 B.C. when men such as Daniel, Shadrach, Meshach, and Abednego were taken away. (2) There was the exile of the "upper class" in

597 B.C. (2 Kings 24:14, 18). (3) There was the general exile in 586 B.C. at which time the temple and city were burned. It was only after Cyrus the Persian king overtook the Babylonians (538 B.C.) that the Israelites were allowed to return and rebuild in 536 B.C. Three returns are recorded: Zerubbabel, Ezra, and Nehemiah. Major events during this period would be the fall of Jerusalem (Jeremiah 39), Shadrach, Meshach, and Abednego thrown into the fiery furnace (Daniel 3), Daniel thrown into the lions' den (Daniel 6), and Nehemiah rebuilding the wall (Nehemiah 3-6).

The Dark or Silent Years—This period of approximately 400 years represents the time between the Old and New Testament. It was during this period that the synagogue system was established. It was also during this era when the Hebrew language was replaced by Aramaic.

Christ on Earth—This is the period in which Jesus Christ reigned on earth and taught His disciples. With His death He nailed the Old Law to the tree (Colossians 2:14; Ephesians 2:15), instituting a new and better covenant. Major events during this period were the birth of Jesus (Matthew 1-2), John baptizing Jesus (Matthew 3), Jesus preaching the Sermon on the Mount (Matthew 5-7), Jesus calling His twelve disciples (Matthew 10), John the Baptist beheaded (Matthew 14), the transfiguration with Peter, James, and John present (Matthew 17), the triumphal entry (Matthew 21), Jesus instituting the Lord's Supper (Matthew 26), Jesus tried and crucified (Matthew 26-27), and Jesus risen from the tomb and seen by others (Matthew 28).

> *It was on this occasion, on the day of Pentecost, that the church of Christ was established.*

Formation of the New Church and Expansion of Christianity—In Acts 2 we find Peter preaching the first Gospel sermon. It was on this occasion, on the day of Pentecost, that the church of Christ was established. Wayne Jackson records, "The first century Church spans approximately seventy years (from 30 A.D. to 100 A.D.) and may be viewed in the following historical segments: (1) the

Jerusalem Church (from the founding of the Church on Pentecost to the death of Stephen—five years), (2) the expanding Church (from the death of Stephen to the council at Jerusalem—fifteen years), (3) the Church spread to the Gentiles (beginning when Peter preached to Cornelius).

Admonition to Established Churches—The remainder of God's Word represents the closing years. Primarily Paul's letters to various churches, this period deals with church growth and church conflict. This is the period in which churches had some of Paul's letters but not the complete Bible. It also represents the transition from a period of miracles to the possession of God's inspired Word.

Easy Summary of God's Word

Atheists and Christians alike are familiar with the two divisions of the Bible: the Old and New Testament. In order to comprehend a "simplified" summary of the Bible, consider placing a new division in Genesis 3. Prior to Genesis 3, man is in a covenant relationship with God—something we can't truly comprehend today. However, after having God walk through the Garden of Eden in the cool of the day (Genesis 3:8), man's relationship to God was shattered by sin. In Genesis 3 we find the dissolution of this covenant relationship. And in Genesis 3:15 we read of the first Messianic prophecy—the fact that Jesus would one day crush the head of Satan. From Genesis 3 all the way through the book of Revelation, the Bible is trying to tell us how to get back into that covenant relationship, ultimately through Jesus Christ.

Questions:
1. Why is important to know where things fit on a historical timeline?
2. What are some stumbling blocks for people accepting a relatively young age for the earth?
3. Which of the 12 Biblical periods lasted the longest?
4. What are some major world events that you could add to the timeline?
5. Oftentimes Christians write off the opening chapters of Genesis as a fable. Why is this compromise dangerous?

Scriptures to Study:
Romans 1:20 • *Exodus 20:11* • *Exodus 31:15-17* • *Genesis 1*

Additional Resources:

Hobar, Linda (2007), *The Mystery of History* (Vol. 1 Creation to Resurrection) (Cheswold, DE: Bright Ideas Press).

Jackson, Wayne (1986), *A Study Guide to Great Bible Knowledge* (Stockton, CA: Christian Courier).

Jones, Dr. Floyd Nolen (2005), *The Chronology of the Old Testament* (Green Forest, AR: Master Books).

References:

Jackson, Wayne (1986) *A Study Guide to Greater Biblical Knowledge* (Apologetics Press). Stockton, CA:

Smith, Charles (1928), *Third Annual Report of the American Association for the Advancement of Atheism*, p. 15.

"So the people shouted when the priests blew the trumpets. And it happened when the people heard the sound of the trumpet, and the people shouted with a great shout, that the wall fell down flat. Then the people went up into the city, every man straight before him, and they took the city."

– Joshua 6:20

Over the past century archaeologists have discovered and excavated Jericho, proving the walls fell outward.

Chapter

Archaeology and the Bible

There it is—in the same place it has been since before he could remember. The family Bible sits on a bookshelf in the living room. Unlike the other books that stand upright, the Bible lies flat where visitors can view the entire cover. When he was younger, he would flip through the opening pages, read the births and baptisms of distant relatives, and then flip over to the back and look at the pictures and maps at the end. Today he finds himself home from college on fall break—literally shaking his head at the dusty, old leather cover. While the sight of that old family Bible brings a warm familiarity, the contents inside cause this young man confusion and trepidation. He is currently enrolled in a World Religions class in which the teacher has claimed all religions are the product of man and that ultimately there is not much difference in any of them. In fact, he was assigned a paper on religious myths and legends, comparing and contrasting several different religions. In the past, the Bible before him brought comfort as he was taught the precepts therein. But today he finds no peace as it is "just another book." No one can point to physical evidence that supports its claims. It's just another book of religious myths. Or is it?

Documents in the Dust

Skeptics have attacked the Bible for centuries. Using a myriad assortment of tactics, they have called into question just about every facet of the inspired Book. You would expect if there really were errors that they would be widely known and would

have long ago discounted the inspiration of God's Word. Yet, the critics rage on, desperately trying to plant seeds of doubt and place a wedge in man's relationship with God.

One such skeptic, William Mitchell Ramsay, was a professor of classical archaeology at Oxford University. He received his formal training in archaeology—but he also became a well-known New Testament scholar. Ramsay employed his scientific skills in an effort to debunk the accuracy of the Bible, specifically the New Testament book of Acts. His choice of Acts was brilliant. In the book of Acts, Luke mentions 32 countries, 9 Mediterranean islands, and 54 cities. Surely, if there were errors to be found, it would be in this book so packed with geographical details. And so, Ramsay set out to disprove the validity of God's Word.

Ramsay took many research journeys to areas such as Greece and modern-day Turkey and became renowned for his knowledge in the geography and topography of this area. Throughout his research, he became an expert in Paul's missionary journeys. What Ramsay found was not discrepancies or contradictions—but rather the truth that Luke had described the geographical details beautifully. Luke was so accurate that Ramsay found himself becoming a believer of the truths contained in the Bible. In his book *The Bearing of Recent Discovery on the Trustworthiness of the New Testament,* Ramsay declared:

> The present writer takes the view that Luke's history is unsurpassed in respect of its trustworthiness.... You may press the words of Luke in a degree beyond any other historian's and they will stand the keenest scrutiny and the hardest treatment, provided always that the critic knows the subject and does not go beyond the limits of science and of justice... (1979, p. 81, 89).

In every circumstance in which Ramsay was able to check, Luke, the author of Acts, recorded the details perfectly. Ramsay then went on to proclaim:

> ...Acts may be quoted as a trustworthy historical authority.... Luke is a historian

of the first rank; not merely are his statements of fact trustworthy; he is possessed of the true historic sense; he fixes his mind on the idea and plan that rules in the evolution of history; and proportions the scale of his treatment to the importance of each incident. He seizes the important and critical events and shows their true nature at great length, while he touches lightly or omits entirely much that was valueless for his purposes. **In short, this author should be placed along with the very greatest of historians** (p. 222, emp. added).

What Ramsay found was not discrepancies or contradictions—but rather the truth that Luke had described the geographical details beautifully.

If the Bible truly is inspired, one should not be surprised at the praise given to its writers. Every time a trowel unearths artifacts in the Middle East, we can rest assured that they will not contradict facts already recorded in God's Word. But even beyond that, many of the discoveries archaeologists have found further validate the Biblical narratives. Not only do they not contradict the Bible, but on many occasions they describe and give additional support to Biblical accounts.

The Science of Archaeology

Most young children enjoy playing in the dirt. There is just something about being able to use your imagination and go to unknown distant lands, all the while feeling that cool warmth that quickly builds under your fingernails. While most people give up this habit before reaching puberty, others make a career out of it. The academic pull of digging in the dirt to uncover past civilizations holds a strong fascination for many—and likewise their discoveries are equally as fascinating to the rest of us.

No one is certain when the discipline of archaeology began; however, its foundation as a field of science was laid down under the enlightenment period (17th & 18th century). While there is not a single definition that is accepted by all scientists, the general understanding is that archaeology is the scientific study of the past—cultures, places, people—and the way people lived based on what they left behind.

As techniques and equipment become more and more specialized, this relatively new field of study has enabled men to peel back the curtain on the past of mankind to verify certain facts about our history.

One of the greatest travesties of all time is that the ongoing stream of discoveries supporting the Bible has all but been **ignored** by our modern mainstream media. In our postmodern era, these findings are not considered newsworthy. Yet, time and time again researchers uncover structures, writings, and artifacts that continue to demonstrate the accuracy of the inspired Scriptures. Were these discoveries that supported atheism or evolution, they would immediately garner the media spotlight and be heralded in all the major newspapers. For instance Dan Brown's books *The Da Vinci Code* and *Angels & Demons* were both released into major motion pictures. These works of fiction focus on secret groups like the Illuminati and Masons as they take viewers down into buried crypts and hidden catacombs to uncover "secrets" buried in the dirt. One wonders how many young people will have their faith shaken from Hollywood's perverse version of the truth.

The evidence is clear. Secrets that were buried for literally hundreds of years now cry out loudly in defense of God's Word. Coins have been found supporting Biblical history. Clay and stone tablets or prisms have been unearthed that speak of rulers and war victories that coincide with Biblical accounts. Additionally, cultural aspects that were mentioned in the Bible have been verified by archaeological discoveries. How does the mainstream media explain the walls of Jericho falling outward that were unearthed or the Babylonian flood account given in the *Epic of Gilgamesh* that resembles the Noahic Flood? Consider these select examples provided by archaeology:

Mud Brick of Ramesses II

There is no question the Bible indicates that the Israelite slaves used straw in manufacturing bricks. In Exodus 5:7-8, Moses wrote, "You shall no longer give the people straw to make brick as before. Let them go and gather straw for themselves. And you

"The tombs of Egypt, the palaces of Assyria, and the royal records of Moab, have been compelled to speak, and now, in different languages, they bear testimony for God and His truth."

– James M. Freeman, (1996), *Manners and Customs of the Bible.*

shall lay on them the quota of bricks which they made before. You shall not reduce it. For they are idle; therefore they cry out, saying, 'Let us go and sacrifice to our God'" (see also 5:15-18). In the British Museum, there is a brick discovered in Thebes, Egypt. As one might suspect, this brick does not draw the crowds that other exhibits draw— as countless thousands scurry past this simple "brick." However, this brick contains a faint cartouche of the great Ramesses II and provides strong evidence for Israelite history. The brick is composed of straw and mud from the Nile and is dated around 1300 B.C. From the size of the brick and the imprint of Ramesses name, it is likely this brick was used not in a common home but rather in official royal construction. But this is not the only brick evidence in existence. In the book *Lost Treasures of the Bible*, Clyde Fant and Mitchell Reddish noted, "Another example of a mud brick stamped with a cartouche of Ramesses II can be seen in the Oriental Institute Museum of the University of Chicago. This brick (OIM 1347; Egyptian Gallery) was found at

Thebes where it had been used in the construction of the pharaoh's mortuary temple (the Ramesseum)" (2008, p. 54). [The mummy of Ramesses II was also discovered and is on display in the mummy room of the Egyptian Museum in Cairo.]

Moabite Stone (a.k.a. Mesha Stele)

In 1 Kings 16:23 we learn that "Omri became king over Israel" (see also v. 28-29). In 2 Kings 3:4-6 we learn that Mesha was king of Moab and that he rebelled against the king of Israel. In August 1868, this Biblical account was confirmed on some black basalt stone. F. A. Klein, a German missionary in Jerusalem, discovered the stone, which had been broken into pieces. However Charles Simon Clermont-Ganneau had obtained a squeeze (paper-mâché impression—BH), allowing he and others to recover and reconstruct the Moabite stone. The stone describes how Moab was indeed conquered by Omri, king of Israel. In addition, both the stone and 2 Kings 3:4-6 list Mesha as king of Moab. It also records Mesha's victories over Omri's son (not mentioned by name), over the Israelite tribe of Gad at Ataroth, and at Nebo and Jehaz. Consider also that this stone records the Israelite God as *Yahweh*, further confirming God's Word.

Sargon's Palace

The Old Testament is replete with rulers, battles, and victories. In Isaiah 20:1 the writer chronicled, "In the year that Tartan came to Ashdod, when Sargon the king of Assyria sent him, and he fought against Ashdod." For many centuries this was the

only indication of Sargon—until an archeologist's pick brought Sargon's name back to life. Sargon II erected a palace in a new capital city, which he called Dur-Sharrukin ("the fortress of Sargon"), known today as Khorsabad, Iraq. Between 1842 and 1844, French archaeologist Paul-Emile Botta uncovered the palace of Sargon. The very event recorded in Isaiah 20 regarding the battle against Ashdod was recorded on the palace walls. One of Sargon's inscriptions reads, "In my first year I captured Samaria. I took captive 27,290 people. People of other lands, who never paid tribute, I settled in Samaria."

Sennacherib's Prism

Sargon II's son was Sennacherib. In the mid-1830s, Colonel R. Taylor found a hexagonal clay prism in Nineveh (the capital city of Assyria). Also known as Taylor's Prism, this 15-inch high vessel contains six well-preserved paragraphs of cuneiform written in the Akkadian language. In 1924, Daniel David Luckenbill of the University of Chicago translated the text. Luckenbill's work uncovered the following statements recorded on **Sennacherib's Prism:**

> I had completed the palace in the midst of the city of Nineveh for my royal residence.... I laid siege to 46 of his strong cities, walled forts and to countless small cities in their vicinity, and conquered them.... [Hezekiah] I made a prisoner in Jerusalem, his royal residence, like a bird in a cage.

"[Hezekiah] I made a prisoner in Jerusalem, his royal residence, like a bird in a cage."

It also identified "Hezekiah, the Judahite." This exact siege on the strong cities on Jerusalem during the reign of Hezekiah by King Sennacherib is clearly documented in three books of the Bible: 2 Kings (see 2 Kings 18:13-16), 2 Chronicles, and Isaiah. In Isaiah 36:1 we read, "Now it came to pass in the fourteenth year of King Hezekiah that Sennacherib king of Assyria came up against all the fortified cities of Judah, and took them." Given that this prism was discovered after centuries in the dirt, one should not doubt the precision and accuracy of Biblical accounts as described by inspired writers.

Ebla Tablets

In 1973 Italian archaeologists discovered the ruins of the ancient city of Elba in northern Syria. Several years later as excavators were digging through the ruins of the city palace, they came across more than 15,000 cuneiform tablets dated around 2200 B.C. The tablets contain what many believe is the **earliest known reference to Jerusalem.** While the majority of these tablets deal with commerce, there is also

"A substantial proof for the accuracy of the Old Testament text has come from archaeology. Numerous discoveries have confirmed the historical accuracy of the Biblical documents, even down to the obsolete names of foreign kings on occasion."

– **Norman L. Geisler, William Nix**
A General Introduction to the Bible
5th Edition (Chicago, IL: Moody Press 1983) p. 253.

valuable information about the culture and life of this ancient city that many Biblical scholars believe further validates some of the details (names and places) found in the Patriarchal Age. Additionally, some scholars recognize the name *Canaan* in the Ebla tablets, a name that skeptics once claimed was not used at that time and as such, was used incorrectly in the early chapters of the Bible.

The Hittites

In Genesis 23 we find Abraham buying a cave in which to bury his beloved wife Sarah. Abraham ends up buying the land from Ephron **the Hittite**. (See also references to the Hittites in Deuteronomy 20:17, Judges 3:5, 1 Kings 11:1-2, 1

Kings 9:20-21, 2 Chronicles 8:7). The Bible references the Hittites approximately forty times, and yet for many centuries there was no physical evidence of the Hittites. Skeptics claimed this civilization never existed. However, in 1906, archaeologist Hugh Winckler unearthed the Hittite capital in present-day Boghaz-Koi, Turkey. All told, they discovered more than 10,000 cuneiform tablets in what was considered the ancient city's library. These tablets contain detailed laws and penalties for their society that are believed to have been in effect for 500 years. As Jack Lewis observed,

> The Hittite documents included legends, myths, historical annals, and a law code. Of considerable interest is a peace treaty between the Hittite king Hattusilis III and the Egyptian Pharaoh Ramses II [sic]. There is also extant an Egyptian copy of this oldest known peace treaty in history. In addition, there is a form of hieroglyphic Hittite whose documents have been deciphered within the last generation (Lewis, 1975, p. 10-11).

Centuries earlier the Bible had recorded it and now archaeologists have verified it.

Cyrus the Great Cylinder

In Isaiah 44 we discover the prophet Isaiah naming Cyrus as a future anointed king of Medo-Persian Empire. This prophecy occurred approximately 150 years before Cyrus was born, and yet we know Isaiah's prophecy was confirmed and recorded in 2 Chronicles 36:22-24 and Ezra 1:1-4. Cyrus would be the leader who would defeat the Babylonians and eventually allow the Jews to return and rebuild their homeland (Isaiah 13; 21:1-10). In 1879, Hormuzd Rassam found what has become known as the Cyrus the Great Cylinder—also called the first bill of human rights. This baked clay cylinder describes the Cyrus' conquest of Babylon in 539 B.C. As a result of his conquest, Cyrus gave permission for the exiled Jews in Babylon to return to Jerusalem. The cylinder records, "I [Cyrus] gathered all their [former] inhabitants and returned [to them] their habitations." This event was described in the book of Ezra 1:1-11.

In 1879, Hormuzd Rassam found what has become known as the Cyrus the Great Cylinder—also called the first bill of human rights.

Pool of Siloam

On December 23, 2004, archaeologists unearthed a pool that had Biblical era coins with Jewish writing on them. Upon further inspection, they realized they had uncovered the Pool of Siloam. Archaeologist Eli Shukron declared, "The moment that we revealed and discovered this four months ago, we were 100 percent sure it was the Siloam Pool" ("Archaeologists...," 2004). One of the excavators, Roni Reich of Haifa University, observed, "We have excavated it and dated it very accurately with coins found in the cement which the pool was built of" (as quoted in Tostevin, 2004). This is the same pool in which Jesus Christ healed a man who had been blind from birth (John 9). John recorded that Jesus initially anointed the man's eyes with clay and then told him, "Go, wash in the pool of Siloam" (v. 7). Having followed Jesus' command, the blind man was healed.

Pilate Inscription

The Bible records the name Pontius Pilate in a variety of instances in the New Testament (see Matthew 27:1ff; Luke 3:1; Mark 15; Acts 4:27). Skeptics questioned whether Pilate was a real person—a question which would bring doubt upon the crucifixion of Jesus. In 1961 a limestone block was discovered that put an end to the skeptics' charges. Deemed the "Pilate Stone," it is a brick discovered in an excavation of an ancient theater (built by decree of Herod the Great c. 30 B.C). The inscription on the stone reads, "The prefect of Judaea, Pontius Pilate, erected the Tiberium (temple in honor of Tiberius Caesar) to the August Gods." This single discovery not only demonstrates that Pilate was indeed a real person, but it also records his full name.

> *Skeptics questioned whether Pilate was a real person—a question which would bring doubt upon the crucifixion of Jesus.*

Spikes of Crucifixion

Few scholars would argue that the Romans used crucifixion as a means of capital punishment. But were victims truly nailed to the cross as the Bible indicates was the case for Jesus Christ, or were they merely lashed onto the cross with ropes? Following His resurrection, Jesus appeared to His disciples and showed them His hands and feet (Luke 24:39-40), indicating the nail holes were still visible. In John's account, Jesus tells doubting Thomas, "Reach your finger here, and look at My hands; and reach your hand here, and put it into My side. Do not be unbelieving but be believing" (John 20:27). Clearly the Bible indicates that Jesus was nailed to the cross. This testimony fits perfectly with the evidence. In 1968 Vassilios Tzaferis discovered a large spike traversing through the right heel bone of a crucified victim. Consider that this discovery was found in a Jewish ossuary—which bore the Hebrew inscription "Jehohanan the son of HGQWL"—and contained a seven-inch spike piercing the remains of two heel bones, with a piece of olive wood at the point (Haas, 1970). Archaeological data reveal that the spikes used during the time of Christ's crucifixion were tapered iron spikes five to seven inches long with a square shaft roughly three-eighths of an inch across (Tzaferis, 1970; Haas, 1970). Ossuary findings indicate that not only was nailing the hands and feet carried out, it may have been the preferred method by the Romans (Tzaferis, 1970; Haas, 1970)—just what would be expected given the Biblical testimony of the death of Jesus.

Conclusion

While these are just a few examples (due to limited space), one can already comprehend the weight of such evidence. The Web site for the Society for Historical Archaeology proclaims, "So historical archaeology is more than just a treasure hunt. It is a challenging search for clues to the people, events, and places of the past" (http://www.sha.org/EHA/default.htm). Archaeology provides strong evidence for the inspiration and validity of God's Word. In an article titled "An Old Story," Jack Schwartz, a New York newspaper editor, declared, "The evidence of a Jewish civilization going back more than two millennia is overwhelmingly borne out in the archaeology of the region. The heritage of the Jews in Palestine is documented" (http://www.israelactivism.com/factsheet/258/). How does this strike a real truth seeker? Professor and archaeologist Nelson Glueck once stated, "I have excavated for thirty years with a Bible in one hand and a trowel in the other, and in matters of historical perspective I have never found the Bible to be in error." Christians can rest assured that no one ever will.

Questions

1. Why is it vital that future generations are familiar with archaeological evidence that supports the Bible record?
2. In Luke 3:1 (cf. Acts 4:27), who was named governor of Judea? What proof exists?
3. In 1 Kings 16:23, 28-29 and 2 Kings 3:4-5, who is recorded as king over Israel and what was the name of his son who succeeded him? What physical proof exists that supports this Scripture?
4. How can things like coins testify for the accuracy of the Bible?
5. Give two reasons you believe this scientific information is often ignored by the mainstream media.

Scriptures to Study

Joshua 2-6 • Luke 23

Additional Resources

Fant, Clyde E. and Mitchell G. Reddish (2008), *The Lost Treasures of the Bible* (Eerdman's Publishing Company).

Hoeth, Alfred and John McRay (2006), *Bible Archaeology: An Exploration of the History and Culture of Early Civilizations* (Baker Books).

Price, Randall (1997) *The Stones Cry Out: What Archaeology Reveals About the Truth of the Bible* (Harvest House Publishers).

References:

"Archaeologists Identify Traces of 'Miracle' Pool" (2004), Associated Press, MSNBC, [On-line] URL: http://www.msnbc.msn.com/id/6750670/.

Fant, Clyde E. and Mitchell G. Reddish (2008), *The Lost Treasures of the Bible* (Eerdman's Publishing Company).

Haas, N. (1970), "Anthropological Observations on the Skeletal Remains From Giv'at ha-Mivtar," *Israel Exploration Journal,* 20:38-59.

Ramsay, Sir William M. (1979), *The Bearing of Recent Discovery on the Trustworthiness of the New Testament* (Grand Rapids, MI: Baker Book House) Reprinted from the 1915 edition.

Tostevin, Matthew (2004), "New Finds Unearthed at Reputed Jesus Miracle Site," Reuters, [On-line], URL: http://www.reuters.com/newsArticle.jhtml?type=topNews &storyID=7169637.

Tzaferis, V. (1970), "Jewish Tombs at and Near Giv'at ha-Mivtar, Jerusalem," *Israel Exploration Journal,* 20:38-59.

"For in six days the Lord made the heavens and the earth, the sea, and all that is in them, and rested the seventh day. Therefore the Lord blessed the Sabbath day and hallowed it."

– Exodus 20:11

Chapter

9

A Day or a Million Years?

"In the news this morning, scientists have discovered a fifty million-year-old bird fossil. This fossil could reveal secrets of how birds evolved from dinosaurs. And in other news, reporters have discovered that the leading political candidate actually believes in creationism. American scientists have said electing this official would move America back 10,000 years." Putting down his coffee cup, the man grabs his coat and briefcase and heads for the door. He knows his friends at the office will point out this latest evolutionary discovery as proof that they are right. His mind starts churning as to how everything really could have happened. He wonders: Is there room for evolution? He definitely believes that God created the heavens and earth. But lately, he wonders if maybe God created everything and then stepped back and allowed evolution to progress the earth to the condition we find it today. Surely all of those news media and scientists couldn't be wrong, could they? As he closes the door to his car, he remembers a verse in the Bible that says, "With the Lord one day is as a thousand years, and a thousand years as one day" (2 Peter 3:8). So maybe his friends were not completely wrong. In fact, maybe today is the day he sides with them and their evolutionary beliefs.

News stories like these are common occurrences in the mainstream media. So common, in fact, that many individuals have bought into the lie that one can be a Christian and embrace evolution. Many are God-fearing individuals are completely convinced that Christianity is compatible with evolution. Having spent literally years studying science and Darwinism, the first point that should be made is that the words *science* and *evolution* are not the same. While the apostles of Darwin speak of evolution being "science," the fact remains that evolution is a theory to explain a process of change. Science, on the other hand, is defined as an area of knowledge that is an object of study. Ironically there are now staunch evolutionists trying to propose that in this situation a theory holds more strength and authority than a fact. Their rationale is that a fact only gives credence to one area—whereas a theory encompasses a broad field of truth. While this may tickle the ears of some, to men who have truly been trained in science this is nonsense. What I've learned through years is that the evidence demands a Designer, and real science often points back to that Designer. So even though the mainstream media commonly portrays a battle between science and the Bible, the fact remains that God is the author of science—they go hand-in-glove.

> *What I've learned through years is that the evidence demands a Designer, and real science often points back to that Designer.*

The real battle is whether the Bible and evolution can coexist. Sir Arthur Keith was given the honor of writing the preface to the 100th anniversary of Darwin's *Origin of Species*. In his preface he acknowledged, "…The conclusion I have come to is this: the law of Christ is incompatible with the law of evolution…. Nay, the two laws are at war with each other…." Having spent years surveying the evidence, I have to concur.

Christians must realize the truthfulness of Keith's statement. The two really are at war. One cannot embrace both and hope to harmonize them together. Michael Ruse wrote a book titled *Can a Darwinian be a Christian?* in which he espoused, "Can a Darwinian be a Christian? Absolutely! Is it always easy for a Darwinian to be a Christian? No, but whoever said that the worthwhile things in life are easy? Is the Darwinian obligated to be a Christian? No, but try to be understanding of those who are." He then went on to conclude, "There are plenty of resources open to the Christian who would **move towards science and away from a literal reading of the early book of Genesis**" (2000, p. 217, emp. added). Again, Ruse here is using the term *science* in reference to evolution. But his message is clear—Christians should abandon the Bible in favor of Darwinian evolution.

"Evolution is unproved and unprovable. We believe it only because the only alternative is special creation which is unthinkable."

– Sir Arthur Keith, as quoted in W.A. Criswell, *Did Man Just Happen?*, 1972, (Grand Rapids, MI: Zondervan), p. 73.

Can a Christian Be an Evolutionist?

Given the popularity of the subject, the average person might be quick to assume that evolution is a proven fact. For instance, in the July 29, 2002, issue of *U.S. News & World Report*, Thomas Hayden ranks its reality right up there with death and taxes. In explaining "how evolution works, and why it matters more than ever," Hayden stated, "It's an everyday phenomenon, a fundamental fact of biology as real as hunger and as unavoidable as death" (2002, 133[4]:43). The message from the secular world is crystal clear: You can question everything else (including your religion), but you cannot question evolution.

Darwin's new apostles have done such an effective job of selling this propaganda that many "Bible-believing" Christians have jettisoned their beliefs of the events in the opening chapters of Genesis. Many of the new "evangelicals" consider God to be the initial Creator, but then evolution brought us to where we are today. They place their allegiance in science and then try to massage God's Word to fit the evolutionary theory. Even many New Testament Christians have bought into this lie. The term given to such "believers" is theistic evolutionists. The word "theistic" originated from the Greek *theos*, meaning "God." Theistic evolutionists therefore believe in the existence of God, but they also have bought into the lies of evolution. As Mark Jennings commented, "Theistic evolution states that God did create and develop the universe and its components, but that He did it by evolutionary processes" (Jennings, p. 3). Theistic evolutionists rationalize their beliefs by declaring, "Yes, God created the heavens and the earth," but then God used evolution to bring about the universe and earth as we find it today.

Given this scenario, theistic evolutionists are stuck with the task of trying to find a place to squeeze millions (actually BILLIONS) of years into the creation account. The only three places they can squeeze that time are: (1) before the creation week, (2) during the creation week, or (3) after the creation week. Most evolutionists and scholars realize the problem associated with putting vast amounts of time **after** the creation week—as it would mean humans have been here for billions of years. But what about the other two options? As a result of their need to account for the vast amount of time required by evolution, theistic evolutionists commonly cling to the Gap Theory, the Day-Age Theory, or Progressive Creationism in an effort to explain their beliefs.

Gap Theory

The Gap Theory is not a newcomer on the scene; Thomas Chalmers of Edinburgh University in Scotland first introduced it in 1814. While gap theorists do not all agree on a strict definition of this theory, the commonly accepted version claims that God created everything—as mentioned in Genesis 1:1—and then there was a massive "gap" of time in which this creation fell under destruction. And then in Genesis 1:2 we read about God "recreating" the earth. This would mean that plants, animals, and even man existed prior to Adam. Many blame this initial destruction on Satan, who they claim rebelled and was cast out of Heaven. This allegedly brought about a war between Satan and God that resulted in the destruction of the planet, which they claim left the earth "waste and void" (Genesis 1:2). Thus, they would say that everything following is a "re-creation" of the original.

> *This would mean that plants, animals, and even man existed prior to Adam.*

Gap theorists defend their beliefs by focusing on two Greek words: *bara* and *asah*. They claim that the word *bara* (which is used in Genesis 1:1, 21, 27) means "to create." Thus, they believe there was an original creation, and then God recreated it following everything being destroyed and left "waste and void." Thus, we are told that the original creation was "created" *(bara)*, and then all references after that refer to things being "made" *(asah)* (i.e., "made over").

Problems with the Gap Theory:
The biggest realization obvious to an unbiased observer is that there is no other Scripture that supports the idea of this pre-Adamic creation. Regarding the words *bara* and *asah*, Scripture refutes this as well, since God's Word uses the words interchangeably. For instance, in Genesis 2:4 Moses wrote, "This is the history of the heavens and the earth when they were **created**, in the day that the Lord God **made** the earth and the heavens" (see also Genesis 1:26-27; 1:21 and 1:25; 1:16 and Psalm 148:5). Second, Moses indicated as he was handing down the Ten Commandments that everything was created in six days. "For in six days the Lord made the heavens and the earth, the sea, **and all that is in them**, and rested the seventh day. Therefore the Lord blessed the Sabbath day and hallowed it" (Exodus 20:11, emp. added). This clearly indicates that **everything** was created in six days. Additionally, Paul describes Adam as "the first man" (1 Corinthians 15:45), ruling out any possibility for men living before Adam.

One should also remember that in Genesis 1:31 the totality of God's creation was pronounced "very good." Had Satan and his followers rebelled in a prior creation, this statement would have been false. Additionally, an earlier creation would indicate that sin and death had entered the world prior to Adam. However, the Bible is clear that sin and death entered mankind through the sin of Adam (see 1 Corinthians 15:21; Romans 8:20-22; Romans 5:12). In his book *Creation or Evolution?*, D.D. Riegle wisely remarked, "It is amazing that men will accept long, complicated, imaginative theories and reject the truth given to Moses by the Creator Himself" (1962, p. 24).

> *"It is amazing that men will accept long, complicated, imaginative theories and reject the truth given to Moses by the Creator Himself."*

So how would one explain the phrase "waste and void"? The phrase "waste and void" literally means **"empty and formless."** These words indicate the earth was not a graveyard of destruction under a curse of judgment. As John Whitcomb wrote in his article "The Gap Theory" published in *And God Created*, "It was simply empty of living things and without the features that it later possessed, such as oceans and continents, hills and valleys—features that would be essential for man's well-being.... [W]hen God created the earth, this was only the first state of a series of stages leading to its completion" (1973, 2:69-70).

Day-Age Theory
Not being able to adequately defend the Gap Theory, many individuals try to squeeze millions (or billions) of years into the creation week. This belief system is commonly referred to as the Day-Age Theory, in which each day of the creation week is suggested to be eons of time. Many people who claim to be Christians view the Day-Age Theory as a way to insert geologic time into the Biblical text, thus allowing them to embrace evolution as a fact. However, the point should not be missed that this is merely a compromise. As John Klotz noted in his book *Genes, Genesis, and Evolution*, "It is hardly conceivable that anyone would question the interpretation of these as ordinary days were it not for the fact that people are attempting to reconcile Genesis and evolution" (1955, p. 87). If anything, the pressure to embrace evolution has grown even stronger in the past fifty years. (**A full refutation follows the section on Progressive Creationists**).

Progressive Creationists
A new group is trying to blend some of these beliefs together. These professed Bible-

believers do not necessarily want to defend organic evolution as correct; nevertheless they accept evolutionary dating methods and must therefore reconcile the old ages. These "progressive creationists" (as they generally prefer to be called), convinced that such dating methods are correct and that the earth is ancient, must then find a way to inject geologic time into the Genesis record. The word *progress* is from the Latin *progredi* (pro-forward + *gradi*-to step) meaning to go forward, proceed, or advance (Traupman, 1981, p. 246). As the name contends, progressive creation affirms a creation by a supernatural intervention by God in natural history—it is a hybrid of the Day-Age Theory and Theistic Evolution. As such, this theory contends that God may have also worked through existing material and natural processes to come to the end result we see today. Progressive Creation-ists also believe that creation is progressive—that is, it proceeded forward in a step-like manner. The last defining characteristic of Progressive Creation is that it happened over unlimited time. Millions of years are inserted by changing the meaning of "day" in the creation account from a single 24-hour rotation of the earth to a long, indefinite period of time and then having God step in and progress creation at various intervals. Thus, believ-ers speculate that creation could have occurred over six literal solar days or over billions of years. This lack of definition of time allows Progressive Creationists to embrace both the Biblical account and evolutionary evidence, which supposedly alleges that the earth is much older than 10,000 years.

Having already proven that the Bible is inspired, let's take a minute and look at the facts:

Fact #1
God Created Everything

Genesis 1:1—"In the beginning God created the heavens and the earth."

Psalm 33:6, 9—"By the word of the Lord the heavens were made, and all the host of them by the breath of His mouth.... For He spoke, and it was done; He commanded, and it stood fast."

Psalm 19:1—"The heavens declare the glory of God; and the firmament shows His handiwork."

Acts 4:24—"So when they heard that, they raised their voice to God with one accord and said: "Lord, You are God, who made heaven and earth and the sea, and all that is in them."

Acts 17:25—"Nor is He worshiped with men's hands, as though He needed anything, since He gives to all life, breath, and all things."

Colossians 1:16—"For by Him all things were created that are in heaven and that are on earth, visible and invisible, whether thrones or dominions or principalities or powers. All things were created through Him and for Him."

Hebrews 1:2—"…Has in these last days spoken to us by His Son, whom He has appointed heir of all things, through whom also He made the worlds."

John 1:1-3—"In the beginning was the Word, and the Word was with God, and the Word was God. He was in the beginning with God. All things were made through Him, and without Him nothing was made that was made."

Fact #2
God Created Everything in Six Days

Genesis 2:3—"Then God blessed the seventh day and sanctified it, because in it He rested from all His work which God had created and made."

Exodus 20:11—"For in six days the Lord made the heavens and the earth, the sea, and all that is in them, and rested the seventh day. Therefore the Lord blessed the Sabbath day and hallowed it."

Exodus 31:15-17—"Work shall be done for six days, but the seventh is the Sabbath of rest, holy to the Lord. Whoever does any work on the Sabbath day, he shall surely be put to death. Therefore the children of Israel shall keep the Sabbath, to observe the Sabbath throughout their generations as a perpetual covenant. It is a sign between Me and the children of Israel forever; for in six days the Lord made the heavens and the earth, and on the seventh day He rested and was refreshed."

Joshua 10:14 (after Joshua's "long day")—"And there has been no day like that, before it or after it, that the Lord heeded the voice of a man; for the Lord fought for Israel."

The words *evening* and *morning* are used together in the Old Testament with the word *day (yom)* over 100 times in non-prophetical literature. Each time the word *day* refers to a literal, 24-hour day.

[Also consider that the green flowering plants were created on Day 3. Many of those flowering plants required pollination in order to reproduce. If each day were millions of years, how did the plants survive millions of years until the flying insects came along on Day 5? Additionally, the sun is not created until Day 4, and yet the plants are already in place. If each day were millions of years, how could the plants survive while waiting on the formation of the sun?]

Fact #3
The Bible Indicates that Man Has Been Here Since the Creation of the World

Mark 10:6—"But from the beginning of the creation, God 'made them male and female.'"

Matthew 19:4—"And He answered and said to them, 'Have you not read that He who made them at the beginning made them male and female.'"

Romans 1:20— "For since the creation of the world His invisible attributes are clearly seen, being understood by the things that are made, even His eternal power and Godhead, so that they are without excuse." [The apostle Paul declared that from the creation of the world the invisible things of God have been: (a) clearly seen; and (b) perceived or understood. Thus, someone had to be there to do the seeing and perceiving "from the beginning" of the creation! Evolution teaches that man is a relative newcomer on the scene.]

Fact #4
The Bible Indicates Adam Was
Indeed the First Man

1 Corinthians 15:22—"For as in Adam all die, even so in Christ shall all be made alive."

1 Corinthians 15:45—"And so it is written, 'The first man Adam became a living being; the last Adam became a life-giving spirit.'" [This first Adam referencing the Adam God made during the creation week, whereas the second Adam refers to Jesus Christ. Consider the dilemma posed when one takes the position that the first Adam was merely a myth—what does that do to the second Adam? Paul referred to both as real individuals.]

Romans 5:12-14—"Therefore, just as through one man sin entered the world and **death** through sin, and thus **death** spread to all men, because all sinned— (For until the law sin was in the world, but sin is not imputed when there is no law. Nevertheless death reigned from Adam to Moses, even over those who had not sinned according to the likeness of the transgression of Adam, who is a type of Him who was to come…" [Paul in writing to the Christians at Rome indicated that Adam brought death into the world].

1 Timothy 2:13—"For Adam was first formed, then Eve." (cf. Genesis 2)

Fact #5
The Bible Gives the Genealogy from
Adam (literal man) to Christ

The genealogy from Adam to Noah's sons is listed in Genesis chapter 5.
The descendants of Noah's son Shem to Abraham are listed in Genesis chapter 11.
The genealogy from Abraham to Christ is given in Matthew 1:1-17 (Joseph's family line).

The genealogy from Christ to Adam is given in Luke 3:23-38 (Mary's family line).

Jude 14 references Enoch as the seventh from Adam **as specified in Genesis 5:18**, indicating there are no gaps in the first seven families.

Fact #6
The Bible Demonstrates the Need for Redemption and a Savior (first mentioned in Genesis 3)

Genesis 3:15—"And I will put enmity between you and the woman, and between your seed and her Seed; He shall bruise your head, and you shall bruise His heel."

1 John 5:11-13—"And this is the testimony: that God has given us eternal life, and this life is in His Son. He who has the Son has life; he who does not have the Son of God does not have life. These things I have written to you who believe in the name of the Son of God, that you may know that you have eternal life, and that you may continue to believe in the name of the Son of God."

Hebrews 6:19-20—"This hope we have as an anchor of the soul, both sure and steadfast, and which enters the Presence behind the veil, where the forerunner has entered for us, even Jesus, having become High Priest forever according to the order of Melchizedek."

Colossians 2:13-14—"And you, being dead in your trespasses and the uncircumcision of your flesh, He has made alive together with Him, having forgiven you all trespasses, having wiped out the handwriting of requirements that was against us, which was contrary to us. And He has taken it out of the way, having nailed it to the cross."

Fact #7
New Testament Writers Believed that Genesis 1-11 Was Historically Accurate

In the New Testament alone, there are at least 200 quotations from—or references to—Genesis. In fact, there are over 100 citations or direct references in the New Testament to the first 11 chapters of Genesis. And every one of those 11 chapters, (except chapter 8) is referred to somewhere in the New Testament.

a. Every New Testament writer refers to the early chapters of Genesis (Genesis 1–11).

b. Jesus Christ referred to each of the first 7 chapters of Genesis.

c. All New Testament books except Galatians, Philippians, 1 and 2 Thessalonians, 2 Timothy, Titus, Philemon, and 2 and 3 John refer to Genesis 1–11.

Reference	Topic	Genesis Reference
1. Matthew 19:4	Created male and female	1:27, 5:2
2. Matthew 19:5–6	Cleave to his wife; become one flesh	2:24
3. Matthew 23:35	Righteous Abel	4:4
4. Matthew 24:37–39	Noah and the Flood	6:1–22, 7:1–24, 8:1–22
5. Mark 10:6	Created male and female	1:27, 5:2
6. Mark 10:7–9	Cleave to his wife, become one flesh	2:24
7. Mark 13:19	Since the beginning of the creation which God created	1:1, 2:4
8. Luke 3:34–36	Genealogies: Abraham to Shem	11:10–26
9. Luke 3:36–38	Genealogies: Noah to Adam to God	5:3–29
10. Luke 11:51	Blood of Abel	4:8–11
11. Luke 17:27	The flood came and destroyed them all	7:10–23
12. John 1:1–3	In the beginning…was God	1:1
13. John 8:44	Father of lies	3:4–5
14. Acts 14:15	Who made the heaven and the earth	2:1
15. Acts 17:24	God made all things	1:1–31

16. Romans 1:20	The creation of the world	1:1–31, 2:4
17. Romans 4:17	God can create out of nothing	1:1–31
18. Romans 5:12	Death entered the world by sin	2:16–17, 3:19
19. Romans 5:14–19	Death reigned from Adam	2:17
20. Romans 8:20–22	Creation corrupted	3:17–18
21. 1 Corinthians 6:16	Two will become one flesh	2:24
22. 1 Corinthians 11:3	Head of the woman is man	3:16
23. 1 Corinthians 11:7	In the image of God	1:27, 5:1
24. 1 Corinthians 11:8	Woman from man	2:22–23
25. 1 Corinthians 11:9	Woman for the man	2:18
26. 1 Corinthians 15:21–22	By a man came death	2:16–17, 3:19
27. 1 Corinthians 15:38–39	To each ... seeds of its own (kind)	1:11, 21, 24
28. 1 Corinthians 15:45	Adam became a living being	2:7
29. 1 Corinthians 15:47	Man from the earth	3:23
30. 2 Corinthians 4:6	Light out of darkness	1:3–5
31. 2 Corinthians 11:3	Serpent deceived Eve	3:1–6,13
32. Ephesians 3:9	Created all things	1:1–31, 2:1–3
33. Ephesians 5:30–31	Cleave to his wife, become one flesh	2:24
34. Colossians 1:16	All things created by Him	1:1–31, 2:1–3
35. Colossians 3:10	Created in His image	1:27
36. 1 Timothy 2:13–14	Adam created first	2:18–23
37. 1 Timothy 2:14	Woman deceived	3:1–6, 13

38. 1 Timothy 4:4	Everything created by God is good	1:10–31
39. Hebrews 1:10	In the beginning God made heavens and earth	1:1
40. Hebrews 2:7–8	All things in subjection under man	1:26–30, 9:2–3
41. Hebrews 4:3	Works were finished	2:1
42. Hebrews 4:4	Rest on the seventh day	2:2–3
43. Hebrews 4:10	Rest from His works	2:2–3
44. Hebrews 11:3	Creation of the universe	1:1
45. Hebrews 11:4	Abel offered a better sacrifice	4:3–5
46. Hebrews 11:5	Enoch taken up	5:21–24
47. Hebrews 11:7	Noah's household saved	7:1
48. Hebrews 12:24	Blood of Abel	4:10
49. James 3:9	Men in the likeness of God	1:27, 5:1
50. 1 Peter 3:20	Construction of the Ark, eight saved	6:14–16, 7:13
51. 2 Peter 2:5	A flood upon the ungodly, eight saved	6:8–12, 7:1–24
52. 2 Peter 3:4–5	Earth formed out of water and by water	1:6–7
53. 2 Peter 3:6	The world destroyed by water	7:17–24
54. 1 John 3:8	Devil sinned from the beginning	3:14
55. 1 John 3:12	Cain killed his brother	4:8, 25
56. Jude 11	The way of Cain	4:8, 16, 25
57. Jude 14	Enoch, the seventh generation from Adam	5:3–24
58. Revelation 2:7	Tree of life	2:9
59. Revelation 3:14	Beginning of the creation of God	1:1–31, 2:1–4

60. Revelation 4:11	Created all things	1:1–31, 2:1–3
61. Revelation 10:6	Who created heaven ... and the earth	1:1, 2:1
62. Revelation 14:7	Who made the heaven and the earth	1:1; 2:1, 4
63. Revelation 20:2	The serpent of old, who is the devil	3:1, 14
64. Revelation 21:4	No more death, sorrow, crying or pain	3:17–19
65. Revelation 22:2	Fruit of the tree of life	3:22
66. Revelation 22:3	No more curse	3:14–19
67. Revelation 22:14	The tree of life	2:9

[Adapted from Dr. Henry M. Morris, *The Remarkable Birth of Planet Earth*, San Diego: ICR; and Walt Brown, *In the Beginning: Compelling Evidence for Creation and the Flood*, Center for Scientific Creation, Phoenix, AZ]

The Bible clearly indicates that God created man on Day 6, the first man was Adam—and that mankind has been here from the beginning of creation. It also indicates Adam is in the genealogical line with Jesus. God's Word teaches the necessity for the redemption of man (through Jesus) in the Garden of Eden because of man's sin. It is also obvious that New Testament writers viewed the accounts in Genesis to be real and historical occurrences.

Conclusion

G. Richard Culp summed it up well when he wrote, "One who doubts the Genesis account will not be the same man he once was, for his attitude toward Holy Scripture has been eroded by false teaching. Genesis is repeatedly referred to in the New Testament, and it cannot be separated from the total Christian message" (1975, p. 160-161). He went on to say, "We stand either with God and His teaching of Creation, or we stand with the evolutionists in opposition to Him. The issues are sharply drawn. There

"It is, in fact, a common fantasy, promulgated mostly by the scientific profession itself, that in the search for objective truth, data dictate conclusions"...."Data are just as often molded to fit preferred conclusions."

– Roger Lewin,
pro-evolutionist as quoted
in *Bones of Contention*, (NY:
Simon and Schuster)
1987, p. 68.

can be no compromise. You are either a Christian or an evolutionist, but you cannot be both." I completely agree.

The two models are at complete odds with one another. In the Biblical account of creation, man starts out as the pinnacle of God's creation and, through sin, falls. The evolutionary account is completely opposite, having mankind start from some amoeba and then after millions of years we evolved our way to the top. There is nothing similar in these two accounts. Consider also that if man truly did not fall as described in the creation account, then what need would there be for Jesus Christ to redeem man?

Robert Taylor put it well when he said:

> *Surely evolution will not have to reverse itself and concede that it reached its zenith with the birth of the Christ child a long, long time ago. Surely this colossal system will not have to concede that it is less able now to produce a greater than Jesus than it did produce two thousand years ago. If evolution is not now able to produce a greater than Jesus, then it seems the system has ceased to be evolution and has become devolution, at least in one sense? (1974).*

Today, this theory appears more like "devilution" than devolution.

While men may occasionally grab 2 Peter 3:8 and claim that a day is a thousand years to God, they have done so by taking that passage out of context. As Guy N. Woods pointed out, this passage simply means that time does not affect the performance of God's promises or threats (1976, p. 146). The context is when Jesus will return, not how long it took to create the heavens and earth.

Honest Bible scholars will admit that only a scant few books in the Bible do not refer back to the opening chapters of Genesis as real and historic. Does this fact mean all other books in the Bible should be cut out or not trusted? Paul in writing to Timothy reminded him, "All Scripture is given by inspiration of God and is profitable for doctrine, for reproof, and for correction, for instruction in righteousness" (2 Timothy 3:16). Can a Christian be an evolutionist? Absolutely not—*indeed the two are at war with one another! A true New Testament Christian realizes the two are incompatible.*

Questions
1. What is the implication of New Testament writers writing about the creation week due to those holding to the evolutionary theory?
2. Why are people hesitant to abandon the old ages of the earth often recounted in the mainstream media?
3. How would a belief in theistic evolution alter one's worldview?
4. Why is 2 Peter 3:8 not a good argument for an ancient earth?
5. What are the strongest arguments against theistic evolution?

Scriptures
Exodus 20:11 • Exodus 31:14-17 • Romans 1:20
Mark 10:6 • Matthew 19:4

Additional Resources

 Fields, Weston (2005), *Unformed and Unfilled* (Green Forest, AR: Master Books).

Morris, Henry (1976), *The Genesis Record* (Grand Rapids, MI: Baker).

References
Culp, G. Richard (1975), *Remember Thy Creator* (Grand Rapids, MI: Baker).
Jennings, Mark (no date), *Theistic Evolution, a tract* (Fort Worth, TX: Star Bible).
Riegle, D.D. (1962), *Creation or Evolution?* (Grand Rapids, MI: Zondervan).
Taylor, Robert (1974), "More Problems for Theistic Evolution," *Gospel Advocate,* January 3.
Whitcomb, John C. (1973), "The Gap Theory," *And God Created,* ed. Kelly L. Segraves (San Diego, CA: Creation-Science Research Center), 2:61-65.
Woods, Guy N. (1976), *Questions and Answers: Open Forum,* (Henderson, TN: Freed-Hardeman University).

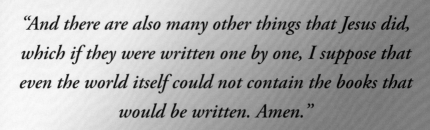

"And there are also many other things that Jesus did, which if they were written one by one, I suppose that even the world itself could not contain the books that would be written. Amen."

– John 21:25

Chapter

10

Jesus on Trial...Again

Heat is rising off the pavement as the thermometer reaches 98°F outside. The three young teens do not really care what they see, they just want to get in from the sweltering heat and have a few hours away from Mom and Dad. So they purchase $10.00 tickets for a movie they have never heard of, buy a $15.00 bucket of popcorn, and settle into the theater seats. After answering some movie trivia and watching a few previews, the screen goes blank and they realize what they paid money to see: a movie called *The Beast*, which claims it has Christianity's best-kept secret—that Jesus Christ never existed. Or maybe it was a movie like *The Da Vinci Code* or *Angels and Demons*. Given Hollywood's love for anti-religious or atheistic themes, the scenario above is far from hypothetical. Year after year, Hollywood releases movies that challenge the existence of God and ridicule the Christian religion. These films often receive enormous press from the mainstream media who love to promote a secular, humanistic worldview. What do these vicious attacks do to the faith of our young people? What happens when our children grow up in a culture that questions the deity of Jesus Christ? What happens when our young people believe there is no evidence for Jesus Christ outside of the Bible?

If one were going to attack the foundations of Christianity, then the very existence of Jesus would be one of the first places to start. Skeptics have questioned whether or not He existed, whether He was in fact the Son of God, and whether or not He was resurrected from the tomb. Director of *The Beast* Brian Flemming stated in an interview on WBAI New York 99.5 FM on April 3, 2005, "I think it is probably correct that Jesus in fact never existed." He went on to note: "Once I started looking at the evidence…I became fascinated by the idea that Jesus Christ never existed…a fact that many people have never even heard at all." Brian Flemming is the same individual who guides viewers through the caustic film *The God Who Wasn't There*, in which he maintains, "Jesus Christ is likely a fictional character, a legend never based on a real human" (see http://www.thegodmovie.com/).

Flemming is far from alone. In his book *The Case against Christianity*, Michael Martin, a professor of philosophy from Boston University, concluded that there was insufficient evidence to establish that Jesus existed. Atheist Bertrand Russell in his book *Why I Am Not a Christian* stated, "Historically, it is quite doubtful whether Christ ever existed at all, and if He did we do not know anything about Him" (see

http://www.classicreader.com/book/1736/1/). Preacher-turned-atheist Dan Barker proclaimed, "The Gospel stories are no more historic than the Genesis creation accounts are scientific…. [I]t is rational to conclude that the New Testament Jesus is a myth" (1992, p. 378). The skeptics' attacks are endless. The mainstream media prides itself in declaring the death of God, Christ, and Christianity. For instance, the April 2009 cover story of *Newsweek* magazine was on "The Decline and Fall of Christian America." The film trailer on *The Beast's* Web site has an image of Jesus with the following propaganda filling the screen: "Centuries ago, a legend was invented…forgery…fraud…coercion…wealth…greed…torture… murder…war…gave it the power to dominate the world." The Web site goes on to claim: "The authors of the Gospels, writing 40 to 90 years after the supposed life of Christ, never intended for their works to be read as biographies. **There are no credible non-Christian references to Christ during the period in which he is said to have lived**" (emp. added). Words are easy to pen—but what does the evidence say?

Messianic Prophecies

One of the strongest evidences for the existence of Jesus Christ (and the inspiration of the Bible) is the numerous prophecies surrounding the coming Messiah—prophecies that were fulfilled in the New Testament. While the media is quick to question

His existence, they never document the prophecies surrounding His life and death. Other books that claim inspiration and elevate men to the level of deity (e.g., the Quran and Mohammed) do not contain the specific predictions and fulfillments that are found in God's Word. Precise details surrounding the birth, life, and death of Jesus Christ were foretold by prophets literally thousands of years before He was born of a virgin. The very first Messianic prophecies is found in Genesis 3:15 as God is handing out His punishment for sin in the Garden of Eden. Throughout the Old Testament we find more than 300 Messianic prophecies—all of which were fulfilled by this man we call Jesus. In order to truly appreciate the specificity of these prophecies one would do well to study Psalm 22 and Isaiah 52-53. Listed below are just a select few of the prophecies and where they were fulfilled in the New Testament.

Topic	Prophecy	Prediction	Fulfillment
Birth and lineage of Jesus	Born of a virgin, named Immanuel	Isaiah 7:14	Matthew 1:18-25
	Born at Bethlehem	Micah 5:2	Matthew 2:1
	From the seed of Abraham	Genesis 22:18	Matthew 1:1
	From the tribe of Judah	Genesis 49:10	Matthew 1:2
	From the house of David	Jeremiah 23:5	Matthew 1:1
Ministry of Jesus	Ministry to begin in Galilee	Isaiah 9:1	Matthew 4:12-13
	He will teach in parables	Psalm 78:2	Matthew 13:34
	He would heal the blind, the deaf, and the lame	Isaiah 35:5-6	Matthew 9:35

	He would enter Jerusalem on a donkey	Zechariah 9:9	Matthew 21:6-11
Arrest and Crucifixion	He will be betrayed by a friend	Psalm 41:9	Matthew 10:4
	Sold for 30 pieces of silver	Zechariah 11:12	Matthew 26:15
	He would be silent before His accusers	Isaiah 53:7	Matthew 27:12
	Hands and feet pierced	Psalm 22:16	Matthew 27:35
	No bones to be broken	Psalm 34:20	John 19:33
	Killed with the transgressors	Isaiah 53:12	Matthew 27:38
	His garments would be parted and cast lots for	Psalm 22:18	Matthew 27:35
	His side would be pierced	Zechariah 12:10	John 19:34
	He would be buried in a rich man's tomb	Isaiah 53:9	Matthew 27:57-60
	He would make intercession for the transgressors	Isaiah 53:12	Luke 23:34

While these prophecies do not prove that Christ walked the earth, they provide powerful testimony to the inspiration of the Scriptures and His deity. However, an atheist is not going to accept the existence of Christ based on a book they do not believe. In order to prove Christ existed, we must take our argument away from the Bible and into the courtroom.

"As the centuries pass, the evidence is accumulating that, measured by His effect on history, Jesus is the most influential life ever lived on this planet."

– Historian Kenneth Scott Latourette

Jesus on Trial

In 2002, Italian atheist Luigi Cascioli accused Enrico Righi, a Catholic priest, of misleading the public by presenting Jesus as a real historical character. That case was eventually thrown out of the court; however, on September 13, 2008, Cascioli raised the stakes by filing a similar suit against a representative of ministers of religion for abuse of popular credulity and impersonation. He contends after years of studying the Bible, "Many of the facts produced and presented as if being true and historical in the so-called 'Holy Scriptures,' are in reality false, first of all the historicization of the figure of Jesus Christ" (see http://www.luigicascioli.eu). Can Christians actually prove that Jesus Christ existed? Are the makers of *The Beast* correct when they suggest there are no credible non-Christian references to Christ? Does sufficient evidence for Christ exist outside the pages of the Bible? Ultimately, who could be called to the stand to testify for Jesus Christ? Consider the following case for the existence of Christ.

Does sufficient evidence for Christ exist outside the pages of the Bible?

Friendly Witnesses

First, I would call "friendly witnesses" to the stand—early non-inspired preachers whose writings testify for Christ.

The defense calls **Clement of Rome** (c. A.D. 30-100) to the stand. Clement served as a bishop in the church at Rome and wrote a letter to Christians in Corinth in which he said:

> The Apostles received the Gospel for us from the Lord Jesus Christ; Jesus Christ was sent forth from God. So then Christ is from God, and the Apostles are from Christ. Both therefore came of the will of God in the appointed order. Having therefore received a charge, and having been fully assured through the resurrection of our Lord Jesus Christ and confirmed in the word of God with full assurance of the Holy Ghost, they went forth with the glad tidings that the kingdom of God should come (*Corinthians*, p. 42).

The defense calls **Ignatius** (A.D. 70-110) to the stand. Ignatius, a bishop of Antioch, wrote letters to churches, three of which specifically referenced Jesus Christ. For instance, Ignatius wrote:

> Jesus Christ, who was of the race of David, who was the Son of Mary, who was truly born and ate and drank, was truly persecuted under Pontius Pilate, was truly crucified and died in the sight of those in heaven and on earth and those under the earth; who moreover was truly raised from the dead, His Father having raised Him, who in the like fashion will so raise us also who believe in Him (*Trallians*, p. 9).

The defense calls **Polycarp** (A.D. 70-156) to the stand. Polycarp was an early Christian leader who was martyred for speaking the Truth. Polycarp wrote:

But may the God and Father of our Lord Jesus Christ, and Jesus Christ Himself, who is the Son of God, and our everlasting High Priest, build you up in faith and truth, and in all meekness, gentleness, patience, long-suffering, forbearance, and purity; and may He bestow on you a lot and portion among His saints, and on us with you, and on all that are under heaven, who shall believe in our Lord Jesus Christ, and in His Father, who raised Him from the dead (*Letter to the Philippians*, Chapter 13).

The defense calls **Justin Martyr** (A.D. 100-165) to the stand. Justin Martyr was an early church leader who many consider one of the greatest early Christian apologists. He wrote a great deal about the New Testament and referenced Jesus as a real person on several different occasions. For instance, he wrote of Jesus "being the first-begotten Word of God, is even God" (*First Apology*, chapter 63). He went on to describe, "Now there is a village in the land of the Jews, thirty-five stadia from Jerusalem, in which Jesus Christ was born, as you can ascertain also from the registers of the taxing made under Cyrenius, your first procurator in Judea" (*First Apology*, 34).

The defense calls **Irenaeus** (A.D. 130-202) to the stand. Irenaeus was also an early church leader who wrote:

> ...this is **Christ, the Son of the living God**. For I have shown from the Scriptures, that no one of the sons of Adam is as to everything, and absolutely, called God, or named Lord. But that He is Himself in His own right, beyond all men who ever lived, **God**, and **Lord**, and **King Eternal**, and the **Incarnate Word**, proclaimed by all the prophets, the apostles, and by the Spirit Himself, may be seen by all who have attained to even a small portion of the truth. Now, **the Scriptures would not have testified these things of Him, if, like others, He had been a mere man** (emp. added, *The Apostolic Fathers*, Chapter 19, available online http://www.ccel.org/ccel/schaff/anf01.toc.html).

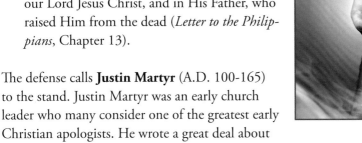

The testimony of these early church leaders may be dismissed by skeptics or atheists—but its existence is irrefutable and speaks loudly of existence of Jesus Christ. Consider the punishment for someone making the claim of deity of another man.

Hostile Witnesses

Additionally, we could seek "hostile" witnesses to take the stand who should not testify for the existence of Christ—but do.

The defense calls Jewish historian **Flavius Josephus** (A.D. 37/38-100) to the stand. In his *Jewish Antiquities* Josephus confirmed:

> And there arose about this time Jesus, a wise man, if indeed we should call him a man; for he was a doer of marvelous deeds, a teacher of men who receive the truth with pleasure. He led away many Jews, and also Greeks. He was the Christ. And when Pilate had condemned him to the cross on his impeachment by the chief men among us, those who had loved him at first did not cease; for he appeared to them on the third day alive again, the divine prophets having spoken these and thousands of other wonderful things about him: and even now the tribe of Christians, so named after him, has not yet died out (*Antiquities of the Jews*, 18:3:3).

> *"And there arose about this time Jesus, a wise man, if indeed we should call him a man; for he was a doer of marvelous deeds, a teacher of men who receive the truth with pleasure."*

The defense calls Roman historian, **Cornelius Tacitus** (c. A.D. 55-117) to the stand. In his historical account, Tacitus mentioned how Nero used Christians as scapegoats for the burning of Rome. He observed:

> Consequently, to get rid of the report, Nero fastened the guilt and inflicted the most exquisite tortures on a class hated for their abominations, called Christians by the populace. Christus, from whom the name had its origin, suffered the

extreme penalty during the reign of Tiberius at the hands of one of our procurators, Pontius Pilatus, and a most mischievous superstition, thus checked for the moment, again broke out not only in Judaea, the first source of the evil, but even in Rome, where all things hideous and shameful from every part of the world find their centre and become popular.

Accordingly, an arrest was first made of all who pleaded guilty; then, upon their information, an immense multitude was convicted, not so much of the crime of firing the city, as of hatred against mankind. Mockery of every sort was added to their deaths. Covered with the skins of beasts, they were torn by dogs and perished, or were nailed to crosses, or were doomed to the flames and burnt, to serve as a nightly illumination, when daylight had expired. Nero offered his gardens for the spectacle (*Annals*, 15:44).

The defense calls Roman historian **Gaius Suetonius Tranquillus** (commonly referred to as Suetonius) to the stand. Suetonius wrote, "Punishments by Nero was inflicted on the Christians, a class of men given to a new and mischievous superstition" (*Lives of the Caesars*, 26. 2), thereby giving us evidence that Christians existed during this time. In his famous work on *The Life of Claudius*, he noted, "Because the Jews at Rome caused continuous disturbance at the instigation of Chrestus, he [Claudius] expelled them from the city" (25:4). [Suetonius simply used a variation on the spelling of Christ, but it is virtually the same as the Latin spelling *Christus*.]

The defense calls **Lucian**, a Greek satirist, to the stand. Lucian scornfully wrote:
The Christians, you know, worship a man to this day—the **distinguished personage who introduced their novel rites**, and **was crucified** on that account.... You see, these misguided creatures start with the general conviction that they are immortal for all time, which explains the contempt of death and voluntary self-devotion which are so common among them; and then it was impressed on them by **their original lawgiver** that they are all brothers, from the moment that they are converted, and deny the gods of Greece, and worship **the crucified sage**, and live after **his laws** (*The Death of Peregrine*, 11-13, emp. added).

The defense calls **Pliny the Younger**, the governor of Bithynia, to the stand. In a letter written about 112 A.D. to Emperor Trajan, Pliny stated,

> They [the Christians] were in the habit of meeting on a certain fixed day before it was light, when they sang in alternate verses a hymn **to Christ**, as to a god, and bound themselves by a solemn oath, not to any wicked deeds, but never to commit fraud, theft, adultery, never to falsify their word, not to deny a trust when they should be called upon to deliver it up (*Epistles* X, p. 96, emp. added).

More evidence could be given, but the case has been unquestionable made that Jesus Christ walked on the earth. His earthly existence can be denied only by those pre-committed to a denial of the evidence and facts. Even the Jews acknowledge His existence.

Questions
1. What happens to the scheme of redemption if Christ is removed from the picture?
2. How does testimony from past historians prove Christ existed?
3. Do other religions recognize Jesus as a historical figure?
4. Given the magnitude of this evidence, what responsibility is placed on the shoulders of those who know the Truth regarding Jesus Christ?

Scriptures to Study
Luke 19:10 • John 1:1-3 • Romans 5:6-8 • Matthew 16:13-18

Additional Resources

Habermas, Gary and Michael Licona (2004), *The Case for the Resurrection for Jesus* (Grand Rapids, MI: Kregel Publications).

McDowell, Josh (1999) *The New Evidence That Demands a Verdict* (Nashville, TN: Thomas Nelson Publishers).

McDowell, Josh (2006), *Evidence for Christianity* (Nashville, TN: Thomas Nelson Publishers).

"By His knowledge My righteous Servant shall justify many,
for He shall bear their iniquities."
— Isaiah 53:11

Chapter

Maniac, Monster, or Messiah?

It was an international bestseller and it was on his summer reading list. The book chronicled the life of religions and their leaders. As a senior in high school, William was not naïve. He knew other men had claimed deity, but he had no idea that these religions had so many followers. According to the author of this book, men like Dali Lama, Zoroaster, Jesus, Buddha, and Muhammad were a dime a dozen. The book compared the similarities and differences of each man. The ultimate purpose of the book was to discount and discredit formalized religion—primarily by taking a hard shot against Judeo-Christianity. The book painted these religious leaders as maniacs or monsters. The author argued strongly that each and every one—including Jesus Christ—was nothing more than a cult leader. Knowing he would be tested on his comprehension of the book, William spent hours digesting the case against the deity of Jesus Christ. As he read the final sentence, he had more questions than answers, but he also had less faith than when he started. Was the entire account of Jesus Christ simply a hoax to justify a religious movement against the Jews?

So Who Was This Jesus?

While Hollywood may try to deny His existence, it is easily provable using historical documents from men of all cultures and backgrounds. The next obvious question is who was this man? Was He a troublemaker or a transformer? In his famous book *Mere Christianity*, C.S. Lewis tried to pinpoint the core principles of Christianity. He took great effort in presenting "an agreed, or common, or central," view of "mere" Christianity (1996, p. 8). These common points were the minimum requirements that Lewis felt one must hold to be considered a Christian. However, in that book he laid the foundation for an argument that Josh McDowell would later refine into the liar, lunatic, or Lord argument. Lewis wrote:

> I am trying here to prevent anyone saying the really foolish thing that people often say about Him: "I'm ready to accept Jesus as a great moral teacher, but I don't accept His claim to be God." That is the one thing we must not say. A man who was merely a man and said the sort of things Jesus said would not be a great moral teacher. He would either be a lunatic—on a level with the man who says he is a poached egg—or else he would be the Devil of Hell. You must make your choice. Either this man was, and is, the Son of God: or else a madman or something worse. You can shut Him up for a fool, you can spit at Him and kill Him as a demon; or you can fall at His feet and call Him Lord and God. **But let us not come up with any patronizing nonsense about His being a great human teacher. He has not left that open to us. He did not intend to**" (1952, p. 40-41, emp. added).

> *Either Jesus was who He said He was – the Son of Man –or else He was a liar or a crazy man.*

Lewis' point is well made. Either Jesus was who He said He was—the Son of Man—or else He was a liar or a crazy man. As McDowell so aptly put it, Christ is either a liar, a lunatic, or Lord.

Was Jesus a liar? How can a liar control the conditions of His birth? Remember that Messianic prophecies had foretold years earlier the conditions of Jesus' birth. These prophecies also described the family lineage from which the Messiah would come. Secondly, liars do not normally endure pain and suffering to perpetuate a lie. Yet, Jesus was scourged, beaten, and crucified. In an article titled "He Showed Himself Alive by Many Proofs," Biblical scholar Wayne Jackson remarked: "While men may die out of religious deception, they do not willingly go to their deaths knowing they are perpetrating a hoax." The label "liar" does not truly fit this man known as Jesus.

"I am an historian, I am not a believer, but I must confess as a historian that this penniless preacher from Nazareth is irrevocably the very center of history. Jesus Christ is easily the most dominant figure in all history."

– H.G. Wells

Was Jesus a lunatic? How many lunatics can come up with such great moral teachings as Jesus Christ (e.g., Don't go one mile, go two. Turn the other cheek.)? Additionally, how many lunatics can live a sinless life? Jesus Christ not only fulfilled all of the Messianic prophecies, but He also did so without sin (1 Peter 2:22; 1 John 3:5). A close inspection reveals Jesus was not a lunatic. Philip Schaff, in his book *The Person of Christ: The Miracle of History*, asked:

> How in the name of logic, common sense, and experience, could an imposter—that is a deceitful, selfish, depraved man—have invented, and consistently maintained from the beginning to end, the purest and noblest character known in history with the most perfect air of truth and reality? How could he have conceived and successfully carried out a plan of unparalleled beneficence, moral magnitude, and sublimity, and sacrificed his own life for it, in the face of the strongest prejudices of his people and ages? (1913, p. 94-95).

The only remaining option is that Jesus was who He said He was—the Son of God. Christ was not a maniac or a monster. Evidence proves this man walked the earth and was the Messiah. The remaining question is did Christ make it out of the tomb?

The Resurrection: Hoax or History?

The profession of disciple did not offer a great life expectancy for those willing to preach and teach in His name. For instance, we know James was killed with a sword (Acts 12); Paul was beheaded; whereas Peter and Andrew were crucified. And yet they preached Christ crucified with boldness. This was not a profession for the faint of heart. The question should be asked: Why would men be willing to give up their lives in exchange to preach the Gospel? The answers lie in a cogent understanding of what the resurrection of Christ really means for mankind.

> *"No intelligent jury in the world could fail to bring in a verdict that indeed the resurrection story is true"*

Humans living in the 21st century do not like buying things "sight unseen"—and I believe this true for the resurrection as well. We want to "kick the tires" and evaluate the evidence. Whether you are a "life-long" Christian or skeptical non-believer, evidence exists that an unbiased heart cannot ignore. While many people still cling to a position of unbelief, a true evaluation of the evidence renders their foundation untenable (see also Butt, 2002). Lord Darling, former chief justice of England, observed, "No intelligent jury in the world could fail to bring in a verdict that indeed the resurrection story is true" (Green, 1968, p. 53-54).

The discipline of science seeks to gain knowledge through observation of the available evidence. When one dissects the resurrection through the eyes of science there are many things one can defend even almost two thousand years removed from that event:

The Evidence Reveals Jesus Lived
A thorough investigation of history reveals Jesus walked this earth. We can read the testimony from early non-inspired preachers whose writings testify for Christ—men

like Clement of Rome (c. A.D. 30-100); Ignatius (A.D. 70-110); Polycarp (A.D. 70-156); Justin Martyr (A.D. 100-165); and Irenaeus (A.D. 130-202). In addition to these non-inspired preachers, there is also extensive documentation from "hostile" witnesses such as the Jewish historian Josephus. He noted: "And there arose about this time Jesus, a wise man, if indeed we should call him a man" (*Antiquities of the Jews*, 18:3:3). For more examples see "hostile witness" section. Considering we date everything by the life of this man Jesus, it is only rational to conclude Jesus lived.

The Evidence Reveals Jesus Suffered Mortal Wounds on the Cross

The Gospel accounts paint a grim picture of the final hours in the life of Jesus. The Romans had perfected the art of torture and slow, painful death. The Bible records that Jesus was beaten, spit upon, scourged, mocked with a crown of thorns, cruci-fied, and then a spear was thrust in His side (see Mark 14-15; Matthew 27; Luke 22:54–23:49; John 19). These statements are confirmed by the testimony of historians such as Josephus. The Jews acknowledge that Jesus lived and even concede in the Talmud (a major text of the Jews only second to the Hebrew Bible) that He was hung. In the Babylonian Talmud they admit:

> On the eve of the Passover Yeshu was hanged. For forty days before the execu-tion took place, a herald went forth and cried, "He is going forth to be stoned because he has practiced sorcery and enticed Israel to apostasy. Any one who can say anything in his favor, let him come forward and plead on his behalf." But since nothing was brought forward in his favor he was hanged on the eve of the Passover! (translated by I. Epstein, London: Soncino, 1935, Vol. III, Sanhedrin 43a, p. 281).

Prior to the crucifixion, Pilate had Jesus scourged. Scourging was a known legal preliminary for every Roman execution, because without it strong condemned men would remain on the cross for several days before finally succumbing to hunger and exposure. Dr. William Edwards and his colleagues described Christ's flogging in the following manner: "Then, as the flogging continued, the lacerations would tear into the underlying skeletal muscles and produce quivering ribbons of bleeding flesh. Pain and blood loss generally set the stage for circulatory shock" (1986, 256:1457). Add to this that John recorded Jesus' side was pierced by a soldier.

The Evidence Reveals Jesus Died

If for no other reason than science has never observed anything that (or anyone who) could escape death, Jesus' death is beyond question. Add to this that the inspired Bible records His death, as do many extra-Biblical sources (see above), and one can logically rationalize that Jesus lived, suffered, and died.

The Evidence Reveals Jesus Was Buried in the Tomb

The Bible is clear that the body of Jesus was placed into a new tomb owned by

Joseph of Arimathea (Matthew 27:57-60; Mark 15:42-46; etc.). Theology professor Wilbur Smith noted, "The word for tomb or sepulchre occurs thirty-two times in the four Gospel records of the resurrection" (1971, p. 38). Archaeological evidence supports the burial practice using tombs and ossuaries during the period under consideration. We also know the body of Jesus was prepared with spices, oils, and linen—a common practice of the day (Mark 15:46-16:1; Luke 23:56). In a letter circulated by the Sanhedrin in the first century, the Jews admit Jesus was crucified and buried in a tomb. "A godless and lawless heresy had sprung up from one Jesus a Galilean deceiver, whom we crucified; but his disciples stole him by night **from the tomb**, where he was laid when unfastened from the cross, and now deceive men by asserting that he has risen from the dead and ascended to heaven" (emp. added) [Mentioned by Justin Martyr in his *Dialogue with Trypho* (A.D. 100-165) and Eusebius (A.D. 265-340)].

The Evidence Reveals Measures Were Taken to Secure the Tomb

A stone was placed in front of the tomb of Jesus (Matthew 27:66). In ancient days this was a protective measure to keep out men and beasts. H. W. Holloman, referencing G. M. Mackie, observed, "The opening to the central chamber was guarded by a large and heavy disc of rock which could roll along a groove slightly depressed at the center, in front of the tomb entrance (1967, p. 38). Additionally Matthew records, "So they went and made the tomb secure, sealing the stone and setting the guard" (27:66). If this were not the case, why would the women who visited after the Sabbath have been concerned with who would "roll away the stone from the door of the tomb for us?" (Mark 16:3). In addition to the stone, they also "sealed the tomb," most likely with a glob of wax imprinted with the signet ring of one of the Romans in authority. Thus, the door could not be opened without breaking the seal—making it a crime. We learn a little more about the "seal" from Daniel 6:17 in which the king sealed a stone with his signet ring. Having given Roman authentication to this seal, a guard was placed in front of the tomb (Matthew 27:65-66). Given that death was the punishment for abandoning a post or neglecting duties while on post, it defies reason that anyone could have easily stolen the body of Jesus. The soldiers' own lives were at stake over the body of Jesus Christ.

> *While Jews agree that a man named Jesus walked the earth, they are unwilling to grant Him the title of Son of God.*

The Evidence Reveals the Tomb Was Found Empty

Scholars agree that the death of Jesus was a major news event in Jerusalem during that time—a focal point that could not be easily ignored. While we think of trials like O.J. Simpson's being a media circus, consider how much attention the death and burial of Jesus received. While it is true Jews and Romans lacked 24-hour news coverage (which might not be a bad thing!), it cannot be overlooked that the trial and death of Jesus would have overshadowed the trial of O.J. Simpson. If Jesus did not make it out of the tomb, word would have quickly circulated among the people. Furthermore, if His body were still in a tomb, His followers would have journeyed to worship that location similar to the way Muslims make their annual pilgrimage today. While Jews agree that a man named Jesus walked the earth, they are unwilling to grant Him the title of Son of God. However, consider their plight—if His bones still existed, no excuses would be necessary regarding who this man was. Yet, the Bible records that the soldiers were bribed to keep quiet (Matthew 28:11-15). Additionally, the *Toledoth Yeshu*, Jewish manuscripts dated to approximately the

6th century, record: "A diligent search was made and **he [Jesus] was not found in the grave where he had been buried**. A gardener had taken him from the grave and had brought him into his garden and buried him in the sand over which the waters flowed into the garden" (emp. added).

The Evidence Reveals the Apostles Preached Boldly After the Resurrection
One of the most convincing pieces of evidence that Jesus came out of the tomb is the change in the Apostles' attitudes following His resurrection. Prior to His resurrection, we learn that His disciples "forsook Him and fled" (Matthew 26:56; Mark 14:50). These were men who were scared. We even find Peter cursing in his denial of knowing Jesus (Matthew 26:69-75; Mark 14:66-72; Luke 22:54-62; John 18:15-18). But after they saw a resurrected Jesus, their fear changed to boldness. We find them teaching throughout the book of Acts with courage and conviction (see Acts 2, 3:14-15, 4, 5:22-32; 10:34-43; 13:26-39, etc.)

> *If Jesus were not resurrected from the dead, then why didn't men speak out during Peter's sermon on the day of Pentecost?*

The Evidence Reveals Jesus Appeared to Many After His Resurrection
The following is a record of whom Jesus appeared to after the resurrection. Once again, if these appearances did not happen, they could have been easily disproven or contested, and yet ancient writings do not contain any challenges to these appearances. If Jesus were not resurrected from the dead, then why didn't men speak out during Peter's sermon on the day of Pentecost (Acts 2)?

Jesus appeared to Mary Magdalene (Mark 16:9; John 20:11).
Jesus appeared to "the other" women at the tomb (Matthew 28:9-10).
Jesus appeared to Peter later in the day (Luke 24:34).
Jesus appeared to two disciples on the road to Emmaus (Luke 24:13-32).
Jesus appeared to ten Apostles (Luke 24:33-49; John 20:19-24).
Jesus appeared to Thomas and the other Apostles (John 20:26-30).
Jesus appeared to seven Apostles by the Lake of Tiberias (John 21:1-23).

Jesus appeared again to all the Apostles (Matthew 28:16-20).
Jesus appeared again to all the Apostles (Acts 1:4-9).
Jesus appeared to 500 brethren on a Galilean mountain (1 Corinthians 15:6).
Jesus appeared to James (1 Corinthians 15:7).
Jesus appeared to Paul (1 Corinthians 15:7).
Jesus appeared at the ascension (Acts 1:3-12).
Jesus appeared to the first Christian martyr Stephen (Acts 7:55).
Jesus appeared to John at Patmos (Revelation 1:10-19).

If these appearances didn't happen, then why were they never refuted?

Is Jesus the Only Way?

Jesus claimed to be the Son of God–the Redeemer of man. However, it should be no surprise that in an environment of tolerance, the mainstream media has embraced the idea that all belief systems are acceptable and that truth is relative. In addition, the majority of the public believes that there are multiple ways to God—multiple ways to get to Heaven. One of the most influential people in our society—Oprah Winfrey—is promoting this twisted concept and urging her viewers to read books like Eckhart's Tolle's *A New Earth*. Consider the following discussion that took place on her highly rated talk show:

Oprah: One of the mistakes that human beings make is believing that there is only one way to live—and that we don't accept that there are diverse ways of being in the world, that there are millions of ways to be a human being.

Audience Member: Then how do you please God?

Oprah: And many ways, many paths to what you call God. And her path might be something else. And when she gets there she might call it the light, but her loving, and her kindness, and her generosity, if it brings her to the same point that it brings you it doesn't matter if she called it God along the way or not. There couldn't possibly be just one way.

"A man who was com-
pletely innocent, offered
himself as a sacrifice for the
good of others, including his
enemies, and became the
ransom of the world.
It was a perfect act."

— Mahatma Gandhi

Audience member: What about Jesus?

Oprah: What about Jesus?

Audience member: You bring Him up in this whole discussion and you say there isn't only one way. There is one way and only one way and that is through Jesus.

Oprah: There couldn't possibly be only one way for the millions of people in the world.

Winfrey may be a media mogul and a wealthy individual, but her voice and opinion have no authority in this discussion. Jesus Christ, the Son of God, plainly said: "I am the way, the truth, and the life. No one comes to the Father except through Me" (John 14:6). God, in His infinite wisdom, provided a way of salvation for sinful men through His Son, Jesus Christ. **And now we have reached the pinnacle of arrogance in which one of the most influential people in our society claims, "There couldn't possibly be only one way."** Maybe the question we should be asking is why did He even provide one way? Are we so arrogant that we presume that the gift of God's Son was not enough?

Conclusion

Anyone can choose to ignore evidence. In fact, some scientists are guilty of throwing out evidence that doesn't agree with their preferred results. But overlooking or discounting evidence does not reduce its importance or make it simply "go away." The facts remain. Last year I interviewed Gary Habermas, *a world-renowned scholar on the resurrection. During our time together, he noted: "[Y]ou don't need the inspired New Testament or even a highly reliable translation of the Bible to get a resurrection. If all you had were the historical facts that the vast majority of critical scholars regularly concede, you can make a very strong case for the resurrection using only their data." Given the mountainous accumulation of evidence for the resurrection, one wonders why more humans have not conceded this Truth and humbly analyzed what it means to their own existence. One also wonders why men are not proclaiming His death, burial, and resurrection today as boldly as the Apostles once did?*

Questions

1. Why is the bodily resurrection of Jesus Christ a foundational plank for the Christian faith?
2. How does testimony from past historians prove Christ existed?
3. Do other religions recognize Jesus as a historical figure?
4. Given the magnitude of this evidence, what responsibility is placed on the shoulders of those who know the Truth regarding Jesus Christ?

Scriptures to Study
Luke 19:10
John1:1-3
Romans 5:6-8
Matthew 16:13-18

Additional Resources

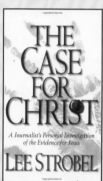

Strobel, Lee (1998), *The Case for Christ* (Grand Rapids, MI: Zondervan).

McDowell, Josh (1987), *More Than a Carpenter* (Living Books).

McDowell, Josh (2006), *Evidence for Christianity* (Nashville, TN: Thomas Nelson Publishers).

References

Barker, Dan (1992), *Losing Faith in Faith* (Freedom from Religion Foundation).
Butt, Kyle (2002) "Jesus Christ – Dead or Alive?", *Reason & Revelation*, Feb.
Edwards, William D., Wesley J. Gabel, and Floyd E. Hosmer (1986), "On the Physical Death of Jesus Christ," *Journal of American Medical Association*, 256:1455-1463, March 21.
Green, Michael (1968), *Man Alive* (Downers Grove, IL: Intervarsity Press).
Holloman, Henry (1967), *An Exposition of the Post-Resurrection Appearances of Our Lord,* Thesis, Dallas Theological Seminary.
Lewis, C.S. (1996), *Mere Christianity*
Smith, Wilbur M. (1971), "The Indisputable Fact of the Resurrection," *Moody Monthly*, May.

"And the Lord God formed man of the dust of the ground, and breathed into his nostrils the breath of life; and man became a living being."
– Genesis 2:7

Chapter

12

Where Did Man Come From? (Part 1)

She's only in the sixth grade. But already at the tender age of twelve, this young girl has seen the classic image that shows a monkey on one end and a human at the other, with all kinds of transitional creatures in between. The ape-like creature is shown walking on all fours, and eventually this series shows the creature evolving an upright stance and possessing biped location like modern man. She has also viewed pictures of ape-like men on the cover of news magazines lying around her house. The artists' reconstructions are in full color, show fine details, and look as if someone walked out into the bush-land of Africa and greeted these alleged "missing links" in person. Given the artists' images and the important-sounding scientific names (most of which she can't pronounce), this young lady accepts it as true. And little by little, her worldview is reshaped away from a beginning in which God created Adam and Eve to a beginning that had ape-like creatures roaming the continent of Africa millions of years ago. Without her consciously knowing it, that single shift has already begun to erode her faith.

Where did man come from and does it matter? The evolutionary theory demands that man evolved his way of from some common ancestor, whereas God's Word indicates man was the pinnacle of God's creation. Evolution presupposes that death brought man into the world. The creation model indicates that man brought death into the world. Both cannot be correct. Because of the over-abundance of propaganda supporting creatures like Neanderthal man, Lucy, *Homo habilis*, and *Homo erectus*, many assume that there is no question regarding the origin of mankind. Having viewed images in textbooks, popular magazines, and news accounts, many individuals—

including Christians—assume there is no debate. As such, many Christians have tried to mesh the evolution of man into God's Word, never realizing that their compromise is incompatible with the text found in the Bible. (e.g., In Mark 10:6 Jesus said: "But from the beginning of creation God made them male and female." The indication being that man was around from the beginning of creation.)

In the Genesis creation account, the Bible describes that all land-dwelling creatures were created on Day 6, with man being the pinnacle of God's creation. In chapter 2 of that same book, Moses describes the creation of man and woman in detail, informing readers: "And the Lord God formed man of the dust of the ground, and breathed into his nostrils the breath of life; and man became a living being" (Genesis 2:7). In verse 20 of that same chapter we find Adam giving names to "all cattle, to the birds of the air, to every beast of the field," indicating that he possessed the intelligence to name animals and understand instructions from God. The Darwinian theory describes man evolving from some primordial soup, initially carrying a club and living in a cave with not much intelligence. These two theories of origins could not be more diametrically opposed.

> *The Darwinian theory describes man evolving from some primordial soup, initially carrying a club and living in a cave with not much intelligence.*

So which is correct?

Scientific knowledge regarding the origin and antiquity of man is primarily based on fossil discoveries made by anthropologists, such as the world-famous Leakey family. Scientists would uncover fossilized bone fragments and then speculate as to what features the original creature possessed and precisely where it fit on the evolutionary tree of life. Each new discovery was heralded as a major scientific contribution—no matter how fragmented the fossil, or how few remains were actually discovered. But as more and more fossils were unearthed, many scientists took delight in designating their finds as entirely new species, providing the scientist with the privilege of designating a new scientific name. While being able to name a new "species" of hominid was beneficial to one's career, the real advantage came in announcing the discovery of the **oldest** upright-walking hominid fossil. The race was on to find the "missing link" that led back to a common ancestor that humans allegedly shared with the apes.

If man evolved from ape-like creatures then the fossil record should record the transition from ape to human. Entire books have been written about alleged missing links. But what does the **evidence** really show? While we don't often think of it in this manner, creationists and evolutionists have the exact same evidence or data. The question becomes how we interpret that data and what biases we bring into that interpretation. A fossil can tell a scientist only so much. It can obviously tell scientists that the creature is now dead. But much of what is presented in textbooks and secular magazines goes beyond the true knowledge into the realm of speculation. For instance, fossils do not shed light on how much hair an alleged ape-like creature would possess. Additionally, fossils do not shed light on skin color, eye color, or intelligence.

Given the frequency that alleged missing links are reported in the media, many are lead to believe that there are numerous fossilized remains that support the gradual evolution from apes to humans. The truth, however, is that the human fossil record is still amazingly sparse. John Reader, author of the book *Missing Links*, wrote in *New Scientist*, "The entire hominid collection known today would barely cover a billiard table" (1981:802). Lyall Watson, writing in *Science Digest*, further admitted: "The fossils that decorate our family tree are so scarce that there are still more scientists than specimens. The remarkable fact is that all the physical evidence we have for human evolution can still be placed, with room to spare, **inside a single coffin**" (1982, 90 [5]:44), emp. added). While additional discoveries have been found since these statements were made, the point is still abundantly clear—missing links are still missing.

The saying that "a picture is worth a thousand words" should not be overlooked in this controversy. Oftentimes textbooks or magazines present images that appear as if a photographer walked out into the African bush country and took a picture of these ape-like creatures, when in reality the image is simply an artist's interpretation—

"At any rate, modern gorillas, orangs and chimpanzees spring out of nowhere, as it were. They are here today; they have no yesterday…"

– Donald Johanson, 1981,
Lucy: The Beginnings of Humankind p. 363.

usually built from a few bone fragments and a couple of teeth. For instance, the October 2008 cover story of *National Geographic* was titled "The Last of the Neanderthals." The brutish images of these alleged missing links captivated the eye and painted the story *National Geographic* was trying to sell. Inside that issue staff writer Stephan Hall posed the question of why they vanished and then laid the blame at the feet of modern man. (See http://ngm.nationalgeographic.com/2008/10/neanderthals/hall-text). One should not fail to notice that many of the fossils for these alleged creatures come from several different locations, having been collected over a period of years. Bone fragments are then glued together, a scientific illustrator is called in, and speculations and assumptions are made on the general anatomy and appearance of the creature.

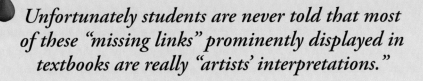

Unfortunately students are never told that most of these "missing links" prominently displayed in textbooks are really "artists' interpretations."

Unfortunately students are never told that most of these "missing links" prominently displayed in textbooks are really "artists' interpretations." Oftentimes from just a few bone fragments and teeth, a totally new "missing link" is derived. Even then, many of these have been discredited through the years. For instance, consider the following alleged missing links in evolution's "Hall of Shame":

Nebraska Man—This alleged missing link was featured on the front cover of the June 24, 1922, issue of the *Illustrated London News* from an artist's interpretation of a man and woman. **What was the evidence for this missing link?** A single tooth received by Henry Fairfield Osborn, head of the department of vertebrate paleontology at New York's American Museum of Natural History. Osborn was a Marxist and a prominent member of the American Civil Liberties Union, and he believed the tooth would serve as prominent evidence for a test case for evolution. Osborn felt the best showcase would be a trial held in 1925 at Dayton, Tennessee (known as the Scopes "Monkey Trial"). The trial was an arranged affair in an effort to promote evolution, but the tooth was never brought into evidence, as there was dissension among those familiar with it.

Again, this alleged missing link was completely "manufactured" from **one tooth**. An artist engaged in a great deal of creative license and created this creature (and his family) from that single tooth. After much controversy a further search was made at Snake Creek (the site of the original discovery), and in 1927 it was concluded that the tooth belonged to a species of *Prosthennops*, an extinct genus of a wild pig. Although the truth of this discovery did not make front-page headlines, it did appear in *Science* (see Gregory, 579). The 14th edition of the *Encyclopedia Britannica* (1929, p. 767) admitted the mistake, revealing that the tooth belonged to a "being of another order." Creationist Duane Gish observed: "This was the first time a pig made a monkey of an evolutionist" (1985, p. 188).

Piltdown Man—

For more than forty years, this fossil find was touted as "the missing link" that connected humans with the apes. Textbooks were published teaching multiple generations that this discovery—from archaeological site in Piltdown, England, between 1908 and 1912—was evidence for evolution. The only problem was that it was a complete **fraud!** Many prominent scientists like Sir Arthur Smith Woodward, Sir Arthur Keith, and Grafton Elliot Smith proclaimed this discovery genuine. So exactly how did these bone fragments fool some the best scientific minds of the time? Perhaps the men were blinded by the desire to be part of a "great discovery." Forty years after it was announced, it was discovered that scientists had taken a modern human skull and combined it with the jawbone of an orangutan (even filing down the back teeth of the orangutan to make them look more humanlike). They dipped the whole thing in acid to give it an aged appearance and presented it to the world as our "missing ancestor." Sadly, someone had even buried a tooth fragment from an elephant molar, a tooth from a hippopotamus and a canine tooth from a chimpanzee fossil to make the Piltdown quarry where this alleged fossil man was discovered appear more significant! In 1953, Piltdown Man was exposed as a forgery and the truth became public knowledge.

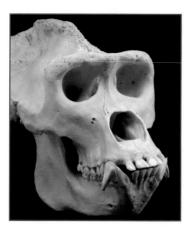

Australopithecus afarensis—**Lucy**

On November 30, 1974, Donald Johanson and graduate student Tom Gray loaded up in a Land Rover and headed out to plot an area of Hadar, Ethiopia, known as Locality 162. There they unearthed a fossilized skeleton that was nearly 40% complete. Dr. Johanson named his discovery *Australopithecus afarensis* meaning "the southern ape from Ethiopia's Afar depression in northeastern Ethiopia." The creature earned the nickname "Lucy" from the Beatles song "Lucy in the Sky with Diamonds" that was playing in the camp the night of the discovery. While there was a great deal of pomp and circumstance offered by the mainstream media when Lucy was first announced, her star does not shine as brightly today. In fact, having over 20 years to examine the fossils, there are several problems with Lucy. For instance:

"To attempt to restore the soft parts is an even more hazardous undertaking. The lips, the eyes, the ears, and the nasal tip, leave no clues on the underlying bony parts....These alleged restorations of ancient types of man have very little if any scientific value and are likely only to mislead the public.... So put not your trust in reconstructions."

– Anthropologist Earnest Hooten, (1931)

Up From The Ape,
p. 332.

A. She has curved fingers and ape-like limb proportions (see Stern and Susman, 1983, *J. Phy. Anthrop.*, 60:280) that point toward her being an ape.

B. She has locking wrists—a trait identified in quadrupeds (see Richmond & Strait, 2000, *Nature*, 404:382-385). Maggie Fox reported in the March 29, 2000, *San Diego Union Tribune*: "A chance discovery made by looking at a cast of the bones of 'Lucy,' the most famous fossil of *Australopithecus afarensis*, shows her wrist is stiff, like a chimpanzee's, Brian Richmond and David Strait of George Washington University in Washington, D.C., reported. This suggests that her ancestors walked on their knuckles" (Fox, "Man's Early Ancestors Were Knuckle Walkers," 2000, *Quest Section*, March 29).

C. The microwear on the teeth indicate this creature was tree fruit eater (see Johanson and Edey, 1981, p. 358). Alan Walker, a professor of anthropology and biology at Penn State University, believes he might be able to reconstruct ancient diets from paleontological samples. In speaking of Alan Walker's material, Johanson noted:

> Dr. Alan Walker of Johns Hopkins has recently concluded that the polishing effect he finds on the teeth of robust *australopithecines* and modern chimpanzees indicates that australopithecines, like chimps, were fruit eaters.... If they were primarily fruit eaters, as Walker's examination of their teeth suggests they were, then our picture of them, and of the evolutionary path they took, is wrong (Johanson and Edey, 1981, p. 358).

D. Lucy's rib cage is conical like an ape's, not-barrel shaped like a human's (see Leakey and Lewin, 1992, p. 193-194). Peter Schmid, a paleontologist at the Anthropological Institute in Zurich, Switzerland, received a replica of Lucy and noted,

> When I started to put the skeleton together, I expected it to look human. Everyone had talked about Lucy being very modern. Very human. So I was surprised by what I saw. I noticed that the ribs were more round in cross section. More like what you see in apes. Human ribs are flatter in cross section. But the shape of the ribcage itself was the biggest surprise of all. The human ribcage is barrel shaped. And I just couldn't get Lucy's ribs to fit this kind of shape. But I could get them to make a conical shaped ribcage, like what you see in apes (Peter Schmid as quoted in Leakey and Lewin, *Origins Reconsidered*, 1992, p. 193-194).

> *"The human ribcage is barrel shaped. And I just couldn't get Lucy's ribs to fit this kind of shape."*

E. The semicircular canals of *Australopithecines* resemble an ape's, not a human's or a transitional creature's (see Spoor et al., 1994, *Nature*, 369:645-648).

F. The pelvis of Lucy is not large enough to give birth leaving one to wonder if she is really a "he" ["Lucy or Lucifer?"] (see Hausler and Schmid, 1995, J. *Human Evol.* 29:363-383).

This doesn't stop textbooks or museums from perpetuating the lie. For instance, at the "Living World" located in the Saint Louis Zoo they have built a shrine to Charles Darwin. As you walk into the "Introduction to the Animals" hall, you are immediately confronted by a life-size animatronic version of Charles Darwin. The area also features a life-size replica of the alleged *Australopithecus afarensis* (Lucy) proclaiming: "This life-sized model shows a likely ancient ancestor of the human family." However, there were never any feet or hand fossils discovered. The question becomes how can they be so sure about what this creature looked like? According to David Menton from Washington University, the statue is "a complete misrepresentation. And I believe they know it is a misrepresentation." When asked how in good conscience they could display a creature possessing feet and hands without fossilized evidence, Bruce L. Carr, the zoo's director of education, declared, "Zoo officials have no plans to knuckle under. We cannot be updating every exhibit based on every new piece of evidence. We look at the overall exhibit and the impression it creates. We think the overall impression this exhibit creates is correct" (*St. Louis Post Dispatch*, July 22, 1996, p. 1). In other words, the impression supports evolution—let's just forget what the evidence shows. Donald Johanson admitted:

> There is no such thing as a total lack of bias. I have it; everybody has it. The fossil hunter in the field has it.... In everybody who is looking for hominids there is a strong urge to learn more about where the human line started. If you are working back at around three million, as I was, that is very seductive, because you begin to get an idea that that is where *Homo* did start. You begin straining your eyes to find *Homo* traits in fossils of that age.... Logical, maybe, but also biased. **I was trying to jam evidence of dates into a pattern that would support conclusions about fossils which, on closer inspection, the fossils themselves would not sustain** (Johanson and Edey, 1981, p. 257, 258, emp. added).

He went on to state: "It is hard for me now to admit how tangled in that thicket I was. But the insidious thing about bias is that it does make one deaf to the cries of other evidence" (p. 277).

Questions:
1. Why is important for parents to monitor the textbooks and media influences their children watch?
2. What are the implications if man evolved from some ape-like creature?
3. What are some proactive steps Christians can take before visiting a museum or zoo that promotes evolutionary propaganda?
4. Was the plan of redemption given for animals?

Scriptures to Study
Psalm 144:3
Proverbs 1:5
Matthew 4:4
Romans 1:28

Additional Resources

Lubenow, Marvin (1992), *Bones of Contention* (Grand Rapids, MI: Baker Books).

Harrub, Brad et al (2003), *The Truth About Human Origins.* (Montgomery, AL: Apologetics Press).

References
Gish, Duane T. (1985), *Evolution: The Challenge of the Fossil Record,* (El Cajon, CA: Creation-Life).
Gregory, W.K. (1927), *"Hesperopithecus Apparently not an Ape nor a Man,"* Science 66: 579-581, December.

Hausler, Martin and Peter Schmid (1995), "Comparison of the Pelvis of Sts 14 and AL 288-1: Implications for Birth and Sexual Dimorphism in *Australopithecines*," *Journal of Human Evolution,* 29:363-383.

Johanson, Donald C. and Tim D. White (1979), "A Systematic Assessment of Early African Hominids," *Science,* 203[4378]:321-330, January 26.

Johanson, Donald, Lenora Johanson, and Blake Edgar (1994), *Ancestors: In Search of Human Origins* (New York: Villard Books).

Leakey, Richard and Roger Lewin (1992), *Origins Reconsidered: In Search of What Makes Us Human* (New York: Doubleday).

Lemonick, Michael D. and Andrea Dorfman (2001), "One Giant Step for Mankind," *Time,* 158[3] (2001): 54-61, July 23.

Reader, John (1981), "Whatever Happened to *Zinjanthropus?*" *New Scientist, 8*9: 802, March 26.

Richmond, Brian G. and David S. Strait (2000), "Evidence that Humans Evolved From a Knuckle-Walking Ancestor," *Nature,* 404:382-385, March 23.

Spoor, Fred, Bernard Wood, and Frans Zonneveld (1994), "Implications of Early Hominid Labyrinthine Morphology for Evolution of Human Bipedal Locomotion," *Nature,* 369:645-648, June 23.

Stern, Jack T. Jr., and Randall L. Susman (1983), "The Locomotor Anatomy of *Australopithecus afarensis*," *Journal of Physical Anthropology,* 60:279-317.

Watson, Lyall (1982), "The Water People", *Science Digest* 90[5]: 44.

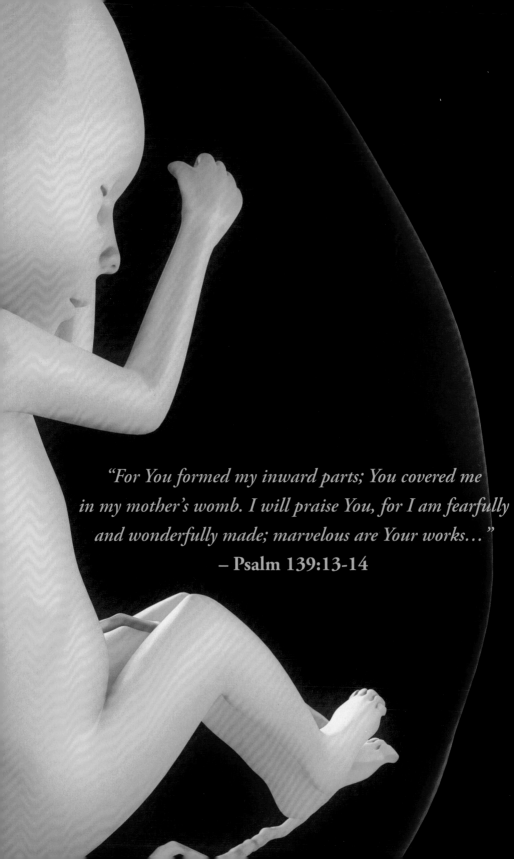

"For You formed my inward parts; You covered me in my mother's womb. I will praise You, for I am fearfully and wonderfully made; marvelous are Your works…"
– Psalm 139:13-14

Chapter

13

🢃

Where Did Man Come From? (Part 2)

Most young people are familiar with the image that depicts an ape at one end and a human at the other—with all kinds of intermediates in between. Students are asked to memorize their names and the period in which they allegedly lived. While the pictures sell a convincing story, the facts prove otherwise. Few students learn how many different locations the bones were collected from, how many bone fragments are included, and how many alleged missing links are simply variations of known species. Consider these examples:

Neanderthal Man—Neanderthal man is one of the most well known of all the alleged missing links. While most people have heard of this alleged creature, many are quite unaware that at the International Congress of Zoology (1958), Dr. A. J. E. Cave said that his examination of the famous Neanderthal skeleton found in France over 50 years ago proved that it was an old man who suffered from arthritis. Consider that most of the Neanderthal fossils have been "discovered" in European countries that don't get a great deal of sunlight. Humans utilize sunlight to make sufficient quantities of vitamin D. In turn, vitamin D aids in the absorption of calcium to maintain strong bones. A deficiency of vitamin D leads to bone disorders and would reconcile perfectly with the fossils found in that particular region. In fact, most of the alleged Neanderthal fossils are easily explained by skeletal variations (still common in humans today) and bone disorders such as rickets or arthritis. After examining the famous Neanderthal skull, Dr. Cuozzo said, "You must understand that this skull really cries out disease. The teeth are badly decayed, and the bones of the vault of the skull are extremely thick. There are many features that testify…of acromegaly or excess secretion of growth hormone in adulthood…" (1998, p. 72). Bone variation from sickness does not prove organic evolution.

Java Man—This discovery was made by Dutch anatomist Eugene Dubois. In 1887, Dubois journeyed to the former Dutch Indies, working as a health officer. A childhood interest in geology and paleontology led him to search for fossils in Sumatra and Java. Once in Java, Dubois supervised the collection of more than 12,000 fossil fragments around the mountain of Lawu. His discovery unearthed fossils from fish to elephants to hippopotami; however, fossils of "early humans" were conspicuously absent. By 1890 Dubois had focused his attention on the banks of Solo near the village Trinil. In a bend of this river, excavators discovered a human-like fossilized tooth in September 1891. After removing about

10,000 cubic meters of dirt, workers uncovered the tooth (September 1891), then later a skull cap (October 1891). The fossilized skullcap was thick and had a cranial capacity revealing that its brains could be only half as big as the brain of a modern human. Initially Dubois believed that the fossils belonged to a large, extinct chimpanzee. A year later he discovered a femur (August 1892) about fifteen meters upstream, and then one more tooth (October 1892). Unlike the ape-like skull, the femur possessed human-like characteristics. Dubois recognized this bone belonged to an upright-walking creature. And he mistakenly attributed the teeth, skullcap, and femur to one individual—an upright-walking specimen of an extinct species he dubbed as *Anthropopithecus erectus* (i.e., the erect-walking, human-like anthropoid). Thirty-five years later, it was revealed that the femur is human and that the skullcap was from a giant gibbon (monkey)!

Rhodesian Man—Found in a zinc mine in 1921, this fossil was displayed prominently in the British Museum of Natural History. The find consisted of the bones of three or four family members: a man, a woman, and one or two children. The fossils were originally discovered and dug out by a mining company, not by an experienced scientist, so a great deal remains unknown about the circumstances of the death and lifestyle of their owners. Upon reaching the British Museum of Natural History, the first staff member to examine the bones was Sir Arthur Smith-Woodward. This was the same scientist who earned fame as the co-discoverer of what has since become known as one of the most blatant scientific frauds of modern times—Piltdown Man. Museum employees unfamiliar with human anatomy reconstructed this "ape-man." The hipbones were smashed, and W.P. Pycraft, one of the Museum's ornithologists (a specialist in birds) and "assistant keeper" of the Museum's department of zoology, was placed in charge of the reconstruction of Rhodesian Man's bones. Why would a **bird** specialist be assigned to reconstruct **human** remains? Pycraft fashioned the fossil as stooped over, and scientists named it *Cyphanthropus* (nickname: "stooping man"). The facial bones compelled Smith-Woodward to admit they possessed "very human characteristics" in his own paper written in 1921 for *Nature*. Many years later after the hipbones were re-examined, "Rhodesian Man" was shown to be nothing more than a modern man.

> *"Rhodesian Man" was shown to be nothing more than a modern man.*

Ardipithecus ramidus kadabba—The front cover of the July 23, 2001, issue of *Time* proclaimed somewhat authoritatively, "How Apes Became Humans," and asserted that a new *Ardipithecus* hominid discovery reveals to scientists "how our oldest ancestors stood on two legs and made an evolutionary leap." Named *Ardipithecus ramidus kadabba*, meaning "the ground root basal ancestor of humanity," this creature was dated at 5.8-5.2 million years old (using evolutionary dating methods). However, on page 57, staff writers Michael Lemonick and Andrea Dorfman admit that the discoverers of the fossils under discussion, Yohannes Haile-Selassie and his colleagues, "haven't collected enough bones yet to reconstruct with great precision what *kadabba* looked like" (1999). One wonders why they would put an image on the cover of *Time* and also in a two page spread if researchers had not collected enough bones to reconstruct what this creature looked like with great precision? This admission underscores that the majority of what was presented in this article was made up from an artist's imagination and speculation. So what evidence exists for this alleged fossil man? The scientists admit: "We found these bones over a period of five years from five different locations." Exactly what did they find? Researchers unearthed a fragment of a right mandible (jawbone), one intermediate hand phalanx (finger bone), a fragmented

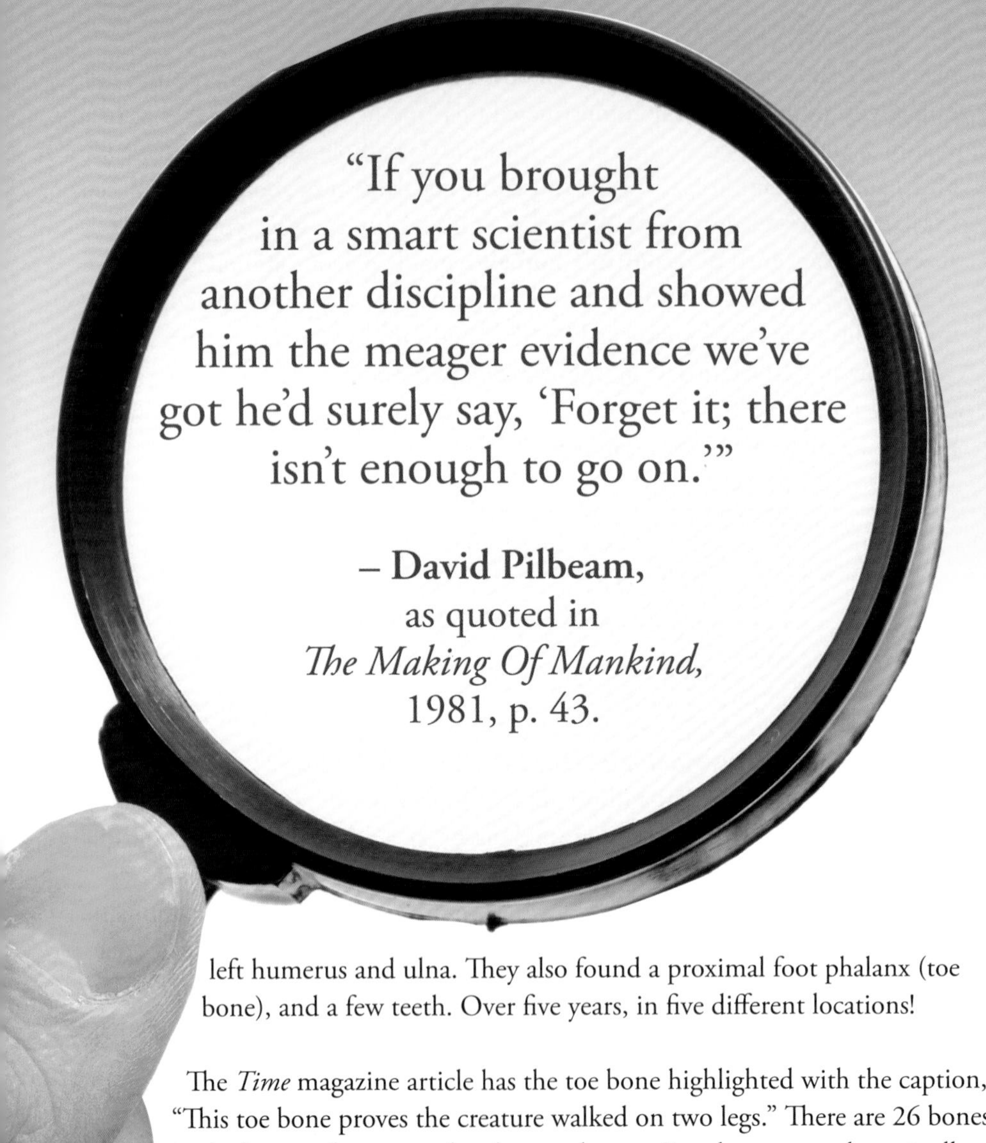

"If you brought
in a smart scientist from
another discipline and showed
him the meager evidence we've
got he'd surely say, 'Forget it; there
isn't enough to go on.'"

– David Pilbeam,
as quoted in
The Making Of Mankind,
1981, p. 43.

left humerus and ulna. They also found a proximal foot phalanx (toe bone), and a few teeth. Over five years, in five different locations!

The *Time* magazine article has the toe bone highlighted with the caption, "This toe bone proves the creature walked on two legs." There are 26 bones in the human foot—yet they have only one. But that one toe bone is all that is needed in order to get this creature upright and walking. Consider an admission made by the authors regarding this single toe bone: **"...not only is it separated in time by several hundred thousand years, but it was also found some 10 miles away from the rest"** (p. 61). So ten miles away researchers dug up a toe bone and placed it together with this collection of bone fragments. They then had the audacity to proclaim, "This toe bone proves the creature walked on two legs." Are we expecting logical people to believe this is a missing link?

And this is literally just the tip of the iceberg. A close inspection of the fossil record proves that it relies heavily on speculation and it provides no real support to the idea that men evolved from ape-like creatures. So what does the fossil record show us? I'm going to let writer Jeremy Rifken describe it, because he characterized it quite well. Rifkin noted:

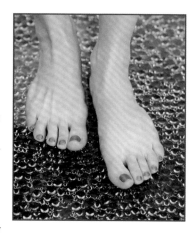

> What the "record" shows is nearly a century of fudging and finagling by scientists attempting to force various fossil morsels and fragments to conform with Darwin's notions, all to no avail. Today the millions of fossils stand as very visible, ever-present reminders of the paltriness of the arguments and the overall shabbiness of the theory that marches under the banner of evolution (1983, Rifkin, *Algeny*, p. 125).

Racism and the Fossil Record

If the evolutionary theory of "survival of the fittest" is correct, then the animals living today are "the fittest" (a tautology). In essence, this godless theory teaches we get better over time. Now apply this theory to mankind. According to evolutionists, mankind evolved out of Africa and eventually migrated to Europe and Asia. **And yet, how does every single form of media portray early "Neanderthal"-like creatures?** Has *National Geographic* ever depicted an "early man" or ape-like creature with fair skin? The common theory being taught in classrooms today is that dark skinned people evolved out of Africa and eventually gave rise to fair skinned populations in Europe and Asia. **A cursory glance will quickly reveal that early man is always depicted with dark skin.** Mankind supposedly got "fitter" and "lost" that color. Allegedly, Caucasians evolved from the Negroid race—thus, fair skinned people are allegedly a more evolved, and thus, more fit superior or race.

Now consider that this is the only legalized theory of human origins in public classrooms today. Students all across America are being shown images of dark skinned, ape-like creatures that supposedly paved the way for white men. Ironic, is it not, that the ACLU, an organization that is supposed to advocate "individual rights by litigating, legislating, and educating the public," is defending a theory that undermines the core of their mission. The ACLU is defending an atheistic theory that by its very definition demands that there is an inferior race.

> *The ACLU is defending an atheistic theory that by its very definition demands that there is an inferior race.*

On college campuses all across this country, Charles Darwin's infamous *Origin of Species* has become a staple of required reading. But how many people are aware of the full title of Charles Darwin's book? While new editions have deleted the subtitle, Darwin's original work was titled *The Origin of Species by Means of Natural Selection—or The Preservation of Favoured Races in the Struggle for Life.* The phrase "favored race" implies that there is a race that is not favored. In his second book, *The Descent of Man*, Darwin noted:

> At some future period, not very distant as measured by centuries, the civilized races of man will almost certainly exterminate and replace the savage races throughout the world…. The break between man and his nearest Allies will then be wider, for it will intervene between man in a more civilized state, as we may hope, even than the Caucasian, and some ape as low as the baboon, instead of as now between the Negro or Australian and the gorilla (2nd ed., New York: A. L. Burt Co., p. 178).

Evolutionist Thomas Huxley, Darwin's famous "bulldog" observed:

> No rational man, cognizant of the facts, believes that the average Negro is the equal, still less the superior, of the white man. And if this be true, it is simply incredible that, when all his disabilities are removed, and our prognathous relative has a fair field and no favor, as well as no oppressor, he will be able to compete successfully with his bigger-brained and smaller-jawed rival, in a contest which

is to be carried out on by thoughts and not by bites (*Lay Sermans, Addresses and Reviews*, New York: Appleton, 1871, p. 20).

More than fifty years after Darwin released *The Origin of Species*, paleontologist Henry Fairfield Osborn remarked:

> The Negroid stock is even more ancient than the Caucasian and Mongolian, as may be proved by an examination not only of the brain, of the hair, of the bodily characters.... The standard of intelligence of the average Negro is similar to that of the eleven-year-old youth of the species *Homo sapiens* ("The Evolution of the Human Races," *Natural History*, 1980, April 89:129; reprinted from *Natural History*, 1926).

While modern day Darwinians would argue that this belief reflects an ancient philosophy, the tenets remain steadfast today. Consider a book released in 2004 titled *Race: The Reality of Human Differences*, in which the authors categorized people according to race, thereby reinforcing the contemporary ideas of racial hierarchy. There can be no doubt; public schools are teaching our children that there is a dark skinned inferior race, as well as a fair skinned superior race. By mandating evolution in the classroom, we are reinforcing the ideals of racism in the hearts and minds of young people. The Bible speaks of one race – the human race.

Could We Have All Come From Adam and Eve?

The human genome project demonstrated different populations of humans share 99.9% similar genetic content. We know today that skin color is caused by a biological pigment known as melanin. The amount of melanin in the skin is determined by the genetic endowment of our parents. Knowing this, geneticists have come along and used special letter combinations to designate how much melanin someone has in their skin (e.g., AABB). For instance, a capital "A" and "B" indicate dominant genes—which can produce large quantities of melanin. Whereas a small "a" and "b" indicate recessive genes —which are unable to produce quite as much melanin. Thus, the designation AABB = **darkest** skin possible, and aabb = **lightest** skin possible.

Using this information, we can build a punnet square to tell us the "genes" (and color) of the offspring. So is it possible to take two people (say Adam and Eve) and explain all of the beautiful colors we see around us today?

AABB x AABB = AABB If Adam and Eve were both very dark skinned all of their children would be very dark skinned.

aabb x aabb = aabb If Adam and Eve were both very light skinned then all of their children would be very light skinned.

However, if God had created Adam and Eve with a mixture (AaBb), say a beautiful "mocha" color, the following possibilities would result:

	AB	Ab	aB	ab
AB	AA BB	AA Bb	Aa BB	Aa Bb
Ab	AA Bb	AA bb	Aa Bb	Aa bb
aB	Aa BB	Aa Bb	aa BB	aa Bb
ab	Aa Bb	Aa bb	aa BB	aa bb

(Adapted from Apologetics Press)

We can get all of these possibilities from just two individuals. And yet eight walked off of Noah's ark. Is it possible to explain the rainbow of colors we see around us today using God's Word? Definitely!

"Unfortunately,
the fossil record is somewhat incomplete as far as the
hominids are concerned, and is
all but blank for the apes."

– Richard Leakey, 1981
The Making Of Mankind,
p. 43.

An Imaginary and Fragmented Evolutionary Tree of Life

Organic evolution teaches that all creatures evolved from a common ancestor. As such, textbooks are quick to show elegant pictures of the evolutionary tree of life. In an interview with Jonathan Wells, author of *Icons of Evolution*, he remarked:

> One [icon] they will certainly see, because you can't teach Darwin- ism without it, is the evolutionary tree of life. That is the branching trees diagram that supposedly shows how all living things are descended with modi- fication from a common ancestor. That's the root of the tree. So, you see, in any biology textbook you will see a version of this, purportedly showing how all the animals descended from this organism or all the mammals descended from that

or all the horses or something like that. These trees are without exception hypothetical. They are really just restatements of Darwin's theory in pictorial form. What you have is a series of fossils or living organisms so you draw lines between them to show how they are related to one another. That's where the hypothesis starts and the evidence ends" (personal interview).

A close inspection of the fossil record proves that it relies heavily on speculation and it provides no real support to the idea that men evolved from ape-like creatures. The alleged missing links can be easily assigned to one of two categories: ape or man. No amount of artist's interpretation or imagination is going to change that.

Conclusion

Consider the worldview that is currently molding the beliefs of future generations. The constant barrage of speculations that men evolved from ape-like creatures begins very early in life and it never recedes. By early adolescence, most children already have a subconscious image of early man as a dumb, club-carrying, long-armed creature living in a cave. High school science books reinforce this notion with pictures of Neanderthal man, and by college most students have accepted this evolutionary progression of man as fact. As such, man's existence and his status in the universe are placed on a level just slightly above the animals. The current generation views man as little more than an educated ape who arrived here by chance. All of our actions and behaviors are now viewed simply as "carryovers" from our ape-like ancestors. With fragmentary skulls of the alleged missing links in hand, evolutionists smile as they permanently remove any lingering doubts about a possible Supernatural Creator.

However, when one clears away the smoke and mirrors to closely examine the available evidence and bone fragments that allegedly make up the evolutionary tree of life, it becomes obvious that there are many factors that this theory cannot explain.

In examining where man came from, it is important to remember the first five words in God's Word—"In the beginning God created." For indeed, man's existence, intelligence, artistic expression, compassion, and sense of morality only make sense in light of the creative activities of an Intelligent Designer. It is apparent from the text of Genesis 1 and 2 that the creation of man differed markedly from that of all other life on earth. A quick examination of the text reveals that a divine conference preceded the forming of man. God said, "Let Us make man in Our image, after Our likeness" (Genesis 1:26, emp. added). Such never is said of the birds, fish, or creeping things. As Feinberg noted:

> *...[M]an is the apex of all creation. Man's creation by God comes as the last and highest phase of God's creative activity.... Now there is counsel or deliberation in the Godhead. No others can be included here, such as angels, for none has been even intimated thus far in the narrative. Thus the creation of man took place not by a word alone, but as the result of a divine decree (The Image of God, 1972, p. 238).*

Does it really matter whether man evolved from some ape-like creature or was made in the image and likeness of God? It does when we examine the evidence and recognize that we will one day stand before the Creator in whose image we were created.

Questions:
1. Why is the fossil record so convincing for many young people?
2. How does evolution and alleged ape-like creatures promote racism?
3. What are some problems that evolution has difficulty explaining?

Scriptures to Study
1 Corinthians 15:45 • Hebrews 2:6-7 • 1 John 3:2 • Romans 8:16-17

Additional Resources:

Cuozzo, Jack (1998), *Buried Alive: The Startling Truth About Neanderthal Man* (Green Forest, AR: Master Books).

Gish, Duane (1995), *Evolution: The Fossils Still Say No!* (El Cajon, CA: Institute for Creation Research).

Well, Jonathan (2002), *Icons of Evolution* (Washington D.C.: Regnery Publishing Inc.).

Werner, Carl (2007), *Evolution: The Grand Experiment* (Green Forest, AR: New Leaf Publishers).

References:
Cuozzo, Jack (1998), *Buried Alive: The Startling Truth About Neanderthal Man* (Green Forest, AR: Master Books).
Darwin, Charles (1952), *The Descent of Man*, 6th Edition, edited under *Encyclopedia Britannica*, Great Books of the Western World, Vol.49, (William Benton Publishers).
Feinberg, Charles Lee (1972), "Image of God," *Bibliotheca Sacra*, 129:235-246, 1972, July–September.
Lemonick, Michael D. and Andrea Dorfman (1999), "Up from the Apes." *Time*, 154[8] 50-58, August 23.
Rifkin, Jeremy (1983), *Algeny* (New York: Viking Press).

"*O Timothy, keep that which is committed to thy trust, avoiding profane and vain babblings, and oppositions of science falsely so called.*"
– 1 Timothy 6:20, KJV

14

Evolution: Fact or Fiction?

He has bought into the lie. Now completing the first semester of his sophomore year, this young man has endured three semesters in general science classes. When he initially entered the university, he held mixed feelings about the origin of mankind and the origin of the universe. However, he has been so fully indoctrinated in the evolutionary theory in his classrooms that "origins" no longer remain a question. On several different occasions, this young man has sat at the feet of professors who claim that organic evolution is a "fact." They have convinced him that science does not make sense except in the light of evolution. Rarely is a subject taught without it somehow being tied back to the evolutionary theory. His textbook is filled with examples that stand as proof for the evolutionary theory. Using intellectual intimidation, the professors have successfully indoctrinated yet another generation of students. So after only three semesters in college, his mind is made up and his worldview has been altered to fit his mindset.

Having sat through a two-week-long videotape series on the life of Charles Darwin in my freshman biology class, the scenario above is not foreign to me. Week after week, my fellow students and I were educated in the sciences from a distinctly evolutionary perspective. What once was only taught as a theory in a general biology class setting has now infected basically every field of science. Many professors believe that one cannot discuss the parts of a plant, the anatomy of a mammal, a bacterial culture, or Mendelian genetics without touching on evolution or evolutionary history. It has successfully permeated all branches of science. Charles Darwin—the man recognized as the Father of the Evolutionary Theory—was heralded as a world-renowned scientist and was elevated to almost "sainthood" status in many of my classrooms. It was only upon further investigation and research that I learned the truth about this man and his theory.

Charles Darwin: Cheater, Preacher, and Scientist

Most parents have told their children: "Cheaters never win." But history has recorded that, at least on earth, that is not always the case. In science, unlike many other disciplines, dates hold great meaning and power. The scientist who first publishes a particular finding is given credit for that discovery from that point forward. This places a great deal of pressure on researchers to publish their findings, and has even resulted in the advent of "advanced online publishing," as scientists literally race to have their names as the first to publish new findings. It also has caused some scien-

tists to cheat and try to out-publish a rival in order to receive attention or fame. One such race has all but been forgotten in the annals of science—and sadly, the cheater was never truly rebuked. Instead, today he is honored and even elevated as one of the greatest scientists who ever walked the earth.

On February 12, 1809, two individuals would be born who would both change the history of the world. Abraham Lincoln was born in Hardin County, Kentucky, and he would go on to serve as president and lead the United States through its greatest internal conflict—the Civil War. On that same day, Charles Robert Darwin was also born at his family home The Mount in Shrewsbury, England, and he would go on to alter the landscape of science. Two different men living as contemporaries took two very different paths and left two very different legacies.

Darwin's Early Years

Darwin was the fifth child of Dr. Robert and Susannah Darwin. His mother died when he was just eight years old, and so her influence was short-lived in his life. This tragedy, combined with the fact that his father was an extremely busy physician, probably played a large role in why Darwin was hungry for attention and would often manipulate people for his benefit. Darwin's father ran one of the largest medical practices outside of London. His grandfather Erasmus Darwin was also a physician and the author of *Zoonomia*, or *The Laws of Organic Life*. These men definitely helped shape Darwin's worldview, and their influence would eventually mold Darwin into someone who longed for status.

Aside from the death of his mother, Charles Darwin led a fairly easy childhood. His father had him baptized as an infant in the Anglican Church—even though the family normally attended the Unitarian Church with their mother while she was living. At the tender age of sixteen, Darwin was sent to the University of Edinburgh to study medicine. Everyone assumed he would follow in the footsteps of his prominent father and grandfather. However, when he was subjected to watching surgical procedures performed without anesthesia, Darwin realized he was not cut out for medicine. Simply put, he could not handle the "occasions when the surgeon's assistant held down the shrieking patient by main force." Even though he craved the attention that position would give him, Darwin neglected his studies and could not stomach that career.

> *How ironic is it that Darwin was trained as a preacher and yet many evolutionists today ridicule preachers and condemn religion.*

Trained as a Preacher

In an effort to save face and the family reputation, Darwin was shipped off to Cambridge University where he studied—of all things—divinity. At this time in his life, Charles Darwin adhered to the conventional beliefs of the Church of England. But that was all about to change. During his tenure at Cambridge, Darwin met a group of Cambridge priests who enjoyed science—led by John Steven Henslow. Henslow, like Darwin, enjoyed collecting various specimens they found along their walks together.

In 1831 Darwin graduated from Cambridge with a degree in **divinity**—the only degree he would ever receive. While many consider him one of the greatest scientific minds ever to have walked the earth, the reality is this man was trained in the theology. How ironic is it that Darwin was trained as a preacher and yet many evolutionists today ridicule preachers and condemn religion.

It was John Henslow's recommendation to Captain Robert FitzRoy that landed Charles Darwin a volunteer position as a naturalist aboard the H.M.S. *Beagle*. A voyage that originally was scheduled to last two years eventually lasted five, during which time Darwin would record meticulous notes and collected hundreds of biological specimens. And it was that voyage that eventually took him to the Galapagos Islands where he found creatures that caused him to ponder the origin of living things.

Five Years of Seasickness

Darwin and the crew of the H.M.S. *Beagle* sailed out of Plymouth, England, on December 27, 1831, on a surveying expedition. Before they set sail, FitzRoy gave Darwin the first volume of Charles Lyells's book *Principles of Geology*, urging him to read it "but not believe it." It would be this book that introduced Darwin to the theory that landforms were the result of gradual processes over huge periods of time. Lyell's book would later play an important role in molding Darwin's beliefs about gradualism and its role in plant and animal development.

During his time on the *Beagle*, Darwin learned two things. First, life at sea did not agree with him as he often suffered from severe bouts of seasickness. At one point he caught a fever in Argentina and spent an entire month in bed. Second, he proved gifted at collecting and recording specimens as he honed his skills along the way. He spent a great deal of time sending Henslow, his mentor, letters of descriptions of his various observations. During this trip he collected enough material to write three books on South American geology. Henslow, meanwhile, often read Darwin's letters before the Cambridge Philosophical Society and the Geological Society of London—an act that brought Darwin "celebrity"

"...I am quite conscious that my speculations run beyond the bounds of true science.... It is a mere rag of an hypothesis with as many flaw[s] and holes as sound parts."

Charles Darwin to Asa Gray,
cited by Adrian Desmond and James Moore,
Darwin, (New York: W.W. Norton and Company, 1991)
p. 456, 475.

status in scientific circles even before his return. The stage was set for this seasick naturalist to garner attention as a leader in the scientific community. This one journey would set up Darwin as a scientist and would shape the rest of his life. One wonders where the world would be had he never stepped onboard.

Married with Children

On January 29, 1839, Darwin married his cousin Emma Wedgwood. Emma served as a nurse for much of Darwin's life as his health suffered throughout much of his adulthood. All told, they were blessed with ten children. Two of those died as infants. But the death of his ten-year-old daughter Annie in 1851 probably affected him more than anything. Many have speculated that this was the keystone event that caused Darwin to completely turn his back on God.

Many have speculated that this was the keystone event that caused Darwin to completely turn his back on God.

Cheater and Author

On June 18, 1858, Darwin received a manuscript that would forever change his life. The author Alfred Russell Wallace had penned his own theory regarding natural selection and evolution. Darwin was literally holding in his hand a paper that would record Wallace's name in the annals of history. Had Wallace sent the manuscript to any scientific journal rather than to Darwin, history would have given honors for the advent of evolution to Wallace, and Darwin's name would be castigated to the heap of forgotten names in science. In an unprecedented and clearly selfish move, Darwin sent Wallace's paper on to Charles Lyell to be considered for publication, but the plot was hatched to co-publish. Wallace's family was suffering from scarlet fever and he was left to trust Darwin, Charles Lyell, and Joseph Hooker. However, his trust was misplaced. Charles Lyell and Joseph Dalton Hooker schemed to read and publish Wallace's essay in conjunction with some of Darwin's unpublished writings before the Linnaean Society and published both in the Society's journal. In Darwin's material they included a letter to the American botanist Asa Gray that **predated** Wallace's essay. This would forever place Darwin's name ahead of Wallace, even though scholars who have compared their articles commonly agree that Wallace's contributions are more significant than often thought.

Mechanism and Micro vs. Macro Evolution

With that under his belt, Darwin hastily put together a book titled *The Origin of Species by Means of Natural Selection—or The Preservation of Favoured Races in the Struggle for Life*. It was this book that helped launch the organic theory for evolution. In his book *Origin of Species* Darwin laid out how he viewed evolution to work:

1. Inheritance of acquired characteristics (borrowing some from concepts developed by naturalist Jean-Baptiste Lamarck)
2. Adaptation
3. Natural selection

Two of these "mechanisms"—inheritance of acquired characteristics and adaptation—have been thoroughly discounted by scientists. Darwin's main driving force for evolution was natural selection, often described as "survival of the fittest." Darwin believed that the surviving species would improve over time and evolve into a completely new species. Most honest scientists will admit natural selection does not work above the level of microevolution. Researchers today also realize this is a tautology—meaning that the fit survive, and the ones that survive are fit. Sadly, there are still some scientists today who accept organic evolution because they know microevolution to be authentic.

Microevolution is true—and is defined as small changes within limited parameters (ex. dogs bred for different traits). **Macroevolution** (or organic evolution) **is false** and has never been proven in a lab. According to the macroevolution model, the universe is completely self-contained. That is to say, the universe is all that exists and thus everything descended from a common ancestor—which itself came from an inorganic form. There is no "First Cause," no "superintending intelligence," no "divine guidance" that is responsible for what we see around us. Organic evolution maintains that all life descended from a common ancestor (ex. dog to a fern or giraffe). Textbooks often teach the truth about microevolution, and then try to slip in macroevolution—that all species evolved from a common ancestor, something that has never been experimentally proven. **Darwin was teaching and espousing macroevolution.** Young people need to know the difference. As Hugo de Fries once noted: "Natural selection may explain the **survival** of the fittest, but it cannot explain the arrival of the fittest" (1905, p. 825-826, emp. added). Respected Swedish biologist Sören Lövtrup observed:

> Micromutations do occur, but the theory that these alone can account for evolutionary change is either falsified, or else it is an unfalsifiable, hence metaphysical, theory. I suppose that nobody will deny that it is a great misfortune if an entire branch of science becomes addicted to a false theory. But this is what has happened in biology.... **I believe that one day the Darwinian myth will be ranked**

"And
the salient fact is this:
if by evolution we mean macroevolution (as we henceforth shall),
then it can be said with the utmost rigor that
the doctrine is totally bereft of scientific sanction.
Now, to be sure, given the multitude of extravagant
claims about evolution promulgated by evolutionists
with an air of scientific infallibility, this may indeed
sound strange. And yet the fact remains that there
exists to this day not a shred of bona fide scientific
evidence in support of the thesis that
macroevolutionary transformations have
ever occurred."

– **Wolfgang Smith, 1988**
Teilhardism and the New Religion
(Rockford., Ill.: Tan Books)
p. 5-6.

the greatest deceit in the history of science. When this happens, many
people will pose the question: How did this ever happen? (1987, p. 422,
emp. added).

Darwin was completely wrong on inheritance of acquired characteristics.
While he recognized some of the problems with Lamarck's original theory,
Darwin still believed the environment might have the ability to change an
organism. Today scientists know that changes that occur in body cells are
not passed on to the DNA in reproductive cells. Scientists know today that
body cells, whether it be muscle tissue or skin tissue, do not have an effect
on sperm and egg cells. Adaptation is ill defined and is not a mechanism for

change. Scientifically speaking, the mechanism Darwin put forth for evolution is not tenable.

> *"I believe that one day the Darwinian myth will be ranked the greatest deceit in the history of science."*

Darwin devoted two chapters of *Origin of Species* to the fossil record. One might think that with two chapters, Darwin had a great deal to say in evaluating the available evidence, yet a careful examination reveals that he spent most of these chapters carefully apologizing for a lack of evidence. Darwin was therefore left to speculate and predict that eventually the fossil record would bear out his theory. Scientists have collected and cataloged approximately 200 million fossils in museums worldwide since that time. Yet, Darwin's elusive transitional fossils are still missing. The world may hail him as king, genius, or even a god. But the evidence reveals a frail man who studied theology, garnered attention from a boat ride, and was willing to cheat in order to place his name first. True scientists have abandoned true Darwinism for "neo-Darwinism" as his mechanism was untenable. And this is a man who textbooks and the mainstream media continue to honor, endorse, worship, and praise?

The Gradual Shift Toward Religious Evolution

Scientists have not always espoused atheistic ideals and evolutionary origins. In fact, many famous scientists were deeply devoted to religion and were not ashamed to espouse their beliefs in God (e.g., Pasteur, Newton, Lister, Lord Kelvin, etc.). However, the advent of the evolutionary theory caused a shift away from God and towards man-made theories. But a scientific theory alone is not enough to pull a society away from its religious moorings. Evolutionists needed a founder they could worship and a vocal spokesman to trumpet the cause. Charles Darwin and Thomas Huxley fit the bill perfectly. Those familiar with New Testament Christianity understand the important role the apostle Paul played in helping spread the Gospel during the first century. We know that Paul was responsible for writing many of the New Testament epistles and furthering the borders of the Church. But evolutionists have their own "apostle Paul" who was responsible for spreading the "gospel" of naturalism and materialism. In a revealing article titled "Is Evolution a Secular Religion?" staunch evolutionist Michael Ruse noted:

> Darwin himself was an invalid from the age of 30, and any profession building had to be done by his supporters, in particular by his "bulldog," Thomas Henry Huxley. In many respects, Huxley played to Darwin the role Saint Paul played to Jesus, promoting the master's ideas (2003, 299:1523).

This is a significant concession coming from a man who is a serious candidate to "pick up" where the late Stephen Jay Gould left off, and one who can pack more

anti-creationist propaganda into a single sentence than Huxley ever could. While Ruse denies any link between evolutionary theory and morals, he owns up to an accusation that many creationists have pointed out for years—that **evolution is not defended by many of its leading advocates as a science but as a religion.**

Ruse points out that the history of the evolutionary theory falls naturally into three parts. He notes, "The first part took place from the mid-18th century up to the publication of Charles Darwin's theory of natural selection as expounded in his *Origin of Species* published in 1859" (299:1523). Ruse maintains that before this time evolution was little more that a "pseudo-science on a par with mesmerism (animal magnetism) or phrenology (brain bumps)" (p. 1523, parenthetical items in orig.). It was during this period that Erasmus Darwin, Charles Darwin's grandfather, wrote evolutionary poetry, including *Temple of Nature*, where he wrote:

> *Imperious man, who rules the bestial crowd,*
> *Of language, reason, and reflection proud,*
> *With brow erect who scorns this earthly sod,*
> *And styles himself the image of his God;*
> *Arose from rudiments of form and sense,*
> *An embryon point, or microscopic lens!* (1803, lines 309-314).

The next phase of evolutionary history came as a result of Huxley's hard work. Even after Darwin's Origin of Species and Huxley's initial attempts to gain evolutionary "clients," Ruse noted:

> [E]volution still had no immediate payoff. Learning phylogenies did not cure belly ache, and it was still all a bit too daring for regular classroom instruction. But Huxley could see a place for evolution. The chief ideological support of those who opposed the reformers—the landowners, the squires, the generals, and the others—came from the Anglican Church. **Hence, Huxley saw the need to found his own church, and evolution was the ideal cornerstone.** It offered a story of origins, one that (thanks to progress) puts humans at the center and top and that could even provide moral messages…. Thus, evolution had its commandments no less than did Christianity (299:1524, parenthetical item in orig., emp. added).

> *Evolution is not defended by many of its leading advocates as a science, but as a religion.*

In detailing the history of this religion, Ruse notes that Huxley preached "evolution-as-world-view at working men's clubs, from the podia during presidential addresses, and in debates" (p. 1524). To Huxley's chagrin, the theory was still excluded from mainstream universities and was not being taught to students (something desperately needed if this theory was ever to take root and survive on its own.) Thus, things remained this way until the third phase, which Ruse notes began around 1930.

It was during this era that mathematicians fused Darwinism with Mendelian genetics, thus giving a scientific footing to evolution. Men such as Ronald Fisher and J.B.S. Haldane were able to help "professionalize" evolution in such a way that it now appeared politically correct to "study" it. Ruse noted, "Rapidly, the experimentalists and naturalists—notably Theodosius Dobzhansky in America and E.B. Ford in England—started to put empirical flesh on the mathematical skeleton, and finally Darwin's dream of a professional evolution with selection at its heart was realized" (p. 1524).

Questions
1. What is the difference between macro-and microevolution?
2. Who came up with the concept of natural selection at the same time of Charles Darwin?
3. Why are evolutionists so protective of their beloved theory?
4. How can macroevolution alter a person's worldview?

Scriptures to Study
Psalm 33
Psalm 8
Jeremiah 4:13-28
Jeremiah 51:15-16

Additional Resources

Johnson, Philip E. (1993), *Darwin on Trial* (InterVarsity Press).

Harrub, Brad (2009) *In the Footsteps of Darwin* (DVD) (Brentwood, TN: Focus Press).

References
Darwin, Erasmus (1803), *The Temple of Nature* (London: J. Johnson), volume 1, canto 1.

Ruse, Michael (2003), "Is Evolution a Secular Religion?," *Science,* 299:1523-1524, March 7.

de Vries, Hugo (1905), *Species and Varieties: Their Origin by Mutation,* ed. Daniel Trembly MacDougal (Chicago, IL: Open Court), p. 825-826.

Lovtrup, Soren (1987), *Darwinism: The Refutation of a Myth* (London: Croom Helm).

"*For the time will come when they will not endure sound doctrine, but according to their own desires, because they have itching ears, they will heap up for themselves teachers.*"
– 2 Timothy 4:3

Chapter

15

🌢

Evolutionary Hoaxes Uncovered

Over one-third of her freshman biology textbook dealt with evolution in some manner. Her class spent close to twelve solid weeks discussing how evolution shaped biology, and how "all of science was incomprehensible without it." The teacher taught entire class periods on examples of "evolution in action" or "proofs of evolution." This information, combined with shows on the Discovery channel and *National Geographic* magazine left more than just a few questions in this young girl's mind. Oh, how she wanted to believe in God and His creation. But the evidence seemed to be stacked against it. Conversations with her friends revealed that they were struggling too, and were beginning to place their allegiance in science. Were all of these evolutionary examples legitimate?

Textbooks abound with what appears to be "evidence" for the evolutionary theory. Yet many of the icons that evolutionists routinely uphold as proof for their beloved theory have serious problems. While the mainstream media and many in academia are familiar with the icons, they are unfamiliar with the problems or truth regarding this alleged evidence. Young and old alike should make themselves familiar with these icons as well as the errors associated with them. Listed below are some of the more common icons used as evidence. I encourage you to look through your children's science books and teach them the truth regarding these evolutionary hoaxes.

Haeckel's Embryos
In 1874, German biologist Ernest Haeckel published a series of drawings that have influenced thousands of biology students. He admitted that the changing point in his life was reading Charles Darwin's book *On the Origin of Species.*

Haeckel believed that humans evolved, and as such, hypothesized that during our embryological development humans allegedly go through successive stages of the animals from which we supposedly evolved (e.g., fish to amphibian to reptile to lower mammal). Biology students today recognize this belief as "ontogeny recapitulates phylogeny." To support this idea, Haeckel, an established artist, drew a series of images depicting embryos from several different species at various stages of development. In his drawings, an early stage human embryo looked similar to the fish, salamander, turtle, bird, pig, etc. This series of drawings seemed to be the perfect evidence evolutionists were seeking to prove the descent of all animals from a common ancestor.

> *Haeckel was rebuked by the scientific community for his fraudulent drawings, but they have continued to be published for decades.*

The only problem was the images were 100% faked. Haeckel altered the illustrations to portray this alleged similarity. Haeckel was rebuked by the scientific community for his fraudulent drawings, **but they have continued to be published for decades.** This hoax is persistently used by textbook writers to convey the idea of common ancestry. One of the most popular examples that originated from Haeckel's embryos is the theory that humans have gill slits as they are growing in the womb. This concept spawned from a set of fabricated drawings. We know today that human embryos never possess gill slits in the womb, and yet, textbooks continue to promote this lie. (Haeckel's embryos also served well in the 1970s for abortion-rights activists who asserted that the "thing" growing in the womb was not human, because it resembled the reptiles, fish, and amphibians. Today we know humans are different!)

Darwin's Finches
Another evolutionary hoax can be laid directly at the feet of Charles Darwin. During his voyage on the H.M.S. *Beagle*, Darwin visited the Galapagos Islands. On these islands he observed thirteen species of finches that possessed differences in bill shape, diet, and the environments in which they lived. Since Darwin's

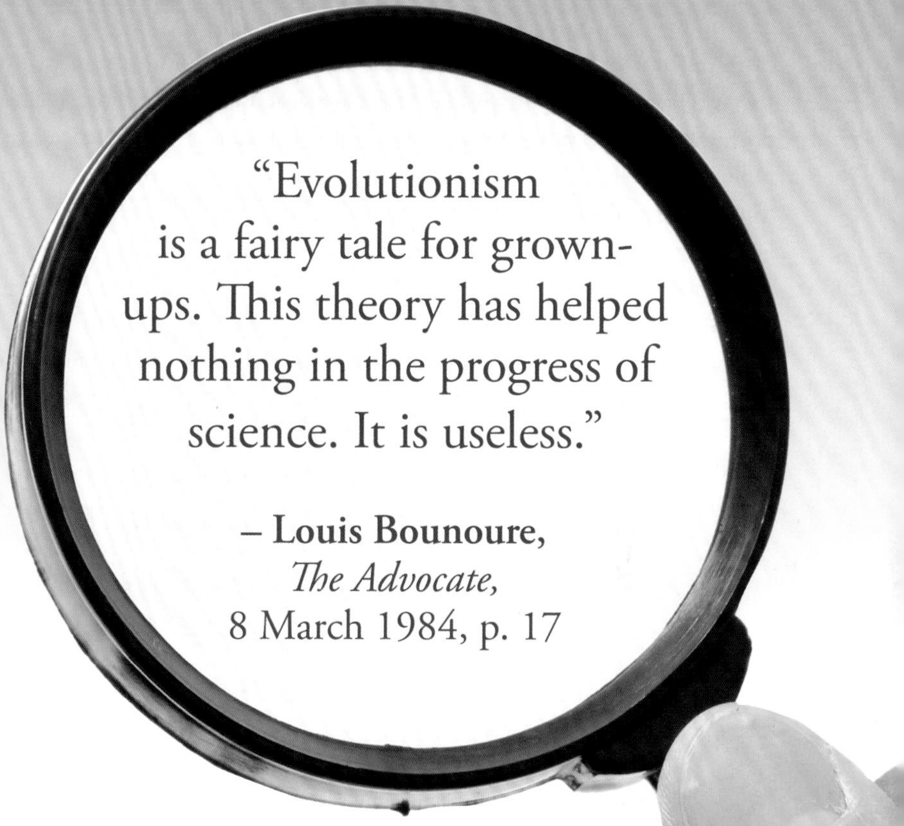

"Evolutionism is a fairy tale for grown-ups. This theory has helped nothing in the progress of science. It is useless."

— **Louis Bounoure,**
The Advocate,
8 March 1984, p. 17

observations, researchers (e.g., Peter and Rosemary Grant) have documented populations of finches changing due to environmental pressure. For example, a drought might result in the primary population of these birds returning to smaller beaks so they could feed on the available plants. The changes documented in these finches have led many evolutionists to proclaim this as example of "evolution in action."

However, the question should be asked: Do differences in beak size result in this species changing into an entirely new species? Microevolution can explain the small changes that are observed among the beaks, but organic evolution does not explain the existence of these birds in the first place. They are still finches—whether a drought existed or not. Also, we know today that these finches can interbreed—which demonstrates they are simply variations of the same species. [Additionally, these changes in beaks actually argue more against evolution. Evolutionists have always argued that evolution is a slow process requiring millions of years. Yet, the changes observed occur in a relatively short amount of time.] A few minor changes in beak size are hardly proof of common descent.

Peppered Moths

Almost everyone who has sat through a biology class can recall seeing a picture of a light-colored moth and a dark-colored moth resting on a tree trunk. Evolutionists proclaimed that prior to the industrial age, 95% of the moths in England

were white, and only 5% were dark colored. They reasoned that the dark-colored moths would be quickly eaten by birds because they stood out against the white lichens of the trees. After the industrial age, the trees took on a darker color from the pollution and soot. The moth population shifted, and 95% of the moths were dark colored and only 5% were white. Evolutionists claimed the dark moths were better camouflaged. Again, they contend this is an example of evolution by natural selection. However, in more than 40 years of research, the moths have only been observed on tree trunks twice! So where did those now-famous pictures come from? They were faked—staged! The moths were glued or pinned to the tree. Additionally, the original research has never been replicated. Lastly, no matter what color they are, the moths are still moths! They have not evolved into a new species. Bob Ritter, a Canadian textbook writer who knew the images were fabricated, noted: "You have to look at the audience. How convoluted do you want to make it for a first time learner? The advantage of this example of natural selection is that it is extremely visual. We want to get across the idea of selective adaptation. Later on, they [high school students—BH] can look at the work critically." In other words, later on they can discern if it is true or not.

Miller-Urey Experiment

All of the biology textbooks in my office contain a discussion of the famous Miller-Urey experiment conducted in 1953. Stanley Miller and Harold Urey put what they believed were the early atmospheric conditions together in an apparatus. They used an electrical spark to simulate lightning. And then they heated up the mixture to see if they could spontaneously generate living material from these non-living gases.

> *Did they create life? No. Did they create proteins? No. What they created was 85% tar...*

Did they create life? No. Did they create proteins? No. What they created was 85% tar—something most textbook writers fail to include. Additionally, we know today that the experiment was carried out in the absence of oxygen, in a reducing atmosphere—something honest scientists will admit is foolishness. (However, Miller and Urey had to do this in order to keep the oxygen from breaking down the desired amino acids.) Additionally, the electrical spark they used was constant, unlike the ever-changing frequency of lightning that would be found in the real conditions of nature. However, they did create trace amounts of a few amino acids. As such, most of these textbooks contain the phrase "scientists have created the building blocks for life"—another embellishment that is used to promote evolution. Routinely, after pronouncing this bold statement, the textbooks will then begin an intensive study of evolution. (Also, make sure children understand that humans have never successfully created living material from non-living material. Life always comes only from other life!)

Vestigial Structures

In 1931, German scientist Alfred Wiedersheim listed 180 human organs as being vestigial or rudimentary in humans. Structures like the appendix, the tonsils, the thymus, etc. were all on the list. Today that list has been abolished due to our increased knowledge. This has not stopped textbook writers from proclaiming that these alleged vestigial structures are "leftover" by-products from our evolutionary ancestors. For instance, a biology textbook published by Holt in 1989 noted, "The vestigial tailbone in humans is homologous to the functional tail of other primates. Thus vestigial structures can be viewed as evidence for evolution: organisms having vestigial structures probably share a common ancestry…." A Glenco biology book noted, "When compared with the caecum of a horse, the caecum and appendix of humans is thought to be vestigial." Today, we know for example that the appendix is a site where immune responses are initiated. Likewise, the tonsils play an immune function in humans. Just because we don't know what something is does not mean it is evolutionary baggage.

Archaeopteryx

Another common icon that evolutionists like to use is the *Archaeopteryx*. They proclaim this to be the missing link between dinosaurs and birds. Yet many scientists recognize this creature for what it truly is—a bird. Colin Patterson, senior paleontologist at the British Museum of Natural History, observed:

[*Archaeopteryx*] has simply become a patsy for wishful thinking. Is *Archaeopteryx* the ancestor of all birds? Perhaps yes, perhaps no: there is no way of answering the question. It is easy enough to make up stories of how one form gave rise to another, and to find reasons why the stages should be favored by natural selection. **But such stories are not a part of science, for there is no way of putting them to the test.** (as quoted in Sunderland, *Darwin's Enigma: Fossils and Other Problems,* p. 102)

In a recent personal email from world-renowned ornithologist Alan Fedducia, he declared, "*Archaeopteryx* was clearly a well-developed bird, with true feathers." This creature is simply a bird—not the desired "missing link."

In 2000, Jonathan Wells authored a landmark book called *Icons of Evolution,* in which he exposed the errors for the arguments for evolution. These icons, many of which were discussed above, are still included in textbooks today. I interviewed Jonathan Wells and asked him to share his thoughts on this crucial subject.

Brad Harrub: For folks who have not read *Icons of Evolution,* could you share what the basic premise is?

"The number of inter-mediate varieties which have formerly existed on earth must be truly enormous. Why then is not every geological formation and every stratum full of such intermediate links? Geology as-suredly does not reveal any such finely gradu-ated organic chain; and this, perhaps, is the most obvious and gravest objection which can be urged against my theory."

– Charles Darwin,
Origin of Species
1902 edition.

Jonathan Wells: The icons of evolution are images that have taken on a life of their own. That is, they go so far beyond the evidence or distort the evidence so seriously that they are no longer the evidence itself. These icons become objects of reverence almost, and they appear in the textbooks recycled over and over. And in fact, most biologists, all they really know about evolution is the icons, because Darwin plays very little role in their work. So they are exposed to the icons in an introductory course, and that's about all they really know.

BH: If you were giving examples to a set of parents of some of the icons they can expect to see in their child's textbooks, what comes to mind?

JW: One they will certainly see, because you can't teach Darwinism without it, is the evolutionary tree of life. That's the branching trees diagram that supposedly shows how all living things are descended with modification from a common ancestor. That's the root of the tree. So you see, in any biology textbook you'll see a version of this, purportedly showing how all the animals descended from this organism or all the mammals descended from that or all the horses or something like that. These trees are without exception hypothetical. They are really just restatements of Darwin's theory in pictorial form. What you have is a series of fossils were living organisms so you draw lines between them to show how they are related to one another. That's where the hypothesis starts and the evidence ends.

> *"These trees are without exception hypothetical. They are really just restatements of Darwin's theory in pictorial form."*

All of these errors and hoaxes may explain why evolutionists are hesitant to "teach the controversy" and allow students to discuss the problems with the Darwinian theory.

Then Why Do They Teach It?

The young man was extremely frustrated. He had come to the seminar as a skeptic, with hopes of debunking much of the material that was being presented. However, during the question and answer period, this college student quickly realized the weakness of his case, and he became angry at having never seen some of the problems of the evolutionary theory and the scientific studies that indicated the earth was relatively young. He asked a few additional questions and began to shake his head. Finally, holding the microphone in both hands, he looked up and asked, "Why haven't they ever taught us this stuff?"

Great question. I suspect the reason many young people are never introduced to the errors associated with the evolutionary theory is that students would quickly realize this theory is foolish and should be abandoned. Add to this the fact this is a godless theory that has ultimately become a religion for those who have stiffened their necks against God, and one can begin to understand why evolutionists are extremely protective about what is taught in the classroom. They don't want anyone loosening the grip they currently have in the academic world.

Textbooks today brashly assert organic evolution as a "fact." Yet, these same textbooks gloss over the fact **that evolution cannot explain:** (1) how non-living material produced living material; (2) from whence matter for the universe originated; and (3) the design found in nature. These are major hurdles for the evolutionary theory, and yet this is the only theory for origins that is legally taught in most classrooms. If we desire young people to be open-minded and critical thinkers, then why are they only exposed to one contaminated theory for the origin of mankind? That is not educating—it's indoctrinating. And our tax dollars are funding it.

In previous years, textbooks correctly taught students the Law of Biogenesis: that life comes only from other life. This **law of science** was established after empirical evidence demonstrated that life cannot spontaneously arise from non-life in nature. This is not a theory or hypothesis, but rather, a **scientific law** that has never been observed to be incorrect. Current textbooks however, have dropped the Law of Biogenesis in favor of abiogenesis—a theory that teaches students the possibility that life can arise from non-life under "suitable circumstances." Do we have any scientific data to back up this new theory of abiogensis? Absolutely not—but at least it doesn't contradict the evolutionary theory. Have we lost the ability to reason? How logical is it to replace a scientific law with an unproven theory?

While evolutionists may have the backing and support of the mainstream media, many Darwinians realize how damaging that spotlight can be when left to shine on their beloved theory too long. Students who are taught to think critically and not swallow whatever is thrown out before them quickly realize Darwin's theory falls short in many areas. For instance:

- Can evolution explain why we laugh/cry?
- Can evolution explain the origin of sex and gender?
- Can evolution explain altruism/charity?
- Can evolution explain the origin of language?
- Can evolution explain the origin of the human consciousness?

"Scientists who go about teaching that evolution is a fact of life are great con-men, and the story they are telling may be the greatest hoax ever. In explaining evolution, we do not have one iota of fact."

– Dr. T. N. Tahmisian
as quoted in *Evolution and the Emperor's New Clothes* by N.J. Mitchell (United Kingdom: Roydon Publications, 1983), title page.

- Can evolution explain the origin of the original matter for the universe?
- Can evolution explain the design found in nature?
- Can evolution explain how we got life from non-life?

But this is only the beginning. Evolutionary theory cannot adequately explain the origin of sex and gender. Think about it for a moment. How do you simultaneously evolve a separate male and female—with all of the necessary internal organs—all the while still being able to reproduce during this evolutionary "transition" period? What good is a partially evolved uterus? Do we have examples of transitional stages between asexual and sexual reproduction? Additionally, if the sole purpose of a creature is to replicate its own genes (e.g., survival of the fittest), then wouldn't asexual reproduction make more sense? Why go to the trouble of "evolving" separate male and female anatomy, when all one would have to do is split or bud off? Evolutionists might argue that sexual reproduction evolved because of the need for diversity—but such speculations are not a part of real science, as no one has successfully demonstrated how this "need" can cause such major physiological changes. Speculations are easy to pronounce, but rarely stand up to the test.

> *Why go to the trouble of "evolving" separate male and female anatomy, when all one would have to do is split or bud off?*

In the Footsteps of Darwin

Just a few months ago, film producer Mark Teske and I set out on a whirlwind journey to follow in the footsteps of Charles Darwin. We concluded that if the islands were the place that set Darwin's mind in motion about the origin of living things, then that's where we should go. Few evolutionists (and even fewer creationists still) have ever actually witnessed firsthand the environment that changed Darwin's life. We wanted to rectify that. So we flew onto Baltra Island and then took boats all around to various islands that Darwin himself surveyed.

During our time there, we witnessed firsthand the finches that made Darwin famous and the blue-footed boobies. Each island had a distinct form of the giant tortoises, and we were able to see many of these in their own natural habit. (We were even able to hold one of the completely spherical eggs at one of the preserves.) It was these same tortoises that years earlier Darwin had eaten while on the islands. In his book *Voyage of the Beagle* (1831-36), Darwin observed:

> As I was walking along, I met two large tortoises, each of which must have weighed at least two hundred pounds: one was eating a piece of cactus, and as I approached, it started at me and slowly stalked away; the other gave a deep hiss,

and drew in its head. These huge reptiles, surrounded by the black lava, the leafless shrubs, and large cacti, seemed to my fancy like some antediluvian animals.

The word *antediluvian* means "before the deluge or Flood." It is commonly used to describe the period between creation and the Flood of Noah's day. Ironic, is it not, that Darwin, a man who many esteem as a god himself, came to the islands and referred back to a Biblical period.

It wasn't until after he returned home from his trip that Darwin began to rethink the origin of living things. He had collected 13 finches from the islands that he examined upon his return and then began to question how these different birds had come into existence. He speculated that rather than being created by God, these birds were probably offspring of a single pair that had flown to the islands years earlier. Darwin failed to realize that this was what we deem today as "micro-evolution," which is simply small changes within limited parameters. It tells us nothing about the source of that particular species. He grew this notion of common ancestry until he reached the point in which he believed all living animals had arisen from a single source—something that has never been observed in a laboratory setting. Having been to the Galapagos Islands, I am even more convicted that there is a Designer behind all of the design we see in nature. I know that the unusual animals we walked with did not arise by chance, but rather they were created by the Creator. Darwin came to the islands and left questioning the existence of a God. We came to the islands and left with a renewed confidence that He lives!

Questions
1. What are some things young people should be taught before leaving for college?
2. How can someone claim evolution has become a religion?
3. What are some typical icons of evolution that students will see in textbooks? What are the problems with them?
4. Why are these icons still in textbooks?

Scriptures to Study
John 18:38
Romans 1:18
Proverbs 1:7
2 Timothy 2:15

Additional Resources

Harrub, Brad (2009),
In the Footsteps of Darwin (DVD)
(Brentwood, TN: Focus Press).

Wells, Jonathan (2002), *Icons of Evolution: Science or Myth,*
(Washington, D.C.: Regnery Publishing, Inc.).

*"Look now at the behemoth,
which I made along with you;
he eats grass like an ox."*
– Job 40:15

Chapter

16

◊

The Dinosaur Dilemma

The sight made me sick to my stomach. Literally nauseous. I was forced to watch as hundreds of school children were being indoctrinated with evolutionary garbage—and all I could think of was that many of them would one day be forfeiting their souls, as they cast aside any belief in the Bible and instead pledged their allegiance to the Darwinian theory. My family and I had stopped at a place outside of Denver known as the Dinosaur Ridge Trail. When I walked up to the first "information station," I asked the guide stationed there to tell me about the site. Just like hitting "play" on a tape recorder, he began reciting how "millions of years ago during the Jurassic period, dinosaurs had walked in this very spot...." As I listened to his canned spiel, I looked up two stations ahead of me and that's when I spotted the school children. Hundreds of young students who had only moments ago listened to this same guide describe "the five dinosaurs that had been uncovered at the Morrison Formation, millions of years before man ever evolved from apes." How many of these children's parents knew that this "field trip" to Dinosaur Ridge was nothing more than propaganda supporting the anti-God theory of evolution? How many of these parents realized the importance of the seeds that were being implanted in the hearts and minds of their children that very day?

Dinosaurs were not extinct from my scientific training. Oftentimes they were presented in the context of the origin of the earth. For instance, they are prominent in high school textbooks today: "Dinosaurs and other interesting animals lived during the Mesozoic Era, which was between 248 and 65 million years ago" (Feather, Snyder, and Zike, 2008 p. 408). Dinosaurs have become the sugar-stick candy that evolutionists offer our young children as they seek to convert them to their anti-God theory—oftentimes indoctrinating them with evolutionary time spans before the children can even read. We can find dinosaur impressions featured on kids' meals, snack crackers, fruit snacks, cereal, sippy-cups, birthday supplies, and a plethora of other products. They are a marketer's dream—as even young two-year-olds become fascinated with these amazing creatures. Our experience at Dinosaur Ridge could be multiplied literally thousands of times as movies, museums, amusement parks, and natural parks continue to promote the false idea that dinosaurs roamed this earth long ages before men. In fact, one would be hard pressed to find a children's book on dinosaurs that does not promote evolution.

Early Indoctrination

By the age of five, most children are already enthralled with the dinosaurs. There are

not too many five-year-olds who are not absolutely amazed by these amazing creatures. Early indoctrination. Our children open up popular books such as the *Magic Treehouse*. In fact, the very first book in that long kids' series starts out with a book about a dinosaur adventure. Upon reading the introduction, the statement is made that "human beings of course had not yet evolved." In fact, when a child opens up that particular book, they are confronted with a timeline that portrays the dinosaurs living through the Triassic, the Jurassic, and the Cretaceous periods. Man doesn't come into the picture until the very end of the timeline. The *Magic School Bus* is another popular children's series. Children open up a particular *Magic School Bus* book to find a young boy holding a picture of a dinosaur chasing a caveman. The boy says, "This story is make-believe." His friend says, "Yes, there were no dinosaurs in the time of cave people" (Joanna Cole, 1994, *The Magic School Bus: In the Time of Dinosaurs*).

But children are not the only ones who are fascinated. Magazines love to put dinosaur pictures on the cover because publishers know when they do so that they are almost guaranteed to increase sales. Month after month, we learn trivia and facts about these creatures—such as the largest dinosaur we have ever discovered is called the *Argentinosaurus*. It is estimated to have weighed 110 tons. (A full-size replica can be viewed at the Fernbank Museum in Atlanta, Georgia, where it stretches literally from one end of the museum to the other). Consider that a child can go to the zoo and see a giraffe, elephant, or rhinoceros—but they can't see a dinosaur. When children turn 12 years old and begin taking school field trips, they visit places like the Smithsonian Institute, the Fernbank Museum, or the Chicago Field Museum to visit a *T. Rex* named Sue. With each one of these trips, young people are confronted with placards giving evolutionary dates about these amazing creatures. So how do young people harmonize that with the Bible? The answer is they don't. Oftentimes what they will do is isolate the two in their brains until they reach 18-19 years old and begin to develop their own belief system. It's at this point they truly recognize the conflict, and sadly many of these young adults place their allegiance in what they learned in museums or in textbooks.

> *...sadly many of these young adults place their allegiance in what they learned in museums or in textbooks.*

The Dinosaur Dilemma

Dinosaurs represent a foundational pillar to evolution. They symbolize 250 million years to staunch evolutionists who believe these creatures walked the earth long before man, and therefore they provide one of the main branches for alleged common ancestry. Consider the dilemma that occurs if dinosaurs coexisted with man. Dr. Philip Kitcher wrote a book titled *Abusing Science: The Case Against Creationism*, in which he claimed that solid evidence for the coexistence of dinosaurs and humans would "shake the foundations of evolutionary theory because of course the dinosaurs are supposed to have been long extinct by the time the hominids arrived on the scene" (1982, p. 121). Evolutionists present a timeline and teach that the dinosaurs died out 65 million years ago. Allegedly, man came along carrying his club and living in caves roughly 3 millions years ago. "Solid evidence" of the coexistence of dinosaurs and man would undermine this entire timeline.

The Bible however, presents a different picture—one in which man would have coexisted with these amazing creatures. In Genesis 1 the Bible indicates man and all land-dwelling creatures (which would include dinosaurs) were literally created on Day 6—the same day. Therefore, if the Biblical account of creation is correct, man and dinosaurs had to coexist! The January 1993 Geoguide page of *National Geographic* starts out by boldly declaring: "No human being has ever seen a live dinosaur" (p. 142). The question is not: "Did dinosaurs exist?" because the evidence reveals conclusively that they did. Their fossilized remains have been discovered on all seven continents. The real question is **when** did they exist?

> *Therefore, if the Biblical account of creation is correct, man and dinosaurs had to coexist!*

A Quick History Lesson

The first dinosaur discovered, as far as recent times is concerned, happened in 1822. An English physician named Gideon Mantell journeyed to visit a sick patient. On that particular day, his wife Maryann decided to join him. They loaded up in horse-and-buggy, and when they arrived at the patient's house, Dr. Mantell went inside to tend to his patient. Maryann decided that she would take a stroll outside. While she was walking, she came across a pile of stones on the side of the road—except one of them did not look like a stone. It looked like a tooth, only it was much too large to be a tooth. She picked it up and took it back to show her husband. Dr. Mantell was amazed. He had never seen anything like it. Being in the scientific community, he showed his colleagues and they had never seen anything like it either. Eventually they went back to the quarry from where those rocks were cut and they found more teeth then more bones. In the year 1825, Dr. Mantell named that long dead creature *Iguanadon*. A few years ago while in Wellington, New Zealand, I was permitted to go into the basement of Te Papa Museum and Natural History and viewed firsthand this fossilized tooth. One could not look at this fossil and not be in awe of the creature to which it once belonged.

This was the beginning of the dinosaur fossil wars between men like Edward Cope and O.C. Marsh, who each unearthed hundreds of dinosaur fossils. The race was on to see who could discover (and as a result name) additional dinosaur species. It would be roughly 20 years later in 1841 when Sir Richard Owen would coin the term *dinosaur* using two Greek words *deinos sauros*, translated by him as "fearfully great lizard." Owen believed that there was once a huge tribe of these reptile-like creatures with shared common characteristics that once roamed the earth. These key discoveries really began our current fascination with these massive creatures. What does the evidence reveal about when they lived?

Evidence for the Coexistence of Dinosaurs and Humans

Dinosaur Found in Mammal's Stomach

Most evolutionary timelines have the mammals evolving from reptiles. Indeed, the textbook I used in my freshman general biology class noted, "During the Mesozoic Era the reptiles, which had evolved earlier from the amphibians, became dominant and in turn gave rise to the mammals and the birds." Evolutionists consider the last 65 million years of earth history (the Cenozoic Era) to be the "age of the mammals." However, in January 2005 a mammal was discovered that had been fossilized with a small dinosaur in its stomach. Some might look at this and question its relevance, but recall the evolutionary theory has mammals arriving on the scene millions of years **after** the dinosaurs. The Associated Press reported, "Villagers digging in China's rich fossil beds have uncovered the preserved remains of a **tiny dinosaur in the belly of a mammal**, a startling discovery for scientists who have long believed early mammals couldn't possibly attack and eat a dinosaur" (emp. added). This discovery was reported in the January 13, 2005, issue of *Nature*.

Ica Stones of Peru

Dr. Javier Cabrera Darquea, professor of medicine at the University of Lima, was given a unique stone as a gift from a local farmer in Peru. He noticed that the stone had elegant carvings on it. Cabrera recalled his father possessing similar stones. Through his investigation, Cabrera determined that these were

"In fact, evolution became in a sense a scientific religion; almost all scientists have accepted it and many are prepared to 'bend' their observations to fit in with it."

– H.S. Lipson, FRS, 1980
(Professor of Physics, University of Manchester, UK),
'A Physicist Looks at Evolution',
Physics Bulletin,
vol. 31, p. 138.

ancient burial stones that the ancient Incans had placed into tombs with their dead. Dr. Cabrera sought to find as many as he could. All told, Cabrera found roughly 11,000 of the stones, of which approximately one-third showed images of dinosaurs on them. And not just dinosaurs, but dinosaurs **and** man. The obvious question arises: How did these early Incans know what to craft into these stones if they did not see them? These are solid evidence for the coexistence for dinosaurs and humans. Evolutionists' only defense is to argue the authenticity of these burial stones.

Lest someone think that these are a recent forgery, there are details the ancient Incas got correct that man has only just recently identified. For instance, prior to the 1990s, scientists did not have any documentation of sauropod dinosaurs possessing dermal frills. However the Ica stones clearly showed dermal frills on the back of sauropod dinosaurs. It would be 1992 when researchers finally unearthed a fossil that conclusively proved the Incans were correct—saurpod dinosaurs did have dermal frills. In an article titled "New Look for Sauropod Dinosaurs," evolutionary paleontologist Stephen Czerkas noted, "Recent discovery of fossilized sauropod skin impressions reveals a significantly different appearance for these dinosaurs. The fossilized skin demonstrates that a median row of spines was present.... Some are quite narrow, others are broader and more conical" (1992 in *Geology* 20:1068). In discussing the dermal spines found in the Howe quarry in Wyoming, Ellen Morris Bishop wrote, "The biggest spines found were about 9 inches long, shaped a little like a shark's dorsal fin. The smallest at the tail-tip were about 3 inches high" (1993, *The Oregonian*, January 14).

How did these early Incans know what to craft into these stones if they did not see them?

Dennis Swift has authored a book titled *Secrets of the Ica Stones and Nazca Lines*. He has made several trips to the area and I had the opportunity to interview him to get his first-hand perspective:

Brad Harrub: How can we be assured the stones are real?

Dennis Swift: Most people are unaware that we have documentation of these stones that dates back to the 1500s. In 1535 Father Simon (a missionary) who was traveling with Pizarro recorded seeing the stones. A few years later, in 1562 Spanish explorers took some stones back with them. A man named Juan de Santa Cruz Llamqui who was from India actually wrote about these stones in the 1500s. So the authenticity is without question.

Additionally, I have come back with about twenty of these stones, some of which are slam-dunks that no one will touch. I have some with saltpeter in their groves. Some of them have mummy blood dried onto them. Others have lichen colonies growing on them. They have found that many of the grooves are covered from patina, indicating heavy weatherizing. Any skeptics that have looked at them have shut their mouths after looking at these stones.

BH: What about people who would claim they are fakes?

DS: Some critics try to say they are faked, saying they don't have enough patina on them, but these critics need to take into account the arid climate that these stones are found in. We know from the American Southwest that in dry climates we would not expect as much patina. This is precisely what we find on the Ica Stones. We have done blind tests on these stones with several universities, and they continue to come back conclusively that these stones are authentic. Now don't get me wrong, there are some fakes stones out there. But any expert can unravel it very quickly and see that they whether they are real. The casual eye can usually tell the fakes.

Dinosaur Figurines from Acambaro, Mexico

Photo from: www.bible.ca

In 1945, German Waldemar Julsrud discovered clay dinosaur figurines buried at the foothills of the El Toro Mountain on the outskirts of Acambaro, Mexico. Today more than 30,000 of these artifacts have been unearthed. Julsrud eventually wrote up his discovery in a booklet titled *Enigmas del Pasado*. The samples have been radiocarbon dated by Isotopes Incorporated of New Jersey, resulting in dates of 1640 B.C., 4530 B.C., and 1110 B.C. These dates, if accurate, would be strong testimony of men coexisting with dinosaurs. Eighteen additional samples were subjected to thermoluminescent testing by the University of Pennsylvania. These came back with dates of roughly 2000 B.C. These dates correspond to other material and pottery that was discovered in the same locale. However, the dates assigned to the material from the dinosaur figurines were later withdrawn when the laboratories learned the material depicted dinosaurs. Both labs basically told them: "We're sorry. We are unable to give you accurate readings on your material." [However in 1990, the University of Arizona dated some dinosaur bone in a blind study. The University Geoscience Department was not aware that the material they were dating came from dinosaur bone. Their test results labeled the material with a date of roughly 9000 years before present.]

800-Year-Old Buddhist Temple in Cambodia

Another example of evidence that refuses to "go away" is an 800-year-old Buddhist temple from the Khmer civilization that was uncovered in Cambodia. The temple had been completely overgrown with vines—making this extremely difficult to fake. When the vines were removed and cut down from Ta Prohm, one of the jungle temples, researchers were able to see the detail artisans had carved into the ancient temple walls. Carved hundreds of years earlier were clear depictions of animals like a monkey and deer—and also a dinosaur. In fact, the carving is so detailed that a 10-year-old child can quickly discern the type of dinosaur (a *stegosaurus*). Two eyewitness accounts from Denny Petrillo and Neal Pollard attest that not only is this temple real, but the carvings are only explained in the light of the ancient men with knowledge of these animals who originally carved this massive structure.

Dinosaur Petroglyph near Blanding, Utah

Located about 40 miles west of Blanding, Utah, there are three sandstone bridges in Natural Bridges National Monument—one of which is called Kachina. On these sandstone bridges, there are numerous petroglyphs and pictographs that date back to the time of the Anasazi Indians. For instance, there are depictions of big horn sheep and men…and also a dinosaur. Francis Barnes, an evolutionist and recognized authority on rock art of the American Southwest, stated, "There is a petroglyph in Natural Bridges National Monument that bears a striking resemblance to a dinosaur" (1995, *Canyon Country Prehistoric Indians—Their Culture, Ruins, Artifacts, and Rock Art*, Wasatch Publishers: Salt Lake City, Utah). Why didn't Barnes just call it a dinosaur? Because as Kitcher said, "Solid evidence of dinosaurs coexisting with man would shake the foundations of the evolutionary theory."

According to evolutionary theory, flying reptiles died out 65 million years ago.

Oh, Those Pesky Flying Reptiles
On those same sandstone bridge walls at National Bridges National Monument were images of flying reptiles. According to evolutionary theory, flying reptiles died out 65 million years ago. And yet, consider these quotes from ancient historians.

Greek historian Herodotus (fifth century B.C.) stated:

> There is a place in Arabia...to which I went, on hearing of some winged serpents; and when I arrived there, I saw bones and spines of serpents, in such quantities as it would be impossible to describe. The form of a serpent is like that of a water-snake; but it has wings without feathers, and as like as possible to the wings of a bat (1850 reprint, *Historiae*, translated by Henry Clay, 2:75 –76).

Herodotus described flying reptiles and knew these were not bats or birds.

Bear in mind both of these historians documented flying reptiles centuries **before** *Charles Darwin or the word* evolution *even came into existence.*

Jewish historian Flavius Josephus also wrote about flying reptiles. Josephus wrote about Moses passing through a particular region because of the presence of flying serpents:

> When the ground was difficult to be passed over because of the multitude of serpents (which it produces in vast numbers...some of which ascend out of the ground unseen and also fly in the air, and do come upon men at unawares, and do them a mischief).... [Moses] made baskets likened the arks of sedge and filled them with ibes (or birds) and carried them along with them; which animal is the greatest enemy to the serpents and imaginable, for they fly from them when they come near them; and as they fly they are caught and devoured by them (N.D. *Antiquities of the Jews* 2:10:2).

Bear in mind both of these historians documented flying reptiles centuries **before** Charles Darwin or the word *evolution* even came into existence. Is one now to toss aside these historical eyewitness accounts because they do not conform to the evolutionary theory?

The Tomb of Richard Bell

What about evidence before the word *dinosaur* was even coined? If you ever get the chance to visit the Carlisle Cathedral in Carlisle, England, ask them to roll up the carpet in the main hall. Below the carpet is the tomb of Richard Bell— a bishop who served that church in the 15th century and died in 1496. The rolled-up carpet will reveal an elegant marble tomb that is inlaid with brass. Carved into the brass are a variety of animals such as an ell, a dog, a pig, a bird…and two long-necked dinosaurs. Bear in mind that Bell died roughly 350 years before the word *dinosaur* came into existence.

Burial Cloths and Pottery

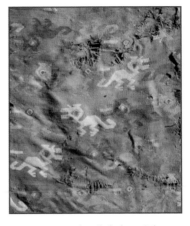

Textiles have been unearthed from Nazca tombs that clearly show dinosaur-like creatures on them. There is also pottery from South America depicting dinosaurs on it that was discovered in tombs. Additionally, an urn from Caria, located in Asia Minor (Turkey), was discovered with the picture of a *mosasaurus* on it. This artifact is described in Thomas H. Carpenter's 1991 book *Art and Myth in Ancient Greece: A Handbook*. Estimated to be from 530 B.C., it portrays the *mosasaurus* along with several known sea creatures such as seals, an octopus, and a dolphin. The image on the urn compares extremely well with the *mosasaurus* skeleton, possessing the thick jaws, big teeth, large eyes, and positioning of the flippers. There are also burial clothes from the Nazca culture in Peru that have clear depictions of dinosaurs on them. Again, the implication being these ancient cultures had first-hand knowledge (or were at least told by individuals who knew) of these amazing creatures. This indicates they were still alive when the ancient Peruvians saw them.

Doheny Expedition

Dr. Samuel Hubbard was the honorary curator of archaeology in the Oakland, California Museum of Natural History. He believed the American Indians had been on the North American continent much longer than historians were giving them credit for. So Hubbard set out on an expedition to prove that fact. His expedition traveled down into the Grand Canyon—off one of the side canyons called the Havi Supai canyon. Hubbard was looking for things like ancient pottery or clothing, anything that would prove the American Indians had previously been in that area. Dr. Hubbard was right. He uncovered their clothing and he found their pottery. But he also stumbled across cave art etched into the canyon walls centuries ago. These were images that had taken men literally hours to carve out. Mixed in with the images of buffalo, sheep, and men was also an image of a dinosaur. Dr. Hubbard said:

> Taken all in all, the proportions are good. The huge reptile is depicted in the attitude in which man would most likely see it—reared on its hind legs, balancing with the long tail, either a feeding or a fighting position, possibly defending itself against a party of men (1954, *Strange Prehistoric Animals and Their History*, A. H. Brill, L. C. Page & Co., Boston, p. 155).

Hubbard went on to proclaim:

> The fact that some prehistoric man made a pictograph of a dinosaur on the walls of this canyon upsets completely all of our theories regarding the antiquity of man.… The fact that the animal is upright and balanced on its tail would seem to indicate that the prehistoric artist must have seen it alive (1925, *Discoveries Relating to Prehistoric Man by the Doheny Scientific Expedition*, Oakland California Museum of Natural History, p. 5-7).

Ironically, nearby there were dinosaur tracks that had been preserved in stratum that evolutionists identified as the Triassic period. The Doheny Expedition included Dr. Charles W. Gilmore, Curator of Vertebrate paleontology at the United States

National Museum. Given this discovery was made by men of science who concluded this pictograph was a dinosaur, what does this mean to the evolutionary theory that places 65 million years between the extinction of dinosaurs and the appearance of man?

Soft Tissue in a Dinosaur Bone

Or how do evolutionists logically explain the soft tissue that was discovered in a *T. Rex* fossil? I actually communicated with Mary Schweitzer, the lady who made this discovery. She shared that it was really a serendipitous event. Her research team wanted to get the long bone—the femur—of the *T. Rex* back to the laboratory. Having encased it in protective material, they discovered it was too large to fit on the helicopter. The original *Washington Post* account mentioned that the bone was broken when it was moved, which permitted access to the soft tissues. When I asked Mary Schweitzer if that was indeed true, she responded: "Yes and no. It was broken in the field—too heavy for the helicopter in one piece. But that only allowed access to the bone chunks they didn't need to 'rehabilitate' the dino. The soft tissues were not immediately apparent or expected." This allowed researchers to look inside the fossil, where they found (1) soft tissue; (2) blood vessels; (3) and (what Schweitzer suspects may be) blood cells. Ask any molecular biologist worth his salt and he will freely admit soft tissue, blood vessels, and blood cells do **not** stick around for 65 million years. This discovery was reported in the March 2005 issue of *Science*.

> *Ask any molecular biologist worth his salt and he will freely admit soft tissue, blood vessels, and blood cells do **not** stick around for 65 million years.*

Ancient Artifacts

There is a Roman mural from the second century A.D. depicting two long-necked dragons. Bear in mind that this mural is composed of hand-laid tiles that were laid down just after the Bible came to be in the completed form we have it today. We believe the Bible was completed in the year 93 A.D. And yet, around this time men were laying tiles in a mural that featured dinosaur-like creatures.

Additionally, researchers have unearthed a Mesopotamian cylinder seal from approximately 3000 B.C. that looks an awful lot like an *apatosaurus* (Moortgart, Anton, *The Art of Ancient Mesopotamia*, 1969, plate 292). This seal was crafted with details that beg the question how did the artist get those creatures so convincingly right? There is also a stone tablet that was discovered that is attributed to Narmer, the legendary first Pharaoh of a United Egypt. This stone tablet shows two long-necked dinosaur-like creatures. Or consider the Egyptian seal from the Mitry collection. It has a cartouche of Tutmosis III (approx. 1400 B.C.). The seal also depicts a *Sauropterygia*-like animal (type of plesiosaur). Even a casual observation reveals anterior and posterior flippers with the narrow connection to the rotund body of the creature. The seal is of unquestioned authenticity. The physical evidence refuses to go away quietly and is impenetrable to evolutionary spin. The only logical conclusion is that men coexisted with the dinosaurs.

Dinosaurs and the Bible

The question is asked: If dinosaurs and man coexisted, then why is there not a record of dinosaurs in the Bible? That's an unfair question. Recall the word *dinosaur* was not coined until the 1840s. When was the Bible translated into English? Answer: The King James version was translated in 1611. A better question would be: Is there compelling evidence of dinosaur-like creatures in God's Word? That is a fair question. In response to that question, an honest investigator should turn to the book of Job.

> *The question is asked: If dinosaurs and man coexisted, then why is there not a record of dinosaurs in the Bible?*

In the opening chapter of Job, we are introduced to a man who is smitten with all kinds of trials. His flocks were taken away. His children were taken away. And soon thereafter Job is covered in boils from the crown of his head to the bottom of his feet. He is in so much agony that his wife tells him, "Curse God and die!" (Job 2:9). But Job doesn't do that. Very soon after his wife makes that foolish statement, Job's three "friends" come on the scene. I would offer that these are not true "friends" but rather busybodies. They are nosy. They assume Job sinned against God and he is therefore being punished for that sin. These "friends" want to know what Job did. Therefore, the next 25+ chapters detail a running dialogue between Job and these three friends: Eliphaz the Temanite, Bildad the Shuhite, and Zophar the Naamathite. They question Job over and over about what caused all of his grief until finally Job bursts out and requests to speak to God. In Job chapter 13:22, we read: "Then call, and I will answer; or let me speak, then You respond to me." Job is saying, "You can go first or I'll go first, it does not matter to me." In Job 38, we have God's response:

> The Lord answered Job out of the whirlwind and said: "Who is this who darkens counsel by words without knowledge? Now prepare yourself like a man; I will question you and you shall answer Me" (Job 38:1-3).

For the next three chapters, God deluged Joe with question after question—many of which mankind has still not answered today. God asked Job, "Where were you when I laid the foundations of the earth?" He questioned, "Where is the dwelling place of light or what about the eagle and hawk—how do they fly? Or what about snow and hail? How do I make those?" In Job 40:15 God turned His attention to a creature called the behemoth.

> Look now at the behemoth, which I made along with you; he eats grass like an ox. See now, his strength is in his hips, and his power is in his stomach muscles. He moves his tail like a cedar; the sinews of his thighs are tightly knit. His bones are like beams of bronze, his ribs like bars of iron. He is the first of the ways of God (Job 40:15-19).

What is a behemoth? Many Bibles will have a footnote that describes this creature as an elephant or a hippopotamus. However a close look at the description of this creature reveals the strength is in his stomach muscles—in other words, it's got a large stomach. This characteristic is true for elephants, hippos, and dinosaurs. Verse 17 goes on to record that he moved "his tail like a cedar." The "cedar" discussed in this passage would have described some of the largest trees. In fact, a word study on "cedar" in the Old Testament reminds investigators that it was the cedars of Lebanon that were used to build the Temple. These were massive trees! And yet, an inspection of the tail of an elephant quickly reveals it does not resemble a cedar. Neither does the tail of a hippopotamus. However, the tail of a dinosaur is much closer to this description. The text describes this creature as "chief in the ways of God" (KJV). What is the largest land-dwelling creature we've ever discovered on the earth? It's the dinosaur. The text then goes on to describe the very environment in which this creature lived.

Dragons: Myth or Menace?

In the next chapter of Job, we learn about a new creature called the leviathan (Job 41). "Can you draw out leviathan with a hook?" (v. 1). Lest someone discount these creatures as imaginary or figurative, keep in mind the context of what God is doing in this historical scene. God is questioning Job how He created all of these things. Why would He then ask about two "imaginary" creatures? The text goes on to ask, "Can you put a reed through his nose or pierce his jaw with a hook?" (v. 2). Verse 26 declares, "Though the sword reaches him it cannot avail nor does dart or javelin." Verse 29 continues, "Darts are regarded as straw and bronze as rotten wood....his undersides are like sharp pieces of pottery, he spreads pointed marks in the mire (v. 30). Some Bibles describe this animal as an alligator or crocodile. However the true description starts in verse 18:

> His sneezings flash forth light, and his eyes are like the eyelids of the morning. Out of his mouth go burning lights; sparks of fire shoot out. Smoke goes out of his nostrils, as from a boiling pot and burning rushes. His breath kindles coals, and a flame of fire goes out of his mouth (Job 41:18-21).

Were there really dragons? History records dragon stories in the majority of ancient cultures. Consider the entry found under the entry for dragon in *Encyclopedia Britannica*:

> Legendary monster usually depicted as a huge, bat-winged, fire-breathing lizard or snake with a barbed tail. The dragon symbolized evil in the ancient **Middle**

East, and the Egyptian god Apepi was the great serpent of the world of darkness. The **Greeks** and **Romans** sometimes represented dragons as evil creatures and sometimes as beneficent powers acquainted with the secrets of the earth. In Christianity the dragon symbolized sin and paganism, and saints such as St. George were shown triumphing over it. Used as warlike emblems in many cultures, dragons were carved on the prows of **Norse** ships and depicted on royal ensigns in medieval **England**. In the **Far East** the dragon was a beneficent creature, wingless but regarded as a power of the air. In **China** it symbolized yang in the yin-yang of cosmology, and it served as the emblem of the royal family (2006, emp. added).

In other words, countries all across the globe have stories, symbols, and artwork featuring these creatures. This entry strongly resembled the description given thirty-three years earlier from *World Book Encyclopedia*, which noted, "The dragons of legend are strangely like actual creatures that have lived in the past. They are much like the great reptiles which inhabited the earth long before man is supposed to have appeared on earth. Dragons were generally evil and destructive. **Every country had them in its mythology**" (Knox, 1973, p. 265, emp. added).

> *If these creatures never existed, then why did so many different civilizations depict such similar creatures?*

Dragons have also been mentioned by firsthand observers and in historical accounts. We also find depictions of them in ancient artwork. The obvious question one should ask is: If these creatures never existed, then why did so many different civilizations depict such similar creatures? How did these ancient artists know what to draw or carve? For instance, in 1975 a gilded bonze dragon was excavated by Caochangpo and Xi'an from the Shaanxi province of China (Michaelson, 1999, p. 90). The dragon is believed to belong to the Tang dynasty (618-906 A.D.). It stands 13.4 inches tall and weighs just over 6 pounds. It is currently on display in the Shaanxi History Museum. In documenting archaeological artifacts from China's golden age, Carol Michaelson also revealed a rubbing of a dragon found on a brick at Maoling, the tomb of the emperor Wudi, from the Han dynasty, 1st century B.C. (1999, p. 91). This brick was similar to another dragon carving found on a stone slab from the Qianling tomb of Emperor Gaozong from the 7th-8th century A.D. (Michaelson, 1999).

> *With so many countries featuring dragon stories, the question arises: Could all of these various countries have independently "imagined" a creature bearing such a similar description?*

With so many countries featuring dragon stories, the question arises: Could all of these various countries have independently "imagined" a creature bearing such a similar description? While some dragon stories can easily be recognized as fantasy, the fact remains that evidence exists that these creatures once walked the earth. For instance, Marco Polo lived in China for 17 years, and in approximately 1271 A.D., he reported that the Chinese emperor raised dragons to pull his chariots in parades. In 1611, the Emperor initiated the post of "Royal Dragon Feeder." Chinese families are said to have raised dragons in order to use their blood for medicine, highly prizing their eggs. We know the Vikings would carve dragons into their boats. Our literature is filled with dragon stories. There's ancient artwork that supports their very existence.

What Happened to the Dinosaurs?

A question that remains a thorn for both creationists and evolutionists is what happened to the dinosaurs. In all honesty, no one knows for sure. There are many theories out there. In fact, some researchers recently speculated that maybe the dinosaurs had died out from lack of sleep. There are more than 20 theories of what happened to the dinosaur. Creationist Don DeYoung outlined five of the theories in his book *Dinosaurs and Creation*:

1. An asteroid struck the earth causing worldwide fires. The dust from the impact and the soot and ash from the fire blocked out the Sun's rays, causing the temperatures to drop drastically.
2. A nearby supernova (exploding star) flooded the earth with intense

radiation, resulting in fatal mutation for dinosaur offspring.

3. The earth's climate became too warm, too cold, too dry, or too wet for the dinosaurs' health.

4. A change in the dinosaurs' diet resulted in weakened eggshells that broke after being laid.

5. A laxative plant in the dinosaurs' diets disappeared, and they died of constipation (*Dinosaurs and Creation*, Donald B. DeYoung, Baker, Grand Rapids, Michigan, 2000, p. 26-27).

One possibility that is seldom mentioned among scientists is a change in environment and weather patterns following the Global Flood. Personally, I think two things led to their demise: (1) a change in the weather and environment following the Global Flood that greatly affected these cold-blooded creatures; (2) consider also what man has always done to animals that we fear. Oftentimes we hunt and kill them. Recall in Genesis 1:29-30, God said, "See I've given you every herb that yields seed which is on the face of all the earth and every tree whose fruit yields seed to you it shall be for food. Also to every beast of the earth to every bird of the air, and to everything that creeps on the earth, in which there is life, I have given every green herb for food; and it was so." The indication was that  both man and animals were vegetarian prior to the Flood. That helps one to understand how humans and dinosaurs could coexist. In Genesis 9 we find God making His promise to Noah. God states: "The fear of you and the dread of you shall be on every beast of the earth, on every bird of the air, on all that move on the earth and all the fish of the sea. They are given into your hand. Every moving thing that lives shall be food for you. I have given you all things even as the green herbs." After the Global Flood, God allowed man to eat meat. The evidence demonstrates not only that man coexisted with dinosaurs, but that these amazing creatures fit beautifully into a Biblical worldview.

Questions
1. Why are dinosaurs considered the sugar-stick candy evolutionists use with young people?
2. Why does evidence of dinosaurs and humans coexisting pose a problem for the evolutionary theory?
3. What transitional creatures would one expect if modern-day animals evolved from dinosaurs? Have any such creatures been discovered in the fossil record?
4. Why aren't dinosaurs mentioned in the Bible? What other some other examples of animals not specifically mentioned in the Bible?
5. Why is this evidence of dinosaur and humans coexisting not published in textbooks?

Scriptures to Study
Job 40-41 • Genesis 1

Additional Resources

Ham, Ken (2000), *The Great Dinosaur Mystery Solved,* (Green Forest, AR: New Leaf Press).

DeYoung, Donald (2000), *Dinosaurs and Creation,* (Grand Rapids, MI: Baker).

References
Feather, Ralph Susan Snyder, and Dinah Zike (2008), *Earth Science* (Columbus, OH: McGraw Hill Glencoe).
Kitcher, Philip (1983) *Abusing Science,* (The MIT Press).
Knox, Wilson (1973), "Dragon," *The World Book Encyclopedia,* volume 5.
Michaelson, Carol (1999), *Gilded Dragons: Buried Treasure from China's Golden Ages,* (London: British Museum Press).

"You covered it with the deep as with a garment; the waters stood above the mountains. At Your rebuke they fled; at the voice of Your thunder they hastened away."
– Psalm 104:6-7

Chapter 17

Catastrophes: The Global Flood

The hike through the Appalachian Mountains was cleansing. Mike and his scout troop bore heavy packs for the week-long hike, but the experience was proving to be well worth it. The troop had learned to rely on one another, and their friendships had grown much stronger over the past few days. Mike suspected the memories he was making would last a lifetime.

Yesterday, the troop worked their way around Black Balsam Knob. It was there some boys discovered several aquatic fossils preserved in rock. These fossils were a clear indication that this region had been under water at some point in time. How did they get way up there? Although the boys had spent much of their hike in relative silence—saving every ounce of energy for the hike—this discovery had set off a flurry of conversation about how the fossils got there. Mike wondered if the Global Flood mentioned in the Bible could have placed the aquatic fossils on the mountains. The Noahic Flood had come up several times in conversation along the trail, but many of the boys believed the Global Flood was either mythological or simply a local flood. Some of his friends speculated that the mountain they were on used to be the ocean floor, but was pushed up by tectonic activity. Mike kept walking as he pondered a logical explanation for the aquatic fossils.

The Problem for Uniformitarianism

Believe it or not, there is one thing creationists and evolutionists agree on—this earth has not always been the way we find it today. The fossil evidence indicates that there was a time when the earth experienced a more tropical-like environment over the majority of the landmasses. Dr. Alfred Russell Wallace, a contemporary of Charles Darwin who independently arrived at the concept of natural selection, described the early earth in the following manner:

> There is but one climate known to the ancient fossil world as revealed by the plants and animals entombed in the rocks, and the climate was a mantle of spring-like loveliness which seems to have prevailed over the whole globe. Just how the world could have been this warm all over may be a matter of conjecture; that it was so warm effectively and continuously is a matter of fact (1876, 1:277).

In an article titled "Evolutionary Growth Rates in the Dinosaurs," E. H. Colbert stated, "In those days the earth had a tropical or subtropical climate over much of its land surface and in the widespread tropical lands there was an abundance of lush vegetation" (*Scientific Monthly*, 69:71). The evidence for this change places the theory of evolution in an awkward position. Almost all of the evolutionary dating methods are based on uniformitarianism—the idea that the earth has been the same since the beginning.

Almost all of the evolutionary dating methods are based on uniformitarianism—the idea that the earth has been the same since the beginning.

It is a cardinal tenet of evolutionary biology. For instance, geologist Charles Felix observed:

> **Uniformitarianism is the great underlying principle of modern geology!** ...Uniformitarianism endures, partly because it seems reasonable and the principle is considered basic to other fields of study, but it also persists because **this is the only way to arrive at the enormous time-frame required for placement of slow evolutionary processes.** It is probably correct to state that evolution depends on the unqualified acceptance of Uniformitarianism! (1988, p. 29-30).

William Stansfield observed, "Several methods have been devised for estimating the age of the earth and its layers of rocks. These methods rely heavily on the assumption of uniformitarianism, i.e., natural processes have proceeded at relatively constant rates throughout the earth's history"

The Science of Evolution (New York, NY: Macmillian), 1977, p. 614.

The physical evidence rejects uniformitarianism. Honest scientists recognize this earth has experienced catastrophes like the Ice Age. But where did these catastrophes come from? Are there logical explanations that fit the evidence and the Bible? Throughout Scripture, there are events that God has orchestrated (e.g., the Flood, the long day of Joshua, et al.) that cannot be called in any sense of the word "uniformitarian" in nature. These events are important not just because of the immediate impact they had on individuals living during that time, but they are also important for the effects they left behind and the message they send future generations.

The Global Flood

The account of the Noah's Flood is a fascinating piece of history that has forever changed this world. God deemed His original creation "very good" (Genesis 1:31), but a few hundred years later "God looked upon the earth, and indeed it was corrupt; for all flesh had corrupted their way on the earth" (Genesis 6:12). While this narrative remains one of the most scoffed by non-believers, Christians can rest assured that it is an accurate description of how God punished a sinful civilization. The inspired writings from God's Word coincide beautifully with a close scientific examination of this world-changing event. This was not a "local" flood limited to the middle-eastern region of the world. But rather, this was a catastrophic deluge that permanently altered this world and ultimately led to a new chapter in the history of mankind.

Consider, "while the earth remains, seedtime and harvest, cold and heat, winter and summer, and day and night shall not cease" (Genesis 8:22). That promise was given to mankind just after the God had unleashed His fury on a sin-sick world. God made a covenant with Noah that He would never again curse the ground or destroy every living thing as He had done through the Global Flood (v. 21).

Think for a moment about the conditions that preceded that catastrophic event. In a world pronounced "very good," mankind did not yet know the polluting effects of vehicle emissions, factory smokestacks, DDT, or Agent Orange. The water was pristine and the vegetation lush, as both man and animals were instructed to eat "every herb that yields seed which is on the face of all the earth, and every tree whose fruit yields seed; to you it shall be for food" (Genesis 1:29-30).

The Global Flood itself brought forth many changes that ultimately altered the earth's environment. Suddenly, new weather patterns were put into place. Lush environments began to dry up into some of the deserts we have today. A mist no longer watered the earth (Genesis 2:6)—but now the water cycle began to water the earth with rain. Following the devastating flood and new environmental conditions, man found himself once again needing to replenish the earth. While skeptics and critics love to abuse the account of the Noahic Flood, the evidence remains. **Water-dwelling fossils have been found literally all over the world and at all altitudes.** Consider the following charges that are often leveled by atheists and evolutionists:

> *While skeptics and critics love to abuse the account of the Noahic Flood, the evidence remains.*

1. The ark would not have been big enough.

In Genesis 6:15 Moses wrote, "And this is how you shall make it: The length of the ark shall be three hundred cubits, its width fifty cubits, and its height thirty cubits." A cubit is defined as the length of a man's forearm. In ancient times there were "royal" cubits measuring up to 20 inches, and common cubits that measured approximately 17.5 inches. In their classic work *The Genesis Flood*, John Whitcomb and Henry Morris used a conservative 17.5 inch cubit and demonstrated that the total volume on the ark would have been 1.39 million cubic feet of storage—taking into account the three decks mentioned in verse 16. They then demonstrated that an ark of this size would have had the carrying capacity equivalent to that of 522 railroad boxcars! This was not some little Sunday afternoon sailing vessel. This was the largest ship built to that day. Is it not logical to conclude that God—the Creator of the animals—could give the appropriate dimensions for a vessel to house all of the land-dwelling animals He created?

Currently docked near Pier 39 in San Francisco is the S.S. *Jeremiah O'Brien*—the last of a fleet of ships known as the Liberty Ships. These boats were specifically built to carry massive loads through rough seas. However, when I called a retired Navy sailor to discuss this particular ship, **he told me the entire fleet was built to the exact dimensions of Noah's ark!** God was the initial Architect who provided the dimensions for a boat that could carry a heavy load through rough seas.

2. But you still can't get two of every species on the boat!

It is important to point out that nowhere in God's Word does it say Noah had to take two of every "species." The text indicates that he was to take two of each "kind" of animal (Genesis 6:20). For instance, would Noah have had to take two Golden Retrievers, two Labrador Retrievers, two English Setters, two wolves, two coyotes, etc.? Or could he have simply taken two of the dog "kind"? But even when one examines the evidence for the species argument, we realize the ark could have easily done the job.

For instance, in 1980 Ernst Mayr, a very famous evolutionary taxonomist, published a book titled *Principles of Systematic Zoology*. In his book he outlined every creature we knew of that was alive on the earth. According to Mayr's own numbers, Noah would have had to provide protection for:

- 3,700 Mammals
- 8,600 Birds
- 6,300 Reptiles
- 2,500 Amphibians (even though some would like the water)

Thus, 21,100 different **species** would have needed protection aboard the ark. We can multiply this number by 2 because we know he was to take two of every unclean animal. We also know Noah was to take seven pair of the clean, so we can look through the Old Testament and discern which animals were considered clean for sacrificing. If we use the "species" definition, the total number of individual animals that would have needed protection on the ark would be approximately 50,000. If we average these 50,000 animals to the size of a sheep (knowing that most birds, reptiles, and amphibians are much smaller—but there will be cows and elephants much larger), then we can ask the question: Can we get 50,000 sheep-sized animals onboard the ark? Well consider that one boxcar is capable of holding 240 "sheep-sized" animals. Thus, we could place 125,000 sheep-sized animals into 520 boxcars—and yet we only had to get 50,000! That would have left plenty of room for Noah, his family, and all of the food necessary.

3. Noah would not have had sufficient time to build a boat that big.
Many creationists have proposed that Noah hired out men to help him build the ark. The Bible however remains silent on the specifics of how the boat was constructed. Given that Noah and his family were the only ones saved, we can safely assume most people considered this "preacher of righteousness" a raving lunatic. As such, hired hands may have been extremely difficult to come by. However, John Morris and Tim LeHaye wrote a book titled *The Ark at Ararat*,

in which they proved mathematically it could have been accomplished with just Noah and his sons! They described how four men could have cut, dressed, and installed approximately 15 cubic feet of gopher wood per day. Since we know the dimensions of the ark (Genesis 6:15), we can safely assume they would have needed approximately 380,000 cubic feet of wood to complete the ark. If they worked six days per week, these four individuals could have completed the task in only 81 years!

> *The Bible however remains silent on the specifics of how the boat was constructed. Given that Noah and his family were the only ones saved, we can safely assume most people considered this "preacher of righteousness" a raving lunatic.*

4. How could Noah have collected that many animals by himself?

Often we find that those who utter the most complaints against God's Word have usually read it the least. The text never indicates that Noah had to collect the animals. In fact, it says quite the opposite. Genesis 6:20 states: "Of birds after their kind, of animals after their kind, and of every creeping thing of the earth after its kind, **two of every kind will come to you to keep them alive"** (emp. added). Noah simply had to provide the ark of the appropriate dimensions with a door that would allow the animals to enter two-by-two.

5. Well, you may be able to get them all on the ark, but how did Noah feed, water, and clean up after that many animals?

There is a theory that is popular with many creationists suggesting that God put the animals into a state of hibernation. Obviously, atheists would charge that Christians are playing the "God card" to get around answering the question. In 1996, John Woodmorappe wrote a book titled *Noah's Ark: A Feasibility Study* in which he went into painstaking detail to show not necessarily **how** it was done, but rather that it **could** be done. Drawing on previous research and mathematical calculations, Woodmorappe demonstrated how, using 80 man-hours per day, we can account for waste management, feeding, and watering of all the animals.

His research clearly indicates that Noah and his family, working ten hours per day, could have easily taken care of the animals—and this does not take into account the possibility of God miraculously caring for the animals.

6. Where did all that water come from?
The second half of Genesis 7:11 records, "On that day all the fountains of the great deep were broken up, and the windows of heaven were opened." While even young children recognize that it rained for "forty days and forty nights" (Genesis 7:12), the text indicates that the fountains of the deep and the windows of heaven continued to usher water on the face of the Earth for several months (Genesis 7:24-8:2). While most have no problem envisioning fountains of the deep (as we know we have fresh-water springs even in the oceans today [Job 38:16]), the question remains: What does it mean that the windows of heaven were opened?

> ## What does it mean that the windows of heaven were opened?

Part of the answer can be found in Genesis 1:6-7. Moses recorded: "Then God said, 'Let there be a firmament in the midst of the waters, and let it divide the waters from the waters.' Thus God made the firmament, and divided the waters which were under the firmament from the waters which were above the firmament; and it was so." The word translated *firmament* is the Hebrew word *raqij`a*, which refers to an expansion or the heavens. So Moses described waters above and below this firmament. Today we are familiar with waters below the firmament. However, what were these "waters above the firmament"? Many creationists believe that there was once a water vapor or ice crystal canopy around the earth—and when God opened the "windows of heaven," it was the ultimate collapse of this canopy. This presence of the canopy would explain how earlier in the earth's history much of the land was tropical in nature.

7. Just how much water?
Consider that God not only had to cover the earth with water, He had to know how much water to place on the earth. Most individuals living in coastal areas

know that the draft of a boat is how deeply it sits in the water. A speedboat has a shallow draft because its purpose is to move quickly across the water, whereas the draft of an ocean-going freighter is much deeper. Most ship-builders will tell you that the draft of a boat that can withstand the pounding waves of the ocean is ½ its height. In other words, that boat has to be able to settle into the water roughly ½ its own height to keep from capsizing. What about the ark? Was it built for speed? No. It didn't have anywhere to go.

But it did need to be able to withstand the pounding waves. So again, the draft would have been ½ its height. In Genesis 6:15 we learn Noah was to make it 30 cubits high—which means **it would have settled into the water roughly 15 cubits**. That means it would have required 15 cubits of water clearance. Now look at Genesis 7: 18-20: "The waters prevailed and greatly increased on the earth, and the ark moved about on the surface of the waters. And the waters prevailed exceedingly on the earth, and all the high hills under the whole heaven were covered. **The waters prevailed fifteen cubits upward, and the mountains were covered**" (emp. added). God knew precisely how much water He needed to place on the tops of the mountains to keep the bottom of the ark from crashing into them.

8. Then where did all of the water go?

If there were a Global Flood, then where did all of the water go? Genesis 8:1 indicates that God "made a wind to pass over the earth." We know today that trillions of gallons of water are now in our atmosphere in the form of clouds. Additionally, we know that trillions of gallons are stored below the earth's crust in the water table. However, the inspired psalmist informs us that God changed the topography of the earth after the Flood, thus accommodating much of the water. Psalm 104 states: "You covered it with the deep as with a garment; The waters were standing above the mountains. At Your rebuke they fled, at the sound of Your thunder they hurried away. **The mountains rose; the valleys sank down to the place which You established for them.** You set a boundary that they may not pass over, so that they will not return to cover the earth" (Psalm 104: 6-9, emp. added).

9. Were dinosaurs on the ark?

When most people first hear the suggestion that dinosaurs were on the ark, they find this incomprehensible. The visual image of dinosaurs walking up a ramp through the doorway of the ark is not a picture many have ever considered. Two mental stumbling blocks make it especially difficult for the average person to give any consideration to this suggestion: evolutionary teaching and their gigantic size. The mainstream media has done such an outstanding job of convincing the general population that dinosaurs lived millions of years ago that the idea of dinosaurs on the ark seems ludicrous. After all, they would have us believe that humans are separated from the dinosaurs by 65 million years.

The other stumbling block is the size of these great lizards. Oftentimes when we picture dinosaurs, we imagine massive sauropod dinosaurs such as the *Apatosaurus* that easily weighed over 50 tons! How do you get such massive creatures on the ark—and once onboard, how do you feed such enormous creatures? Furthermore, how did Noah's family and domestic creatures share living quarters with ferocious creatures such as the *Tyrannosaurus rex*?

In evaluating what animals were on the ark, it is important to investigate the true description given in God's inspired Word for details. (Remember, this is the **only** inspired book.) Consider the following Truths that can found in the Bible:

A. All land-dwelling creatures were created on Day 6 (Genesis 1:24-26).
It is clear that on the sixth day God created all land-dwelling creatures and man: "Then God said, 'Let the earth bring forth the living creature according to its kind: cattle and creeping things and beast of the earth, each according to its kind'; and it was so…. And God saw that it was good. Then God said, 'Let Us make man in Our image…'" This creative history is emphasized again in Exodus 20:11 which tells us: "For in six days the Lord made the heavens and the earth, the sea, and all that is in them, and rested the seventh day." Clearly, everything—including man and dinosaurs—was created during the six days of creation.

> *Clearly, everything—including man and dinosaurs—was created during the six days of creation.*

B. Noah was to take two of every unclean land-dwelling creature on the ark—which would include dinosaurs (Genesis 6:19-20). Moses wrote, "And of every living thing of all flesh you shall bring two of every sort into the ark, to keep them alive with you; they shall be male and female. Of the birds after their kind, of animals after their kind, and of every creeping thing of the earth after its kind, two of every kind will come to you to keep them alive" (Genesis 6:19-20). God brought every land-dwelling creature to Noah for safekeeping. If dinosaurs were around during this time, then one can reasonably conclude that they too would have required safekeeping.

C. The book of Job describes the "behemoth" (40:15), a creature that fits the description of a dinosaur that was living after the Flood. (Additional scientific evidence exists that these amazing creatures lived after the Flood.) In Job 40:15 God questions Job about a creature He describes as the behemoth. While many (uninspired) footnotes describe this creature as an elephant or hippopotamus, the description better fits a dinosaur-like creature. (How many elephants or hippos have "tails like a cedar," Job 40:17?) While most scholars consider Job to be one of the first books written, the events described therein take place a few centuries after the Flood. Also, there is extensive scientific evidence that men living after the Flood saw these amazing creatures.

D. Genesis 1:29-30 indicates that both man and animals were to eat vegetation before the Flood. It was only after the Flood that God allowed the eating of meat (Genesis 9:3). If it were the case that both man and animals were vegetarian prior to the Flood, then sharing close quarters on the ark would not have presented a problem.

E. The Bible does not specify that Noah had to take adult animals onboard the ark. While many would argue that dinosaurs would have been too large to fit on the ark, we must bear in mind that there are some mysteries that God's Word does not reveal. For instance, why couldn't Noah have taken juveniles? Consider they take up less space, eat less food, produce less waste, and you don't have to worry about reproductive problems! Also, not all dinosaurs were massive in size.

So could dinosaurs have been on the ark with Noah and his family? Absolutely!

Scholars enjoy mocking the Noahic Flood as a ridiculous myth. However, their scorn fails to account for the physical evidence all across the planet that points toward a Global Flood. A serious investigation reveals this earth has changed dramatically. An unbiased examination reveals that Noah's ark would have been more than adequate to do the job God put forth. The laughter of skeptics does nothing to alter the truth laid forth in God's Word. This catastrophe was real—and was the direct result of sin. It was this catastrophe that was responsible for the putting into place the weather patterns we experience today. If God needed a "Noah" today, could He count on you?

Questions:
1. Why is it illogical to conclude that the Noahic Flood was a "local flood"?
2. Why are catastrophes a problem for the evolutionary theory?
3. What was the cause and result of the Flood?
4. How could all of the animals have fit onboard the ark?
5. What are some additional examples of catastrophes?

Scriptures to Study
Genesis 6-9 • Isaiah 59:2 • 1 Peter 3:19-21 • Hebrews 11:6-7 • 2 Peter 2:5

Additional Resources:

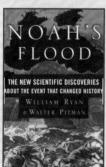

Ryan, William and Walter Pitman (1998), *Noah's Flood: The New Scientific Discoveries About the Event That Changed History* (New York, NY: Simon and Schuster).

Morris, Henry M. and John C. Whitcomb (1961), *The Genesis Flood: The Biblical Record and Its Scientific Implications* (Phillipsburg, NJ: R & R Publishing).

Rehwinkel, Alfred M. (1951), *The Flood* (St. Louis, MO: Concordia Publishing House).

References:
Morris, Henry M. and John C. Whitcomb (1961), *The Genesis Flood: The Biblical Record and its Scientific Implications* (Phillipsburg, NJ: R & R Publishing).
Felix, Charles (1988), "Geology and Paleontology," *Evolution and Faith*, ed. J.D. Thomas (Abilene, TX: ACU Press).
Wallace, Russell (1876), *The Geographical Distribution of Animals*, 1:277, (New York, NY: Harper and Brothers).

*"Have you entered the treasury of the snow,
or have you seen the treasury of hail?"*
– Job 38:22

Chapter

18

🌢

Catastrophes: The Ice Age

It was the trip of a lifetime! Connor and his best friend had scored cheap airline tickets to Alaska and they were now exploring the last great frontier. After landing in Anchorage, they immediately headed northwest to Denali National Park. They spent two days in the park, and finally got a glimpse of Mt. McKinley just before leaving. Already their journey had brought them face to face with bald eagles, several moose, Dall sheep, and two brown bears. They were now journeying down onto the Kenai Peninsula, eager to spend a day fishing for salmon and halibut. As they made their way down to Seward, they passed a sign for Exit Glacier. They were not scheduled to be at the fishing dock for another two hours, so they decided on a quick visit. The glacier was just a few miles off the main road, and they were able to park fairly close, leaving just a short walk to the gigantic glacier. The massive blue ice was impressive—and it was something Connor had never witnessed. The eerie size and color was by far one of the coolest things he had seen thus far, but it also left many questions unanswered. Was there really an Ice Age? How did all of this fit into the Bible? Did the glacier he was standing on give credence to the vast old ages espoused by evolutionists?

Most of us can remember sitting through a history or science class hearing the teacher describe a land bridge that connected Asia with North America. Images of creatures like the woolly mammoth paint a picture in our mind of what we identify as the Ice Age. But was it real? Did the Ice Age really happen? And if so, when? *Encyclopedia Britannica* defines the Ice Age in the following manner:

Also called Glacial Age, any geologic period during which thick sheets cover vast areas of land. Such periods of large-scale glaciations may last several million years and drastically reshape surface features of entire continents. A number of major ice ages have occurred throughout earth's history. The earliest known took place during the Precambrian Time, dating back more than 570 million years ago.

What evidence exists regarding the Ice Age and other climate-changing events?

The Ice Age—a Result of the Flood

Creationists and evolutionists agree that there was once an Ice Age. The difference is in when this event occurred, what caused it, and how long it lasted. The United States Department of Interior/U.S. Geological Survey published a paper titled "The Great Ice Age" that was funded by our tax dollars [see http://pubs.usgs.gov/gip/ice_age/ice_age.pdf]. In that article, the author Louis L. Ray observed: "The Great Ice Age, a recent chapter in the Earth's history, was a period of recurring widespread glaciations. During the Pleistocene Epoch of the geologic time scale, which began about a million years ago, mountain glaciers formed on all continents, the icecaps of Antarctica and Greenland were more extensive and thicker than today."

There can be little doubt that the Ice Age was real. One can hardly look at El Capitan or Half Dome in Yosemite National Park or hike the Continental Divide Trail in Glacier National Park without witnessing firsthand the awesome power of past glaciers. Normal river erosion causes v-shaped valleys. But these advancing ice sheets produced a u-shaped cross profile in many of these areas. As the ice sheets advanced, they would often pick up boulders, soil, loose rocks, which would act as an abrasive polisher for mountain faces in the path of the growing ice sheet.

Those seeking "proof" for the Ice Age can look in three different areas. 1.) Geology—geologists have identified rocks on many continents that have been cut, polished, scratched, or scoured by advancing glaciers. In addition, when the glaciers melted they would often leave deposits such as till (composed of clay, sand, gravel, and boulders) and glacial moraines, and drumlins that are readily identified today, revealing the pathway of past glaciers. 2.) Past temperatures—scientists have studied ice cores and sedimentary rocks in an effort to determine temperatures in the past. Studies have shown that water containing heavier isotopes have a higher heat of evaporation, thus its proportion would be decreased in colder (Ice Age) conditions. By measuring isotopes researchers believe they can reconstruct temperature data from the past. 3.) Migration fossils—scientists have uncovered fossils that help track migration patterns during this period. There are clear indications of animals that could adapt to the cold, whereas some of the animals spread into lower altitudes because they could not tolerate the colder climates. Taken together, sufficient evidence exists that for a time ice and snow covered much of northern United States, as well as Canada, Eurasia, Greenland, and Antarctica.

> *Creationists, on the other hand, recognize that the evidence given above fits a climatic change that would be consistent with the period following the Noahic Flood.*

So what triggered this catastrophic event? While evolutionists are quick to prescribe evolutionary dates to the Ice Age, they are not as quick to provide a cause. In the official government publication on the Great Ice Age, Louis Ray declared: "Many attempts have been made to account for these climatic fluctuations, but their ultimate cause remains unclear." In addition, evolutionists find themselves in the peculiar position of defending multiple ice ages as a cyclic event, even though they do not have a good explanation for why they occurred. Creationists, on the other hand, recognize that the evidence given above fits a climatic change that would be consistent with the period following the Noahic Flood.

Mike Oard retired from the National Weather Service as a meterologist and has written extensively on the Ice Age. He has written several technical papers demonstrating how the Ice Age fits in perfectly with the Genesis Flood. I had the opportunity to interview him regarding his knowledge of the Ice Age.

Brad Harrub: What scientific evidence supports an Ice Age? What was the extent of freezing?

Michael Oard: We see glacial till, a mixture of rocks of all sizes in a finer grained matrix, over much of the northern United States and Canada. Similar features occur over northern Europe and northwest Asia. In fact, 30% of the Earth was glaciated during the Ice Age, while only 10% is glaciated now. These features include moraines, which are hills of debris formed at the edge and in front of a glacier or ice sheet. Many distinctive horseshoe-shaped moraines extend out from mountain valleys of the western United States, for instant the northern Wallowa Mountains in northeast Oregon. We see boulders of distinctive rock carried hundreds of miles from their source. They are called erratic boulders. One very prominent boulder, once weighing about 170 tons, is argillite, a slightly metamorphic shale, found about 40 miles southwest of Portland, Oregon. The nearest source for argillite is northern Idaho and western Montana. This boulder is not going to roll down in Floodwater. It would break apart in a matter of a mile or so in the Flood. But since the area around Portland was not glaciated, this boulder must have been rafted down in the Lake Missoula flood, caused when the edge of the ice sheet in northern Idaho ponded a 2,000-foot deep lake in the valleys of western Montana and then broke. We see plenty of scratched boulders and bedrock in areas formerly glaciated.

> *You must remember that uniformitarian scientists really cannot explain the Ice Age themselves, and the Ice Age is the last major event to impact the earth.*

BH: You have written that the Flood led to the Ice Age. Can you explain how a Global Flood would result in an Ice Age?

MO: The climate today is so warm in the summer, an ice age cannot occur. Since the glacial deposits are post-Flood, the Ice Age must have occurred right after the Flood. That brings up the question of whether the huge catastrophe of the Flood could cause the Ice Age? You must remember that uniformitarian scientists really cannot explain the Ice Age themselves, and the Ice Age is the last major event to impact the earth. There are more than 60 theories, all of which have serious difficulties. David Alt (2001, p. 180) said in his book about the Lake Missoula flood, *Glacial Lake Missoula and Its Humungous Floods:* "Although theories abound, no one really knows what causes ice ages."

As far as how the Flood can cause an Ice Age, we need to first know the requirements of an Ice Age. You must have much cooler summers, much greater snowfall, and the climate change must persist for years. The climatic aftermath of the Flood fulfills those requirements because of all the volcanic dust and aerosols (small particles) trapped in the stratosphere after the volcanism of the Flood. Copious post-Flood volcanism, as seen in ice age deposits, would replenish the dust and aerosols as they fell back to earth. The dust and aerosols cause cooler temperatures because some of the sunlight is reflected back to space. The cooling effect is mainly over mid and high latitude continents in the warm season. Hot water added to the pre-Flood ocean during the Flood and volcanism would have resulted in a warm ocean, from top to bottom and pole to pole. Evaporation is proportional to sea surface temperature. Such warm ocean water at higher latitude would cause huge evaporation that would result in rapid snowfall over land [think "lake effect" snow–BH]. Such a climate, starting right after the Flood, would persist for hundreds of years.

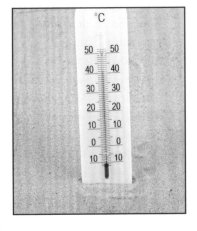

BH: Were there multiple ice ages?

MO: The idea of multiple ice ages is really an assumption, based mainly on the astronomical hypothesis for ice ages, the currently popular hypothesis of mainstream glaciologist. Most areas that were glaciated show only one Ice Age. Those areas that can be interpreted as from multiple ice sheets, mainly along the edge of the former ice sheets, can be explained by one dynamic ice sheet that moves and retreats rapidly because of surges. The Greenland Ice Sheet shows only one Ice Age. Too many assumptions are used in Antarctica for glaciologists to come up with one ice age.

BH: Many would argue that ice cores reveal an ancient earth. What would be your response to someone who claims we can determine the age of the earth through ice core samples?

MO: To make a long story short, glaciologists assume that the Greenland and Antarctica Ice Sheet are old and have been similar in size for millions of years. Based on this they set up standards for measurements that cause old age to be built in. The measurements in ice cores are constrained within these assumptions. So, as they count annual layers going down into the Greenland Ice Sheet (you cannot count annual layers on the high Antarctica Ice Sheet because of the low snowfall), they are correct on the years for perhaps 1,000 feet. But then their wrong assumptions constrain their annual layers and they arrive at 110,000 years down to near the bottom of the ice core. That is still only one Ice Age in their scheme. But with different assumptions of a rapid build up of ice during the Ice Age, the age of the ice can be found to be around 5,000 years old.

My world history textbook, written from an evolutionary perspective, remained silent on cause of the Ice Age. The Bible, how-

ever, does not. In Genesis 7:11 the Bible describes where the water for the Flood came from. Moses wrote, "On that day all the **fountains of the great deep were broken up,** and the windows of heaven were opened (emp. added)." In Genesis 8:2 the text indicates: "The **fountains of the deep** and the windows of heaven were also stopped, and the rain from heaven was restrained" (emp. added). The Hebrew word *mayan*, translated to "fountains," means things like "spring, well, or fountains." Commentators Keil and Delitzsch describe it as "the unfathomable ocean."

Two points should not be missed: (1) the fountains were "broken up" and (2) they were in the great deep. Just the sheer force of breaking these deep layers would have caused massive fissures. This breaking open of the "fountains of the deep" implies that the ocean itself rose up and helped cover the land. Second, recall from geology the temperature of the earth increases as you descend through the layers. The earth is composed of a series of layers we deem the crust, mantle, and core. The crust is the outermost portion of the earth and extends approximately 25 miles down. The mantle extends further down about 1800 miles, and the core makes up the remainder of the earth. If things are breaking open in the "unfathomable ocean" at great depths, does it not make logical sense that the temperature closer to the mantle would have been hotter?

Thus, God's fury upon a sin-sick world would have caused massive earthquakes resulting in large cracks or rifts deep within the earth's crust explosively releasing subterranean water and triggering volcanic activity. We know today from the fossil record that there are volcanic rocks interspersed between the fossil layers that were obviously deposited during or just after Noah's Flood. We also know from ice-core samples that volcanic ash was present. For instance Anthony Gow took 7,100 feet of core samples from nine different Antarctic glaciers and found over 2,000 individual volcanic ash falls embedded within the ice. While I don't agree with Gow's dating of 10,000 - 30,000 years ago (primarily because he uses radio-carbon dating which is based on 7 assumptions that all must be correct), the data for volcanoes during this period is irrefutable [see Gow, Anthony (1972), "Glaciological Investigations in Antarctica," *Antarctic Journal of the United States* 7, no. 4:100-101].

> *Having not witnessed a Global Flood from an angry God, we have a hard time of truly envisioning the devastation God unleashed on that sin-sick world.*

The Perfect Recipe for an Ice Age

Having not witnessed a Global Flood from an angry God, we have a hard time of truly envisioning the devastation God unleashed on that sin-sick world. As tectonic plates shifted below, there would have been tsunamis, volcanoes, and torrential rains as God punished all land-dwelling creatures. The heat released from the "fountains of the great deep" would have undoubtedly warmed the oceans, causing an increase in evaporation and the amount of water in the atmosphere available for precipitation. At the same time, the ash from volcanoes all across the globe would have very effectively blocked out much of the sun's rays, cooling the land. This combination of cool land and increased precipitation would have easily resulted in snowfall that fell much faster than it could melt, allowing ice sheets to build up.

The climatic change of warmed oceans and cooled land would have persisted for a long time even after the Flood waters had abated. The land bridge that my high school World History teacher described was one of the by-products for this time pe-

riod. Consider that following the Flood, the Bible records the Tower of Babel incident. According to the text, people were already making bricks (Genesis 11:3). And then God confused their languages and dispersed them. This ice bridge would have allowed both the descendants of Noah, as well as land-dwelling animals, to easily migrate from America to Asia. Eventually, however the seas would cool, producing less evaporated water, decreasing the snow supply for the continents. Additionally, as the ash from the volcanoes settled, the sun's warming rays would penetrate, causing the ice sheets to melt, resulting in the topography we see today.

Consider the evidence. We know the Ice Age was real. Only one theory has a plausible cause for it. How much faith does it take to continue embracing an evolutionary theory that acknowledges this historical period, but has no explanation for it? The Ice Age was real, and its existence causes problems for uniformitarianism, but fits in beautifully with God's Word.

Conclusion

In late August 2005, Hurricane Katrina ripped through southern portions of Alabama, Mississippi, and Louisiana. While citizens in New Orleans dodged a direct hit from this major storm, the intense rain eventually proved too much for the outlying system of canal levees and substations. For citizens of "The Big Easy," the next few hours would place them on an emotional roller coaster that few will ever forget. After experiencing the joy of having "dodged the bullet," they discovered that the levees broke, and many parishes began to fill with water. Individuals were trapped inside their homes as the water washed away their furniture, along with a lifetime of memories. Up and down the streets people found themselves trapped in upper levels of their homes as cries for help rang out incessantly. There was no way out. People were dying all over the city...and yet the water kept on coming.

This modern-day tragedy was a harsh reminder of the power of Mother Nature. While we can still visualize television images of those who were stranded on rooftops, take a minute and try to imagine the horror and the screams that echoed around the globe when God let loose His fury on a sinful world. In August of 2005, we only heard the screams from the citizens of New Orleans and outlying regions. Thousands of years earlier there were screams heard literally around the world. Literally millions of people perished from the Global Flood that forever changed this earth.

The account of the Global Flood and Noah's ark is one of obedience and righteousness. Similar to the people of Nineveh (Jonah 3:4-10), God gave the people time to repent and change their ways (Genesis 6:3). The desire of the world to pursue their own pleasures allowed God to demonstrate His holy wrath and righteous judgment of a sinful people. But thankfully, Noah found grace in the eyes of the Lord (Genesis 6:8). We read in 1 Peter 3:20, "...When once the divine longsuffering waited in the days of Noah, while the ark was being prepared, in which a few, that is eight souls, were saved through water." In Peter's second letter, he condemns false teachers, reminding them that God "did not spare the ancient world, but saved Noah, one of eight people, a preacher of righteousness, bringing in the flood on the world of the ungodly" (2 Peter 2:5). The scars left behind from the catastrophes of the Global Flood and the resulting Ice Age should be a bold reminder of the evidence of the holiness of God.

Questions:
1. How would the Ice Age affect the dispersal from the Tower of Babel? How would it help explain the American Indians or Ancient Aztecs?
2. What is the recipe for an Ice Age?
3. How does the Global Flood fit into the Ice Age?
4. What evidence exists for the Ice Age?

Scriptures to Study
Genesis 6-9 • 1 Thessalonians 5:21

Additional Resources:

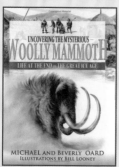 Oard, Michael and Beverly Oard (2007), *Uncovering the Mysterious Woolly Mammoth: Life at the End of the Great Ice Age* (GreenForest, AR: Master Books).

References:
Gow, Anthony (1972), "Glaciological Investigations in Antarctica," *Antarctic Journal of the United States* 7, no. 4:100-101.

"By the word of the Lord the heavens were made,
and all the host of them by the breath of His mouth....
For He spoke, and it was done;
He commanded, and it stood fast."
– Psalm 33:6, 9

Chapter

19

Evidence for a Young Earth

With summer break coming to a close, Steven and his best friend Samuel had finally received permission from Steven's parents to camp outside on their property. The boys spent the day setting up their tent, playing in the creek, and building a fort. As the sun was beginning to set, Steven stumbled across a stone that had a funny looking "bug" embedded in it. He showed Samuel and they identified the fossilized creature as a trilobite. Last year in their science class they had studied these creatures, and their teacher described it as an "index fossil" that lived approximately 500-600 million years ago. The fossil was placed inside their tent as the boys built a small campfire to roast hotdogs and marshmallows. With their stomachs full and their muscles aching from a full day of playing, the two boys crawled into their sleeping bags and began discussing their day and their cool fossil. Steven found himself wondering how this fossil could be millions of years old when his parents had informed him that the genealogies in the Bible indicated that the Earth was only a few thousand years old. How could that be? The evidence was right inside the tent. Were his parents wrong about the age of the earth and how it came to be?

While the above scenario is fictional, many people—young and old—can relate to the dilemma. The "evidence" appears to support an old earth—a conclusion that would support the evolutionary theory. Exactly what does the evidence reveal regarding the age of the earth, and how reliable is the evidence?

Circumstantial evidence can help determine probable cause or proof beyond a reasonable doubt within a court of law. While it is a valuable resource, it is not nearly as valuable as physical evidence. Physical evidence cannot die, lie, quit, forget, or get fired. An abundance of physical evidence is a defendant's nightmare and a prosecutor's dream. The question of evidence is an important factor when considering the validity of the evolutionary theory. What physical evidence remains after all of the speculations, hype, bias, emotions, and occasional outright lies are removed? During my scientific training, we were not introduced to any evidence against the evolutionary theory. It was only in my personal research that I came across numerous anomalies that don't fit into the evolutionary theory. Many geologic anomalies—physical evidence—exist which demonstrate that much of the propaganda reported on the apparent age of the earth is not credible.

Most individuals have heard true accounts about someone finding seashells at extremely high elevations atop mountains. Christians often argue that this is excellent proof for the Global Flood, while evolutionists contend that the seashells simply prove that the topography has "evolved" over millions of years, as tectonic plates crashed together. Other evidence, such as the Great Sphinx, Stonehenge, the Great Pyramid of Giza, the 110-foot tall Colossus at Rhodes, and the Hanging Gardens at Babylon are intriguing because of the tremendous engineering required to carry out such construction projects. How could individuals without modern equipment build such enormous and complex structures? While seashells, Stonehenge, and pyramids present some intriguing unanswered questions, the focus of this chapter will be on anomalies that step beyond the realm of merely puzzling. These anomalies are physical evidence disproving the evolutionary theory.

The Geologic Column

The latest age evolutionists have assigned to the earth is 4.6 billion years old. They would further allege that life arose within the last three billion years, with man being a relatively latecomer, arriving on the scene approximately three million years ago. One of the mainstays of evolutionists is the so-called "geologic timetable" or "geologic column." To many, the geologic column is an impressive argument for an ancient earth. Their spiels and examples (like the Grand Canyon) are so effective that—as students observe those layers of sedimentary rocks piled one on top of another—the only explanation appears to be that vast amounts of time were required. The story they paint teaches that each section of the rock represent a time eons ago and an ancient world that long since ceased to exist.

> *Scientists (and park rangers) subject students to evolutionary descriptions of how the rock layers came into existence over millions of years.*

While it may come as a surprise to many, the standard geologic column actually was devised prior to Darwin's *Origin of Species* by catastrophists who considered themselves creationists (Ritland, 1982). It would be Charles Lyell's book *Principles of Geology* that opened Darwin's eyes to the concept of the geologic column and the earth being shaped over vast periods of time. The timetable is a common staple in most textbooks dealing with geology, biology, paleontology, etc., and proposes to show the development of living creatures, in ascending order from the simple to the complex, from the ancient past to the present. Students are expected to memorize the specific names for the layers as well as the evolutionary times assigned to those layers. This assignment, while viewed by many as simply a "harmless memorization exercise," is often deeply rooted in the minds of youngsters, who then carry an evolutionary timeline with them throughout the remainder of their lives.

Evolutionists have divided the geologic column into a hierarchical system of eons, eras, periods, and epochs. The two major eon divisions are the Precambrian (590 million years to 4.5 billion years ago) and the Phanerozoic (590 million years to the present). The three major eras of the Phanerozoic are the Palleozoic—termed the Age of the Trilobites—(which includes the Cambrian, Ordovician, Silurian, Devonian, Carboniferous, and Permian periods), Mesozoic—termed the Age of the Dinosaurs—(which includes the Triassic, Jurassic, and Cretaceous periods), and Cenozoic—termed the Age of the Mammals—(which includes the Tertiary and Quaternary periods).

A massive problem with this evolutionary staple is that it is based on **circular reasoning**. The strata layers are dated according to the fossils discovered within them, but then the fossils are dated according to the layer "in which they are found." (e.g., a dinosaur bone assumed to be 65 million years old is discovered in a layer of rock and so that age is assigned to the rock layer. The other fossils discovered in that layer are then assigned a date of 65 million years old.) Many have been taught the geologic column "proves" that evolution is true and that the earth is extremely old. While it appears to be good circumstantial evidence, the physical evidence tells a completely different story.

> *Many have been taught the geologic column "proves" that evolution is true and that the earth is extremely old.*

Polystrate Fossils

One of the most crucial pieces of physical evidence against the evolutionary timetable can be found transcending several different layers of the geologic column. Embedded in sedimentary rocks all over the globe are fossils that transcend through several different layers. These are known as "polystrate" (or polystratic) fossils. The term *polystrate fossil* was first coined by N.A. Rupke, a young geologist from the State University of Groningen in the Netherlands (see Morris, 1970, p. 102). An example would be a fossilized tree that goes through several different layers. Morris discussed polystrate fossils in his book *Biblical Cosmology and Modern Science*, where he described:

> Stratification (or layered sequence) is a universal characteristic of sedimentary rocks. A stratum of sediment is formed by deposition under essentially continuous and uniform hydraulic conditions. When the sedimentation stops for a while before another period of deposition, the new stratum will be visibly distinguishable from the earlier by a stratification line (actually a surface). Distinct strata also result when there is a change in the velocity of flow or other hydraulic characteristics. Sedimentary beds as now found are typically composed of many "strata," and it is in such beds that most fossils are found (1970, p. 101, parenthetical items in orig.).

Dr. Morris then went on to explain that "large fossils...are found which extend through several strata, often 20 feet or more in thickness" (p. 102). The physical existence of these fossils violates the idea of a slowly accumulated geologic column. Scott Huse recognized this scientific truth in his book *The Collapse of Evolution*:

> Polystratic trees are fossil trees that extend through several layers of strata, often twenty feet or more in length. There is no doubt that this type of fossil was formed relatively quickly; otherwise it would have decomposed while waiting for strata to slowly accumulate around it (1997, p. 96).

The most widely recognized polystrate fossils are tree trunks that extend vertically through three, four, or more layers of rock—layers that supposedly were deposited during vast epochs of time. However, other examples such as fossilized whales, catfish, and other plants exist all across the globe. Organic material that dies (such as plants or whales) and is exposed to the elements will decay and rot, not fossilize. The evidence demands that these tree trunks must have been preserved very quickly, which indicates that the sedimentary layers surrounding them must have been deposited rapidly—possibly (and likely) during a single catastrophe (see Ham, 2000, p. 138). It is illogical to conclude that the layers built up over millions of years. Consider the explantion given to explain the existence of a baleen whale that was discovered fossilized on its back at a 60-degree angle (with its tail down and its head pointing up). In the January 24, 1977, issue of *Chemical and Engineering News*, Larry S. Helmick, professor of chemistry at Cedarville College in Cedarville, Ohio, wrote that it must have been buried "under very unusual and rapid catastrophic conditions." He went on to describe how "such phenomena cannot easily be explained by uniformitarian theories, but fit readily into an historical framework based upon the recent and dynamic universal flood described in Genesis, chapters 6-9" (1977, 55[4]:5).

The response from the scientific community to Helmick's letter was quick—albeit ridiculous. One scientist, Harvey Olney, wrote in a letter to the editor of *Chemical and Engineering News*:

Dr. Helmick, **how dare you imply that our geology textbooks and uniformitarian theories could possibly be wrong!** Everybody knows that diatomaceous earth beds are built up slowly over millions of years as diatom skeletons slowly settle out on the ocean floor. **The baleen whale simply stood on its tail for 100,000 years, its skeleton decomposing, while the diatomaceous snow covered its frame millimeter by millimeter.** Certainly you wouldn't expect intelligent and informed establishment scientists of this modern age to revert to the outmoded views of our forefathers just to explain such finds! (1976, 55[12]:4, emp. added).

So there we have it. The whale stood on its tail for 100,000 years. Rather than accept the physical evidence at face value and admit that gradualistic, uniformitarian processes simply do not work, Olney expects students to believe that a whale carcass stood on its tail—decomposing all the while—as millions of tiny diatom skeletons enshrouded it over a period of 100,000 years! Physical evidence does not lie (or require unbelievable speculations).

> *So there we have it. The whale stood on its tail for 100,000 years.*

Metallic Vase from Dorchester, Massachusetts

In 1852, *Scientific American* featured an article titled "A Relic of a Bygone Age" that described a discovery that poses a serious challenge to the Darwinian theory. The article stated:

A few days ago a powerful blast was made in the rock at Meeting House Hill, in Dorchester, a few rods south of Rev. Mr. Hall's meeting house. The blast threw out an immense mass of rock, some of the pieces weighing several tons, and scattered fragments in all directions. Among them was picked up a metallic vessel in two parts, rent asunder by the explosion. On putting the two parts together it formed a bell-shaped vessel, 4-1/2 inches high, 6-1/2 inches at the base, 2-1/2 inches at the top, and about an eighth of an inch in thickness. The body of this vessel resembles zinc in color, or a composition of metal, in which there is a considerable portion of silver. On the side there are six figures or a flower, or

bouquet, vine, or wreath, also inlaid with silver. The chasing, carving, and inlaying are exquisitely done by the art of some cunning workman. This curious and unknown vessel was blown out of the solid pudding stone, fifteen feet below the surface. It is now in the possession of Mr. John Kettell. Dr. J.V.C. Smith, who has recently traveled in the East, and examined hundreds of curious domestic utensils, and has drawings of them, has never seen anything resembling this. He has taken a drawing and accurate dimensions of it, to be submitted to the scientific. There is no doubt but that this curiosity was blown out of the rock, as above stated; but will Professor Agassiz, or some other scientific man please tell us how it came there? The matter is worthy of investigation, as there is no deception in the case (*Scientific American*, 1852, p. 298).

At the conclusion of the article, the editors of *Scientific American* stated, "The above is from the *Boston Transcript* and the wonder is to us, how the *Transcript* can suppose Prof. Agassiz is qualified to tell how it got there any more than John Doyle, the blacksmith. This is not a question of zoology, botany, or geology, but one relating to an antique metal vessel perhaps made by **Tubal Cain**, the first inhabitant of Dorchester" (p. 298, emp. added).

After consulting a recent U.S. Geological Survey map of the Boston-Dorchester area, Cremo and Thompson determined that the pudding stone mentioned in the article is considered to come from the Precambrian Age—over 600 million years old (1996, p. 107). According to evolutionary timelines, that would place the vase over 300 million years **before dinosaurs**, and over 590 million years before man allegedly made his appearance on the earth. The physical evidence proves that the vase was blown out of the rock. The date assigned to that rock is not as certain.

Grooved Spheres from South Africa

On February 25, 1996, the late Charlton Heston hosted a one-hour special on NBC titled "The Mysterious Origins of Man." During that show he discussed grooved

spheres that were discovered in South Africa. He noted:

In Klerksdorp, South Africa, hundreds of metallic spheres were found by miners in Precambrian strata said to be a fantastic 2.8 billion years old. The controversy centers around fine grooves encircling some of the spheres. Lab technicians were at a loss to explain how they could have been formed by any known, natural process.

Even though Heston got the city wrong (they were unearthed in quarries closer to Ottosdal, West Transvaal, rather than Kerksdorp), he did get one thing correct: lab technicians (and scientists) are at a loss to explain how these grooved spheres could have been formed by any natural process. David Childress observed:

A curious discovery along these lines was first reported in 1982. According to various reports, including one in the book *Forbidden Archeology*, over the past several decades, South African miners have found hundreds of metallic spheres, several of which have three parallel grooves running their equator. The spheres are of two types—"one of solid bluish metal with white flecks, and another which is a hollow ball filled with a white spongy center" (Childress, 2000, p. 88).

Evolutionists argue that maybe these spheres are metamorphic nodules. But they are left speculating as to why the spheres have grooves and are so hard. As Childress noted:

Roelf Marx, curator of the museum in Klerksorp, South Africa, where some of the spheres are currently being housed said in a 1984 letter, "There is nothing scientific published about the globes, but the facts are: They are found in pyrophyllite, which is mined near the little town of Ottosdal in the Western Transvall. This pyrophyllite ($Al2Si4O10(OH)2$) is a quite soft secondary mineral with a count of only 3 on the Moh's scale and was formed by sedimentation about 2.8 billion years ago. On the other hand the globes, which have a fibrous structure on the inside with a shell around it, are very hard and cannot be scratched, even by hard steel." The Moh scale is a hardness scale using ten minerals as reference points, with diamond the hardest (10) and talc the softest (1) (p. 88).

raised characters. Fortunately, several of the most respectable gentlemen residing in Norristown were called upon to witness this remarkable phenomenon, without whose testimony it might have been difficult, if not impossible, to have satisfied the public, that an imposition had not been practiced by cutting the indentation and carving the letters after the slab was cut off (p. 361).

Is the physical evidence of these letters hard to explain? They are hard to explain if one is tied to the geologic timeline espoused by evolutionists. Once again, the physical evidence of these marble letters is undisputable, but the same cannot be said for the age attributed to the marble slab.

Meister Footprint

According to the Darwinian theory, trilobites evolved at the beginning of the Paleozoic Era (over 500 million years ago) and became extinct during the late Permian period (248 million years ago)—long before dinosaurs or men are alleged to have lived on the earth. These creatures are believed to be extinct, having once flourished in the oceans. According to evolutionary theory, the Cambrian Period is known as "The Age of Trilobites," and these fascinating creatures have become known as "index fossils" for that time period. Evolutionists use the widely distributed index fossils to assist in dating other fossils found in the same sedimentary layer (circular reasoning).

On June 1, 1968, however, evolutionist William J. Meister, an amateur fossilologist, while working near Antelope Springs, Utah, made a discovery that was destined to dispel that incorrect evolutionary supposition. Several of his friends were there to witness this particular discovery. Working their way up the side of a mountain some 2,000 feet to a ledge above, Meister broke open a slab of rock with his hammer to investigate it for fossils. Imagine his astonishment when he "saw on one side the footprint of a human with trilobites right in the footprint itself. The other half of the rock slab showed an almost perfect mold of the footprint and fossils. Amazingly the human was wearing a sandal" (as quoted in Lammerts, 1976, p. 186-187).

In 2004, I was able to examine firsthand the trilobite fossil. There is no doubt that there are trilobites (yes, more than one) embedded in the sandal print of a human being. A close inspection reveals the stitching of the sandal, and the heel is worn on the back outside corner—in exactly the same fashion that modern men wear down the heels on their shoes. Only one explanation has been given by evolutionists to explain away this geologic anomaly. For instance, Glen Kuban has suggested that rather than sandal prints the fossil is really the result of spalling. Interestingly, however, in his effort to explain away this fossil he never indicates that he has actually inspected the print firsthand. The physical evidence is there. The only question is how can 500-million-old trilobites coexist with humans if mankind has only been around for the last 3-5 million years?

Metallic Tubes from Chalk in France

In 1968, molded metallic tubes were found in "Cretaceous Chalk" by Y. Druet and H. Salfati (see Corliss, 1978, p. 652-653; Cremo and Thompson, 1993, p. 809-810). They reported:

We would like to bring to your attention the following facts, and hope you will give our discovery some consideration. As speleologists and investigators, we have studied for several years the Pay d' Auge region of Calvados. During the year 1968 we discovered some metallic nodules in a hollow in an Aptian chalk bed in a quarry being worked in Saint-Jean de Livet. These metallic nodules have a reddish brown color, a form absolutely identical (semi-ovoid), but are of different size. A central section had a form corresponding with the exterior form. These nodules at first seemed to be fossils, but having examined them carefully we became conscious of their entirely metallic nature. Experiments at the forge showed that the carbon content was higher than castings of today. We were lead to consider the hypothesis that they were meteorites, but five pieces were found all of the same nature, which lead us to reject this hypothesis. There remains only an intelligent intervention in the Secondary Era (the end of the Cretaceous) of beings who could cast such objects.

These objects, then, prove the presence of intelligent life on earth long before the limits given today by prehistoric archeology.

P.S.: The Geomorphology Laboratory of the University of Caen is now studying these objects which we have sent them (without great hopes) [as quoted in Corliss, 1978, p. 652-653, parentheses in orig.].

Michael Cremo and Richard L. Thompson described that the chalk bed, exposed in a quarry at Saint-Jean de Livet, France, is estimated to be at least "65 million years old" (1996, p. 117). That would imply that either intelligent beings existed 65 million years ago who could produce these metallic tubes, or the man-made and man-assigned evolutionary dating system is wrong. The physical evidence does not lie.

While shoe prints are not exactly front-page news, a shoe print found in allegedly five-million-year-old rock would be.

Shoe Sole from Nevada

While shoe prints are not exactly front-page news, a shoe print found in allegedly five-million-year-old rock would be. An amateur geologist discovered the fossilized imprint of a shoe complete with thread marks and broken heel in Fisher Canyon, Pershing County, Nevada. On October 8, 1922, the "American Weekly" section of the *New York Sunday American* ran an article titled "Mystery of the Petrified 'Shoe Sole,'" written by Dr. W. H. Ballou.

Some time ago, while he was prospecting for fossils in Nevada, John T. Reid, a distinguished mining engineer and geologist, stopped suddenly and looked down in utter bewilderment and amazement at a rock near his feet. For there, in a part of the rock itself, was what seemed to be a human footprint! Closer inspection showed that it was not a mark of a naked foot, but was, apparently, a shoe sole which had been turned into stone. The forepart was missing. But there was the outline of at least two-thirds of it, and around this outline ran a well-defined sewn thread which had, it appeared, attached the welt to the sole. Further on was another line of sewing, and in the center, where the foot would have rested had the object really been a shoe sole, there was an indentation, exactly such as would have been made by the bone of the heel rubbing upon and wearing down the material of which the sole had been made. Thus was found a fossil which is the foremost mystery of science today. For the rock in which it was found is at least 5 million years old (p. 2).

A five-million-year-old rock containing a well-defined sewn thread? The fossil is physical evidence and is unquestionable. The date assigned to the rock however came from evolutionary assumptions.

Many other anomalies exist. For example, in 1889 while boring a well at Nampa, Idaho, a tiny baked clay figurine was pumped up from a depth of 300 feet. This

figurine was discovered underneath a "Tertiary" lava sheet that would be approximately 12 million years old according to evolutionary dating schemes (see Bird, 1934, p. 17-26; Velikovsky, 1955, p. 90). Again, I am constrained to ask, what human was around twelve million years ago who had the ability to fashion (and bake) a clay figurine?

Another discovery was made near London, Texas. In 1936, a metal hammer with a wooden handle was dug out of Cretaceous limestone—dated by evolutionists at 135 million years old. The hammer's broken handle is 6¾ inches long, and the hammer itself is made of a very strong metal. When the surface oxidation was removed, the metal was still shiny. [Details of this remarkable discovery (including photographs) may be found in Helfinstine and Roth (1994, p. 83, 91-92), and the February 1984 issue of *Creation Ex Nihilo* magazine (see "Ordovician Hammer Report," 2[3]:16-17).]

Errors in Radiometric Dating

Most people have never heard the evidence against an old earth. However, everyone is familiar with dating methods that allegedly prove an old earth. The three common methods used by evolutionists to date fossils are stratiography, radiometric dating (e.g., carbon-14), and index fossils. Many scientists base their entire careers around the dates these methods provide, and thus, they are not quick to admit their flaws. The consequence is that the evolutionary placards remain in place assigning vast old ages to fossils, are very rarely questioned, and are never truly validated by the scientific method.

Again, I am constrained to ask, what human was around twelve million years ago who had the ability to fashion (and bake) a clay figurine?

Stratiography

Stratiography dates the fossils according to how deep they are found and what layer of earth they occur. Allegedly the deeper the rock, the older it is. However, those familiar with strata layers of the Grand Canyon quickly recognize the problem with this method. The upper layers of the canyon actually date older than the layers at the base. Clearly the science of stratiography is not an exact one. A quick survey of strata layers around us reveals that not all of the layers fall neatly into a horizontal fashion. As Charles Leith noted more than 85 years ago, "If rocks remained in their original forms the structural problem would be a comparatively easy one, **but usually they do not**. Often they are folded and faulted and mashed to such an extent that that it is difficult to go behind the superimposed structural features to the original conditions in order to work out the geologic history" (Charles Leith, 1921, *The Economic Aspect of Geology*, p. 5, emp. added).

Radiometric Dating Methods

Radiometric forms of dating are based on seven different assumptions—all of which **must** be true in order for the dating method to be correct. Consider for instance that all radio-metric dating methods require a uniform earth. A quick examination reveals that volcanic explosions such as Mt. Saint Helen's have caused certain areas of the world to possess more radioactivity than others. This can hardly be considered "uniform."

RADIOACTIVE

Radiometric dating is based on measuring the amount of radioactive material in a particular sample and subtracting that amount from what is known to exist in a living organism. For instance, since the present level of carbon-14 in living tissues can be determined, and since the half-life of C-14 is believed to be 5,730 years, then scientists measure the amount of C-14 that is remaining to determine the age of a sample of organic material. Theoretically, this should allow us to "date" material according to how much radioactive decay has occurred. However, scientists must admit that living dinosaur specimens do not exist, so they do not know what the "standard" amount should be. Furthermore, there are environmental factors that can affect the half-life of carbon-14. Radioisotope dating should never be used directly on fossils since fossils do not contain the unstable radioactive isotopes used in the dating process! And yet, the general public is under the false assumption that this dating method is iron clad. Here are assumptions that should be considered for carbon-14:

1. Perhaps the most critical assumption of radiocarbon dating is that the rates of carbon-14 production and decay are in a state of equilibrium, and have been so for millions of years. If this were true, the carbon-12/carbon-14 ratio in living organisms will be the same as the ratio in an organism that lived thousands of years ago. However, we have reason to think that this is not true.
2. Has the half-life of C-14 been accurately determined?
3. Has the decay of C-14 varied in rate?
4. Has there been contamination of the sample by extraneous C-14 (i.e. groundwater, soil, or foreign matter)?
5. Has atmospheric nitrogen, the precursor of C-14, been constant?
6. Has any of the original C-14 been leached out by physical agencies? What effects do environmental factors such as forest fires, volcanic eruptions, have on this system?
7. Is the instrumentation precise and does the technique always yield uniform results?

Ironically, some evolutionists recognize the limitations of radiometric dating. Most evolutionists have completely abandoned radiocarbon dating in favor of potassium/argon or some other element. Commenting on the accuracy of carbon-14 dating, evolutionist Richard Dawkins even admitted: "It is useful for dating organic material on an archaeological/historical timescale where we are dealing in hundreds or a few thousands of years, but it is no good for the evolutionary timescale where we are dealing in millions of years" (*The Blind Watchmaker*, 1986, p. 226).

Consider the following examples of published errors using radiometric dating:

A. A living mollusk was tested by carbon-14 and dated as being 3,000 years old (M.S. Keith and G.M. Anderson, "Radiocarbon Dating: Fictitious Results with Mollusk Shells," *Science*, August 16, 1963, 141:634).

B. Freshly killed seals have been dated at 1,300 years old, and mummified seals, dead only some 30 years, have yielded ages as high as 4,600 years (W. Dort, "Mummified Seals of Southern Victoria Land," 1971, *Antarctic Journal of the U.S.*, 6:210).

C. Muscle tissue from beneath the scalp of a mummified musk ox found in frozen muck at Fairbanks Creek, Alaska, had a radiocarbon age of 24,000 years, while the radiocarbon age of hair from a hind limb of the same animal was dated to be only 7,200 years old (Robert Brown, *Review & Herald*, October 28, 1971, 148:44).

D. Wood taken from actively growing trees has been dated by the C-14 method as being 10,000 years old (Caryl Haskins, *American Scientist*, June 1971, 59:298).

While the mainstream media is quick to point out evolutionary ages, they remain silent on physical evidence that points toward a young earth.

The Evidence Points to a Young Earth

While the mainstream media is quick to point out evolutionary ages, they remain silent on physical evidence that points toward a young earth. For instance, it is a known scientific fact that magnets lose their strength over time. It is also a well-known fact that the earth has a magnetic field (e.g., compasses point to magnetic north). Scientists have documented that the **earth's magnetic strength has declined 6% in the last 150 years** (*Astronomy and the Bible*, Donald DeYoung, p. 18). If one were to extrapolate back, the only conclusion that makes logical sense is the earth is not billions of years old. For another example, the oceans possess 3.6% salt water. The salt is introduced to the oceans through the water cycle. Calculations demonstrate that we could have gone from fresh water to salt water in less than 5,000 years. If the earth were billions of years old, the oceans would be too salty to sustain life. Additionally, the erosion from the water cycle should have long ago worn down the mountains. The runoff from the rivers also poses another problem. For instance, the Mississippi River is depositing sediment at a rate of approximately 80,000 tons an hour day after day. If the earth were billions of years old, the Gulf of Mexico should have long filled in by now. Evidence such as the sun shrinking, or polonium halos, or helium in diamonds may be ignored, but it cannot be silenced. The evidence demonstrates the earth is not billions of years old—and without billions of years of time, the evolutionary theory cannot get off the ground. There is too much physical evidence pointing in an entirely different direction. Yes, God created a mature earth (trees in the Garden already producing fruit!), but His creation does not incorporate billions of evolutionary years. The question is will people turn a blind eye to it or evaluate the evidence with an open and honest mind?

The evidence demonstrates the earth is not billions of years old—and without billions of years of time, the evolutionary theory cannot get off the ground.

Questions:
1. What problems do polystrate fossils pose for the geologic column?
2. How can geologic anamolies be explained using the creation model?
3. What is the difference between a mature creation and an evolutionary creation?
4. Why does evolution require vast amounts of time?
5. How has the earth "aged" in the past 100 years?

Scriptures to Study
Psalm 19:1
Isaiah 42:5
Exodus 20:11
Romans 1:20

Additional Resources:

Ashton, F. John (2001), *In Six Days: Why Fifty Scientists Choose to Believe in Creation* (Green Forest, AR: Master Books).

DeYoung Don (2005), *Thousands Not Billions: Changing the Icon of Evolution, Questioning the Age of the Earth* (Green Forest, AR: Master Books).

Morris, John (2007), *The Young Earth: The Real History of the Earth - Past, Present, and Future* (Green Forest, AR: Master Books).

References:
Ballou, W.H. (1922), "Mystery of the Petrified 'Shoe Sole' 5,000,000 Years Old," *New York Sunday American,* p. 2, October 8.
Bird, A. (1934), *Boise: The Peace Valley* (Boise, ID: Caxton Publishers).
Browne, J.B. (1831), "Singular Impression in Marble," *American Journal of Science,* 19:361.
Childress, David Hatcher (2000), *Technology of the Gods* (Kempton, Illinois: Adventures Unlimited Press).

Corliss, William R. (1978), *Ancient Man: A Handbook of Puzzling Artifacts* (Glen Arm, MD: The Sourcebook Project).

Cremo, Michael A. and Richard L. Thompson (1993), *Forbidden Archeology* (Los Angeles, CA: Bhaktivedanta Book Publishing).

Cremo, Michael A. and Richard L. Thompson (1996), *The Hidden History of the Human Race* (Los Angeles, CA: Bhaktivedanta Book Publishing).

Ham, Ken (2000), *Did Adam Have a Belly Button?* (Green Forest, AR: Master Books).

Helfinstine, Robert F. and Jerry D. Roth (1994), *Texas Tracks and Artifacts* (Anoka, MN: Privately published by authors).

Helmick, Larry S. (1976), "Strange Phenomena," [Letter to the Editor], *Chemical and Engineering News,* 55[4]:5, January 24.

Huse, Scott M. (1997), *The Collapse of Evolution* (Grand Rapids, MI: Baker), third edition.

Lammerts, Walter, ed. (1976), *Why Not Creation?* (Grand Rapids, MI: Baker), p. 185-193.

Morris, Henry M. (1970), *Biblical Cosmology and Modern Science* (Grand Rapids, MI: Baker).

Olney, Harvey O. III (1977), "A Whale of a Tale," [Letter to the Editor], *Chemical and Engineering News,* 55[12]:4, March 21.

"Ordovician Hammer Report" (1984), *Creation Ex Nihilo,* 2[3]:16-17, February.

O'Rourke, J.E. (1976), "Pragmatism versus Materialism in Stratigraphy," *American Journal of Science,* 276:51, January.

Ritland, R. (1982), "Historical Development of the Current Understanding of the Geologic Column: Part II," *Origins,* 9:28-47.

Rupke, N.A. (1973), "Prolegomena to a Study of Cataclysmal Sedimentation," *Why Not Creation?,* ed. Walter E. Lammerts (Grand Rapids, MI: Baker).

Scientific American (1852), "A Relic of a Bygone Age," 7[38]:298, June 5.

Velikovsky, Immanuel (1955), *Earth in Upheaval* (New York: Dell).

"*The heavens declare the glory of God; and the firmament shows His handiwork.*"
— **Psalm 19:1**

Chapter

20

Great Beginnings...or the End: The Big Bang and Starlight

Daniel was supposed to be sleeping. However, on this night he found it impossible. If his parents walked by his room it would appear that he was asleep, and he had the covers over his head. However, buried underneath the covers was a young boy looking through his latest Christmas present—a telescope. With eyes as big as saucers, he pointed it out the window and focused first on the moon, and then the countless stars. Daniel had watched the Discovery channel enough to know that everything he viewed through his scope was supposed to be the product of some Big Bang explosion. He also was familiar with the alleged timeline of the universe, sun, moon, and earth. But that's where the confusion came in. Daniel was having trouble figuring out exactly how God played into all of it. Did God make the Big Bang? And how could the Bible mention the earth being created first, when astronomers suggested that the stars were the first ones on the scene, with planets like the earth coming into existence millions of years later? Daniel looked out at one of the brightest stars in the sky and wondered how long it would take a rocket to reach it. Not knowing much about rockets or intergalactic distances, he guessed 20 million light-years. But how could that be if the earth was as young as his parents had taught him? Wouldn't it take millions of years for the light to reach us here on earth?

How many times has a scenario similar to this played itself out—over and over—as children look up to the skies only to become more confused? Oftentimes, parents either avoid questions on the Big Bang, or they inadvertently provide inaccurate answers that are later found to be untrue. Parents should inform themselves of what is being taught in textbooks and on major network stations, so that they can better "train up" their children with the Truth.

We begin this final chapter at the place many textbooks start—the Big Bang and the origin of the universe. I think it is fitting to end with the material textbooks start with, as by now an honest evaluation will recognize that the evidence put forth in this book has put an end to the evolutionary theory. So what about the Big Bang? What do parents need to know regarding this fanciful theory?

1. What, exactly, was the Big Bang supposed to be?

Often, individuals picture in their mind an explosion of matter that flew through space. Many astronomers would argue, however, that the Big Bang was not an explosion of matter into space, but rather an explosion of space itself. According to the Big Bang theory, the universe began by expanding from an infinitesimal volume with extremely high density and temperature. According to evolutionists, at some point in the distant past, the universe was small enough to fit comfortably in both of your hands. When the "explosion" occurred, allegedly the fabric of space itself began expanding like the surface of an inflating balloon. Astronomers contend that matter (e.g., planets, stars, etc.) simply rode along the stretching space like dust on the balloon's surface. Thus, they would argue that the Big Bang is not like an explosion of matter in otherwise empty space; rather, space itself began with the Big Bang and carried matter with it as it expanded. It may seem like semantics, but how many children have entered a college classroom and heard wild speculation on the origin of the universe, only to

then deduce that maybe mom and dad didn't really understand this thing. One thing astronomers have yet to answer is where that initial matter came from.

2. History of the Big Bang

Most of us have heard the phrase "nature abhors a vacuum." This is especially true with scientific theories. Oftentimes, a worn-out theory will not be completely abandoned until a new theory arrives to take its place. In many ways, this is how the Big Bang theory came into existence. The biggest problem of all theories regarding the origin of the universe was simply their inability to explain the **literal** origin of the universe. For many years during the mid 1900s, evolutionists Fred Hoyle and his colleagues touted the Steady State theory as the answer to this problem. The Steady State theory got around the problem of origins by simply stating that the universe was eternal. However, scientists soon realized that this theory fell into conflict with what they were actually observing. By the mid 1970s scientists knew that the universe was behaving (expanding) in such a way that there must have been a beginning, and they also realized it violated the first law of thermodynamics (which states that neither matter nor energy can be created or destroyed, but can only be conserved). Enter the Big Bang. In actuality, the Big Bang theory was around before the Steady State theory, but it was not given serious consideration until the downfall of the Steady State theory.

> *The biggest problem of all theories regarding the origin of the universe was simply their inability to explain the **literal** origin of the universe.*

3. Can a Christian Still Believe in the Big Bang?

Often, sincere Christians pose the question: "Could God have used some Big Bang to form the universe as we see it today?" I imagine that question has been posed by many parents—either verbally or mentally. After all, if it were true, it might alleviate some headaches that Christian parents confront in explaining the origins of the universe. However, a thorough reading of God's Word documents that there was no Big Bang explosion.

Consider the evidence. In his famous book *First Three Minutes*, Steven Weinberg set the initial temperature 0.02 seconds after the explosion at 1011 Kelvin (the Kelvin scale is 273° higher than the Celsius scale). After three minutes, the temperature allegedly would have been 109 K, a temperature far too hot to sustain any form of life. Weinberg suggests that after 700,000 years the temperature still would be 3000 K (or 3272° C). Given those enormous temperatures, imagine what those early few days would have been like.

Even a small child recognizes the difference between fire and water. God's Word tells us on Day 1 there was water covering the earth (Genesis 1:2). The first two verses of the Bible state: "In the beginning God created the heavens and the earth. The earth was without form, and void; and darkness was on the face of the deep. **And the Spirit of God was hovering over the face of the waters**" (emp. added). How could there be water on the earth if the temperature from the explosion was millions of degrees Celsius? In Genesis 1:1-2, the account records that the earth, from the moment of its creation, was enshrouded with water. Is there a difference between a beginning in fire and a beginning in water? If so, then there also is a difference between the Big Bang theory and the origin that the Bible presents.

> ### How could there be water on the earth if the temperature from the explosion was millions of degrees Celsius?

There are other reasons Christians should not believe in the Big Bang. For instance, the Bible tells us that the heaven and earth were created on Day 1. The sun, moon, and stars did not come along until Day 4. This chronology does not correspond with the Big Bang theory. The Big Bang places stars (and our sun) much earlier in time than the Earth. Also, creation was accomplished through divine fiat, not by a chaotic explosion. God's design, and method, of creation are evident: "By the word of Jehovah were the heavens made, and all the host of them by the breath of His mouth" (Psalm 33:6). God spoke, and by His utterance, creation occurred. Nowhere in the Genesis account (nor anywhere else in Scripture, for that matter) is reference ever made to some sort of "primeval explosion." When God commanded the creation of the sun, moon, and stars on Day 4, the event did not require billions of years, but was completely finished **that very day**. Our children need to understand these major differences between the Big Bang theory and God's inspired Word.

4. Where does man fit in with the Big Bang?

According to Big Bang dogma, a vast period of time separated the origin of the universe from that of mankind. Currently, most evolutionists date the Big Bang back more than 10 billion years ago. Yet, the Scriptures teach that **everything** was created within six days of the Creation week as recorded in Genesis 1-2, (a fact later reaffirmed by Exodus 20:11 and Exodus 31:17). The Scriptures also affirm that the human family came into existence the same week as the universe (Genesis 1; Exodus 20:11; 31:17). Thus, the point is made quite clearly that the Cosmos, the earth, and **all** of the Creation were brought into existence during the same week. Man, therefore, has existed from the beginning of the Creation (cf. Isaiah 40:21; Matthew 19:4; Mark 10:6; Luke 11:50; Romans 1:20-21). It was on the sixth day of Creation, in fact, that God made man and woman. "And God said, 'Let Us make man in Our image, after Our likeness.' ... And God created man in His own image, in the image of God created He him; male and female created He them" (Genesis 1:26-27). Jesus Himself declared "But from the beginning of the creation, God 'made them male and female.'" (Mark 10:6, emp. added). As God's Son, and the Creative Agent through which such events were accomplished (cf. John 1:1ff.), He should know!

Christ thus dated the first humans from the creation week. The Greek word for "beginning" is *arché*, and means "**absolute**, denoting **the beginning of the world and of its history, the beginning of creation.**" Thus Jesus Christ has placed man at the creation. The Big Bang theory doesn't have man coming along until billions of years later.

5. Are there scientific problems with the Big Bang theory?

Currently, many of the scientific data do not support the Big Bang theory. Yet, just like the little Dutch boy who keeps sticking fingers in the crumbling dam, Big Bang theorists continuously figure out modifications and tweaks so that the Big Bang theory is never fully abandoned. (We should teach our children to question any theory that routinely must be modified or reworked when conflicting data come in. Instead of tossing out the data, maybe we should be tossing out some of these pitiful theories.)

One problem with the Big Bang theory involves the density of the universe. Simply stated, there is not enough matter in the universe to explain the composition and expansion that scientists observe. Where is all of this "missing matter"? Scientists do not have the first clue. However, rather than abandon their beloved theory, they have come up with "dark energy" and "dark matter" to explain away the problem. In fact, their theory postulates that 73% of the universe is "dark energy" and 23% is "cold dark matter." That would mean the material we can see (i.e., stars, planets, etc.) only composes 4% of the universe. And yet, even with all of the scientific observations that have been made, there is no evidence to support the existence of dark energy or cold dark matter! Thus, 96% of the universe is allegedly composed of something that we aren't even sure exists!

In referring to the work being carried out by a team of researchers headed by Leonard Susskind of Stanford University, Philip Ball wrote that: "...Physicists have claimed that the prevailing theoretical view of the universe is logically flawed. Arranging the cosmos as we think it is arranged, say the team, **would have required a miracle**" (emp. added). Ball then observed that the apparent incomprehensibility of our situation even has driven Susskind's team to ponder whether "an **unknown agent** intervened in the evolution [of the universe] for reasons of its own" (emp. added). Good question. For it takes far more faith to believe in the Big Bang theory, which relies on 96% of "matter" that has never been scientifically observed, versus a miraculous creation account.

And yet, high school and college textbooks are filled with all kinds of exotic astronomical terms aimed at accounting for this missing matter. Textbooks commonly define terms like: neutrinos, black holes, photinos, gravitinos, solitons, cosmic sheets and strings, WIMPS (weakly interacting massive particles), MACHOS (massive astrophysical halo objects), magnetic monopoles, etc. But the reality is, these are all theoretical. No significant observational evidence has been discovered that even supports their existence.

In addition, evolutionists also have failed to describe how a Big Bang expansion can occur without violating the First Law of Thermodynamics. No matter how far back you take it, and no matter how small you make that initial bit of matter (often called a "ylem" or cosmic egg), **there must still be an explanation for the origin of that matter.** The First Law of Thermodynamics states that matter can be neither created nor destroyed. Yet the birth of galaxies and stars had to come from **something**. (This is discussed in detail in the opening chapters).

> *The First Law of Thermodynamics states that matter can be neither created nor destroyed. Yet the birth of galaxies and stars had to come from* **something**.

Christians should encourage their children to evaluate theories such as this from a purely logical perspective. For instance, if everything really did expand/explode outward from a massive blast, then the law of conservation of angular momentum tells us that all of the material moving away from that blast should be moving in the same direction. [Think of placing four children on a merry-go-round, and spinning it so fast they fly off. They might fly off at different points, but once they came off the merry-go-round they would all be moving in the same general direction.] Yet, that's not what we observe in outer space. We know today Venus and Uranus (and possibly Pluto) rotate backwards from the other planets. In fact, 6 of the 63 moons we have identified in our solar system rotate backwards. Jupiter, Saturn, and Neptune have moons orbiting in both directions! And these irregularities are just the ones we've found in our own solar system—how many more exist in the universe? If everything in the universe expanded outwards from the same initial blast, then how could we have moons orbiting in **both** directions? Obviously, the observed data do not support the beloved theory.

On a somewhat more technical note, there is also a smoothness problem within the universe. If the Big Bang expansion did occur, then one would expect the universe to be "smooth" (homogenous) and isotropic (the same in all directions) in appearance. After all, this Big Bang expansion should be apparent everywhere we look in a centerless universe. And yet, that's not what we have observed. Scientific observations tell us the universe is lumpy. In many places there are great voids, followed by massive clusters of stars or even sheets of galaxies (e.g. the "Great Wall"). Periodic density differences in the universe would be expected, but not the gigantic irregularities that are actually observed. Scientists can't even agree on a specific age (or even a reasonable range, for that matter) for the universe. Estimates range anywhere from 2 to 25 billion years ago. The process that is used to determine the age of the universe is has problems of its own.

> *Periodic density differences in the universe would be expected, but not the gigantic irregularities that are actually observed.*

The Problem of Starlight and Time

I have been asked by Christians and non-Christians alike how one can accept a young earth when we are able to see starlight from stars millions of light years away. Wouldn't that indicate the starlight that we are seeing today left those stars millions of years ago? The assumption is that the light we are witnessing today "must" be millions of years old. The Bible is clear that the stars were created on Day 4 (Genesis 1:16)—an inspired truth that negates the possibility of the Big Bang theory. We also know starlight was visible to the early patriarchs, as God told Abraham that his descendants would be numbered like the stars: "Then He brought him outside and said, 'Look now toward heaven, and count the stars if you are able to number them.' And He said to him, 'So shall your descendants be'" (Genesis 15:5). God's Word also provides man with an idea of the size of the universe when the prophet Jeremiah revealed that the stars cannot be numbered (Jeremiah 33:22). But what about the starlight reaching the earth?

In order to understand this problem, one must understand how distance is measured. The proximity of stars to earth is measured using a method known as stellar parallax. *Webster's Dictionary* defines *parallax* as "the apparent displacement or the difference in apparent direction of an object as seen from two different points not on a straight line with the object; the angular difference in direction of a celestial body as measured from two points on the earth's orbit."

For a simplified analogy of the measurement of displacement consider each one of your eyes representing the earth at two opposite points as it revolves around the sun.

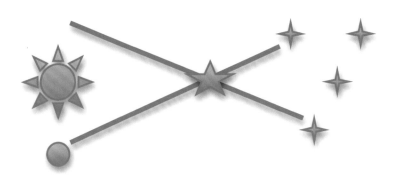

An outstretched hand represents the star to which you want to measure the distance. By covering up one eye, you view your outstretched hand and the background behind it. (The earth being represented by your eyes and your outstretched hand representing the distant star.) You would then place the same hand over the other eye and continue viewing your hand. The background behind your hand appears to shift because of the different viewpoint from each eye. The angle of displacement or difference can be measured, allowing scientists to calculate the distance to the star. Objects in space that are closer to earth have a larger parallax than objects that are far away.

The distance to stars is often recorded in light-years. One light-year is the distance light can travel in a vacuum in one year (approximately 5.88 trillion miles.) Thus, we often read reports of stars being x light-years away. Evolutionists and those who believe the earth is millions of years old argue that it would take millions of years for light from distant galaxies to reach us on earth. However, the "starlight and time" argument has several flaws and assumptions that Christians should be aware of:

1. God created everything mature. We know from Genesis 2 that the trees were already producing fruit, and given that Adam was naming the animals before Eve was created (Genesis 2:19-20), one can logically deduce that God created Adam grown and not as a helpless infant unable to communicate. This same truth can also be applied to the stars and heavenly bodies. When Adam and Eve looked into the sky, they were already able to see starlight, even though stars were only two

days old. While this answer explains some aspects of starlight and time, it doesn't explain how we can see stars exploding or growing in intensity that are millions of light-years away. The reason we see these changes is because light is reaching us on the earth today. This scientific truth demands additional answers.

2. The universe is expanding. This is a scientific fact that can easily be proven by the movement of modern-day stars. This movement indicates the universe is not eternal, but rather is expanding outward. As Robert Jastrow observed, "The lingering decline predicted by astronomers for the end of the world differs from the explosive conditions they have calculated for its birth, but the impact is the same: **modern science denies an eternal existence to the universe**, either in the past or the future" (WW. Norton, (1977), *Until the Sun Dies*, New York, p. 30, emp. added). This constant expansion means that some of the light we are observing today originated from distant galaxies that were closer in the past. In other words, the light we see today must have began its journey when galaxies were closer (and also much smaller and less energetic) than today.

3. It is a scientific fact that gravity plays a role on time, and could also play a role on the speed of light. We know that clocks on top of skyscrapers or mountains run faster than those closer to sea level due to the fact that the lower elevation

is closer to the earth—the source of gravity. Some have suggested that the earth is in a "gravitational well" and is located in the center of the universe. If that were the case, this gravitational well would mean we experience things slower (like the clock at sea level) than things further out in space. Commenting on the possibility of the gravitational well, astrophysicist Jason Lisle remarked, "This term means that it would require energy to pull something away from our position into deeper space. In this gravitational well, we would not 'feel' any extra gravity, nonetheless time would flow more slowly on earth (or anywhere in our solar system) than in other places of the universe" (see http://www.answersingenesis.org/articles/nab/does-starlight-prove).

4. While light travels at a constant speed (186,000 miles per second) on earth, we are not certain how (or how fast) light travels in distant space. In 2000, the Associated Press recounted how scientists had broken the speed of light. The report noted that:

> In an experiment in Princeton, New Jersey, physicists sent a pulse of laser light through cesium vapor so quickly that it left the chamber before it had even finished entering. The pulse traveled 310 times the distance it would have covered if the chamber had contained a vacuum. Researchers say it is the most convincing demonstration yet that the speed of light—supposedly an ironclad rule of nature—can be pushed beyond known boundaries, at least under certain laboratory circumstances (http://archives.cnn.com/2000/TECH/space/07/20/speed.of.light.ap/).

If the speed of light is not the constant that we have always assumed, then our calculations for how far stars are from the earth would be incorrect. Bear in mind no one knows for sure how light behaves in deep space.

> *If the speed of light is not the constant that we have always assumed, then our calculations for how far stars are from the earth would be incorrect.*

5. In addition to the speed of light being variable, it is also unknown as to whether light has traveled at the same speed throughout the **history** of the universe. Dr. Lisle observed:

> At today's rate, it takes light (in a vacuum) about one year to cover a distance of 6 trillion miles. But has this always been so? If we incorrectly assume that the rate has always been today's rate, we would end up estimating an age that is much older than the true age. But some people have proposed that light was much quicker in the past. If so, light could traverse the universe in only a fraction of the time it would take today (see http://www.answersingenesis.org/articles/nab/does-starlight-prove).

Again, if the speed of light has not been uniform throughout the history of the universe then all of our calculations for starlight and time would hold no value. One could safely assume that the starlight we receive today would have covered much greater distances in space in the early years following creation.

6. Some scientists have suggested that time synchronization may play an important factor in the starlight and time problem. This concept is best explained by considering the different time zones across the United States. For instance, on a normal weekend I fly home through the airport in Atlanta, Georgia. Normally the time I leave Atlanta is almost exactly the same time I arrive in Nashville due to a one-hour time change. For instance, I leave Atlanta at 9:00 p.m. and arrive in Nashville at 9:00 p.m. From the perspective of a clock, it appears the trip was instantaneous. However, in looking at the actual time spent on a plane, it is obvious that the trip included an hour of travel. (My body often feels like it has been even longer!). So looking at it this way, the trip arrived at the same time using "local time" (because I was traveling west), but it took an hour using "universal time." Discussing these phenomena Dr. Jason Lisle observed,

> Light traveling toward earth is like the plane traveling west; it always remains at the same cosmic local time. Although most astronomers today primarily use cosmic universal time (in which it takes light 100 years to travel 100 light-years), historically cosmic local time has been the standard. And so it may be that the Bible also uses cosmic local time when reporting events. Since God created the stars on Day 4, their light would leave the star on Day 4 and reach earth on Day 4 **cosmic local time**. Light from all galaxies would reach earth on Day 4 if we measure it according to cosmic local time. Someone might object that the light itself would experience billions of years (as the passenger on the plane experiences the two-hour trip). However, according to Einstein's relativity, light does not experience the passage of time, so the trip would be instantaneous (For more information, see http://www.answersingenesis.org/articles/nab/does-starlight-prove).

Other theories have been given, such as the idea that the universe may be curved and thus light travels quicker along curved pathways. This concept of a curved universe is known as Riemannian Space and was first proposed by Parry Moon and Domina Spencer in 1953. But the evidence is clear that several possibilities exist—and with those scientific possibilities one need not be worried with the puzzle of starlight and time. Rather, one should remember, "The heavens declare the glory of God; And the firmament shows His handiwork" (Psalm 19:1). Rather than doubt or question God, we should stand in awe: "When I consider Your heavens, the work of Your fingers, the moon and the **stars**, which You have ordained..." (Psalm 8:3, emp. added).

Questions:
1. Why does the Big Bang theory not fit the Bible?
2. What are some scientific problems with the Big Bang theory?
3. How can we explain starlight that seems to be millions of light-years away?
4. Why is the Big Bang theory dangerous for Christians?

Scriptures to Study
Psalm 33, 69 • Genesis 1 • 1 Thessalonians 5:20-21 • Colossians 1:16-17

Additional Resources:

Ashton, F. John (2001), *In Six Days: Why Fifty Scientists Choose to Believe in Creation* (Green Forest, AR: Master Books).

DeYoung Don, (2005), *Thousands Not Billions: Changing the Icon of Evolution, Questioning the Age of the Earth* (Green Forest, AR: Master Books).

The Conclusion of the Whole Matter

I can still remember the first time I looked at a nerve cell through a microscope. I was impressed—after all, I knew firsthand the result of injuring a finger or toe—but I was not nearly as impressed as I would become years later as my scientific training progressed. From that first casual glance, I was able to identify various parts of this highly specialized cell, but that glance didn't reveal much about how a nerve cell communicates, or how different nerve cells carry out different tasks. It was easy to forget this was a living structure. My first glimpse into just how complex this little cell was came from a textbook titled *Ionic Channels of Excitable Membranes* written by Bertil Hille. It was during that same semester that I enrolled in a cellular biology class and began learning about molecular machines and intracellular transportation.

Having taken biology and science classes from my undergraduate years, I was extremely familiar with the common labels of "organelles" within a cell. Not many students graduate with a degree in biology without being about to identify the nucleus of a cell and structures such as the endoplasmic reticulum, mitochondria, ribosomes, and Golgi apparatus. But suddenly those labels seemed far too elementary as we began to study these structures in microscopic detail—and how they actually functioned. I spent weeks disseminating information on voltage-gated ion channels that allow the cells to maintain a voltage gradient across the cell membrane. We examined vesicular transport and all of the proteins necessary for normal cellular activity. I had always heard of the word *protein*—primarily in regards to diet, but now I was learning there were countless proteins necessary just to conduct routine cellular maintenance.

And then we jumped off the deep end—into the ocean. By my third year of graduate school we had learned not only how to record electrical activity from specific nerve cells within the brain, but also what was happening to those nerve cells on the microscopic level that allowed them to pass an electric current. Our textbooks went from broad generalities about areas of the human body down to very specific physiology of a single system. For instance, we studied Douglas Junge's classic *Nerve and Muscle Excitation* to fully comprehend synaptic transmission and membrane potentials. And, even though in many cases I was looking at the same type of nerve cell that I initially observed through the microscope, it was no longer just a two dimensional cell with a nucleus and an axon. I was looking at an incredible living machine that itself purposefully created specific proteins and transported them to distinct areas of the cell for specific tasks. This was a three-dimensional cell that conducted electrical current from one end to the other and was able to pass the nerve signal on to a neighboring cell—in less than a second! I'll never forget one of the hardest tests I took was just a single question (and lots and lots of blank paper). My professor wanted us to describe in microscopic detail what happened when a painful stimulus was felt in the leg and the leg moved. That was a test in which we were given several days to complete.

The human body is just like a massive onion in complexity. Every time you peel back an anatomical layer there is a new and even more complex layer underneath. It appears to be unending in layers. So from whence did all of this complexity arise? Is it logical to conclude that everything we see is the product of time + mutations + natural selection? **How many beneficial mutations would it take to make all of the necessary proteins for life?**

That's not even addressing the chicken/egg problem. For instance, within the cell two ribosomal subunits are required to synthesize proteins from amino acids in mRNA. Without the ribosome, proteins cannot be formed—and the cell would die. Yet, those ribosomes are made of large complex **proteins** themselves. How were the original proteins for the ribosome formed if protein assembly is dependent on having ribosomes present? From whence did the original ribosome originate? In thinking of the chicken vs. egg, consider which came first, the heart or lungs—the digestive system or the vascular system? Both are needed to function properly.

How do cells know to become a liver cell, blood cell, or nerve cell? How did they know which **type** of nerve cell to become? How did the cell know how much of each secretory protein or cargo molecules to produce? How did they acquire and store the material needed to make such molecules? How did the proteins know the proper way to fold and unfold? How did the various genes know when to turn on and off? How is each protein programmed with stop codons as polypeptide chains were forming? This is machinery far more sophisticated than the iPhone, and it can last years longer.

Anyone who evaluates the evidence with an unbiased eye is forced to admit that the only logical conclusion is that the human body—just like the universe—demonstrates far too much complexity to have arisen by chance. It shows incredible design and purpose, and many scientists recognize it. During my scientific training, I had the opportunity to spend one-on-one time with many brilliant minds. I talked to neurosurgeons, physicists, anatomists, molecular biologists, etc.—and in almost every case, they would admit that what we were studying was far too complex to have arisen by purely evolutionary processes. However, as soon as another individual walked into the laboratory, the scientist would drop the conversation and always toe the evolutionary party line. After all, in many cases their positions were tethered to an allegiance to naturalism.

How tragic is it that thousands of young people today are growing up under the impression that evolution is a "fact" and that naturalism has an answer for everything. In many cases, they are being intimidated to repeat evolutionary dogma under the assumption that all "intellectual" people believe in evolution. The notion of anything supernatural is considered unscientific—and religion is viewed as a crutch for weak individuals. After all, no respectable scientist would ever posit a belief in some Intelligent Designer. In 1989, Richard Dawkins wrote a book review in the *New York Times* espousing, "It is absolutely safe to say that if you meet somebody who claims not to believe in evolution, that person is ignorant, stupid or insane (or wicked, but I'd rather not consider that)."

I think it is time someone reminded Richard Dawkins of the shoulders he is currently standing on. Dawkins has the privilege of standing on the shoulders of giants who laid the foundations for the scientific fields he studied. Most of those scientific fields—currently taught in major universities—were founded by men who believed that God created everything, similar to the description given in the Bible. Did that mean these men were ignorant or stupid? Did it lessen their discoveries in the scientific community? Consider the following small sample.

Sir Isaac Newton, a man who was perhaps the greatest scientist of all time, who laid much of the groundwork in areas like physics, calculus, mathematics, astronomy, etc. He wrote strong papers refuting atheism and defending creation and the Bible. He said, "I find more sure marks of authenticity in the Bible than in any profane history whatsoever."

Johann Kepler, a man considered by most to be the founder of the field of astronomy, who said his astronomy was thinking God's thoughts after Him. He went on to declare, "I see how God is also gloried, by my endeavors in astronomy for the heavens declare the glory of God."

Blaise Pascal who helped develop hydrostatics and differential calculus. He came up with the famous Pascal Wager in which he asked the question, "How can anyone lose who chooses to be a Christian?"

Samuel B. Morse, inventor of the telegraph and Morse code. The first message he sent was "What hath God wrought?" (Numbers 23:23). He went on to declare, "The nearer I approach the end of my pilgrimage, the clearer is the evidence of the divine origin of the Bible...."

Robert Boyle, a man considered by most to be the father of modern chemistry. He actually conducted mission work, used his own money to translate Bibles into foreign tongues, and set up the Boyle Lectures after his death to defend the Christian religion.

James Clerk Maxwell, a mathematician and theoretical physicist who originated "Maxwell's Equations" and developed the classical electromagnetic theory. Albert Einstein called Maxwell's achievement the most profound and the most fruitful that physics has experienced since the time of Newton. During his life Maxwell mathematically refuted evolutionary "nebular hypothesis" (still being taught in many classrooms today), and scientifically refuted Darwin and other evolutionary philosophers.

These were brilliant men—men who **founded** many of the fields we turn to for answers today. These were individuals who conducted phenomenal science, held a belief in God, and weren't pre-committed to naturalism. Don't let someone tell you that belief in an Intelligent Designer is unscientific. I maintain that those who are so pre-committed to naturalism, who are able to look at the evidence of irreducible complexity and deny the handiwork of God, are either ignorant, stupid, or insane (or wicked, but I'd rather not consider that). The evidence of design is unmistakable.

Many college students will plod along in the same path I took many years ago completely unaware that their fields of study were forged by men who were convicted by their belief in God. Sadly, these students will never be exposed to much of the evidence and information discussed in this book. Instead, they will find themselves placing their allegiance in textbooks that continue to promote humanistic values from an atheistic perspective. I find it incredible that in a field that prides itself on evaluating evidence that many scientists refuse to remove the blinders when the evidence clearly points in a direction they are morally uncomfortable with. The evidence will not go away quietly into the night. While it may be suppressed in the classroom, the truth will continue to confront future generations as we learn even more about the complexity of nature around us. I challenge future scientists to strip away the blinders and report the facts to the world.

I have been asked on many different occasions if spending so much time researching science has weakened my faith. On the contrary, it has strengthened my faith. My faith is firmly founded in evidence. **I am convicted.** The more layers I peel back, the more I recognize the handiwork of God. Having reviewed material from every scientific field, I see a clear pattern. True science—science without the interpretations built on biases from ungodly men—points back toward the Creator.

I hope that future generations will not be quick to "drink the kool-aid" but instead will evaluate the truth for themselves. Young people need to learn to ask questions like:
1. What do you mean by that?
2. How do you know that is true?
3. Where did you get your information?
4. What happens if you are wrong?
These questions, if asked in the right spirit at the right time can really help establish the Truth.

The scientific community is trained to collect data, report our findings, and then draw logical conclusions from our observations. The evidence for God is undeniable. As Paul told the church in Rome, His invisible attributes have been clearly seen since the creation of the world (Romans 1:20). The very existence of matter is a massive obstacle that atheistic or evolutionary theories cannot surmount without a great deal of faith and mental gymnastics. A scholarly investigation of the Bible reveals historical accuracy and unity. These Scriptures that could have only been penned through inspiration of an all-knowing Creator. In addition, there is a plethora of historical and physical evidence that points toward a man named Jesus Christ who walked this earth. Those three factors, when honestly evaluated by an unbiased observer, point to only one conclusion: Man was created by God for a purpose, the Bible is His inspired Word, and Jesus Christ plays an important role in the redemption of mankind.

We started this investigation by asking the major questions of life:

Where did I come from?
Why am I here?
Where am I going when I die?
What is my purpose?

Having thoroughly evaluated the evidence, we are now in a better position to answer those questions. Mankind, as the Bible indicates was the crowning glory of God's creation. We are here, Solomon said to "fear God and keep His commandments" (Ecclesiastes 12:13) and our eternal destiny depends on obedience to His commandments. While many may find comfort in saying "We can't know," the evidence is unmistakable (Romans 1:20). The responsibility is now on your shoulders. This book has demonstrated that faith in God is not based on a "blind leap." The last question for you to consider is: What will you do with that knowledge? My prayer is after a careful study of the evidence that you too will be **convicted**.